MW00576195

NEED TO KNOW

First published in 2024 by 100 Movements Publishing
www.100Mpublishing.com
Copyright © 2024 by 100 Movements Publishing and Boundless Publishing
Text copyright individual contributors.

Library of Congress Control Number: 2024940095

ISBN 978-1-955142-57-1 (print)
ISBN 978-1-955142-58-8 (eBook)

Editorial team: Helen Bearn, Joel Varner, Carolyn Smith, and Allison Mangrum
Cover design and interior design by Jude May

100 Movements Publishing
An imprint of Movement Leaders Collective
Richmond, Virginia
www.movementleaderscollective.com

curated by
DANIELLE STRICKLAND

NEED TO KNOW

Empowering Female Leadership and Why It's Essential for the Future of the Church

Anita Giardina Lee
Inés Velásquez-McBryde
Scot McKnight
Jo Saxton
Dr. Mimi Haddad
Aaron White
Mandy Smith
Alan Hirsch
Janet Munn
Bob Ekblad
Angela Lam
Beth Allison Barr
Rev. Dr. Elizabeth Rios

Dr. Oneya Fennell Okuwobi
Lori Anne Thompson
Dr. Tammy Dunahoo
Carolyn Whatley
Mariah Humphries
Meghann Jaeger
Lisa Rodriguez-Watson
Rev. Dr. Julie Faith Parker
Dr. Natasha Sistrunk Robinson

100 MOVEMENTS PUBLISHING

This book is dedicated to women who have been abused, oppressed, marginalized, silenced, and overlooked by the body of Christ. Your continued faith is staggering to behold, your determined hope for a better future for everyone is unparalleled, and your love keeps overflowing to us all in cascading light that shows us the way. May we have courage to follow.
#untileverywomanisheard

CONTENTS

SECTION FIVE THE FUTURE CHURCH 213

INTRODUCTION

Danielle Strickland

is an author, movement leader, and founder of Boundless Enterprise. From establishing justice departments to launching global anti-trafficking initiatives to creating new movements that mobilize people towards transformational living, Danielle trains, advocates, and inspires people to live differently.

Alan Hirsch

is an award-winning author/coauthor of numerous books on missional spirituality, leadership, and organization. He is a cofounder of Movement Leaders Collective, the Forge Missional Training Network, and 5Q Collective.

You may have heard the story of the two young fish happily swimming around when an older fish passes by and asks: "Good morning, fellas. How's the water?" One young fish turns to the other and asks, "What the heck is water?" This somewhat humorous parable highlights a problem we all face from time to time: We don't notice what we take for granted. Sometimes we need to step back, question the unquestioned, and become more aware of the everyday elements that shape our existence.

Rick Warren is recognized as one of America's most influential spiritual leaders, regularly advising international leaders in the public, private, and faith sectors on the most challenging issues of our time. He founded Saddleback Church (which currently has more than 28,000 attendees)[1] and authored one of the best-selling Christian books of all time, selling fifty million copies of *A Purpose Driven Life*.[2] But recently, Rick tweeted his biggest regret in ministry: that he did not do his own personal exegesis on the four passages used to restrict women in ministry, sooner.[3] Warren has publicly apologized to Christian women for his previous views on church leadership, acknowledging that he was wrong in his ministry assumptions that Scripture prohibits women from preaching and serving as pastors, and apologizing for failing to speak up for women in his years of ignorance.

Wow. A lifetime of Christian leadership, and his biggest regret is how he participated in disempowering women and that he did it without even bothering to do his own research as to why. How did that happen?

In the Western church today—particularly in evangelical spaces—we see the elevation of males in leadership and dominance, the depiction of God as male, and the over-valuing of "masculinity" in the church's promotion of certain character traits. Not only have we allowed these ways of operating to become our norm, they've become enmeshed with our understanding of following Jesus and being the church. It's become the water we swim in—that we breathe in—and we're completely oblivious.

This is the problem we face. Those of us who benefit from the ways we currently operate struggle to identify the impact it is having on the church and its reduction of the kingdom transformation we are called to bring. This is due to what has been called "the stakeholder principle"— the challenge of helping someone understand something when their livelihood or self-identity depends on *not* understanding it. In the church, those of us who benefit from the current status quo (most notably white, cis, heterosexual men) are slow to recognize its pitfalls when we experience better salaries, more leadership opportunities, and fewer menial tasks in our roles. Even when we support the equality of women in the church, it can be difficult for us to fully understand women's experiences and to do the necessary work to improve their situations. Our ignorance isn't necessarily willful; the structures we inhabit have simply become our norm.

Often, I (Danielle) meet with men in leadership who believe they are advocates for women's equality, but they are so used to swimming in the waters of patriarchy that they still "don't know what they don't know" and ignorantly perpetuate the system. Many years ago, I interviewed an influential executive leader about the challenges he experienced in trying to bring health and change within his organization. He offered valuable insights that I still find relevant today. However, he also expressed something of significant concern. He said that as he rose in leadership and influence within his organization he found it increasingly difficult to get an accurate understanding of the situations he faced. Most of the people around him simply provided information they believed he wanted to hear and, as he rose in power, there were fewer dissenting voices offering much-needed, alternative viewpoints. Eventually, he reached a point where he couldn't determine whether his efforts were genuinely making any difference at all. This led him to realize that he needed to break free from the cycle of closed-loop feedback in order to gain a more objective perspective, as well as drive changes with real consequences. What I learned from this man was that it is very hard to expect change from people who benefit from the system as it is. Change requires us to listen to voices outside of what has become our norm.

What you have in your hand are the words of some of those who can bring a different perspective to that of the status quo. What you hold is a book that will highlight the need to change the overwhelmingly male-dominated nature of the church. In the way of the younger fish in the story, and the confession of Rick Warren, the vast majority of leaders in this country are totally unaware of the problems of the prevailing system, because they are its prime beneficiaries. We need to listen to the voices of those who are experiencing abuse in the church, are excluded from certain roles, have their gifts and talents overlooked, are victim-blamed or even encouraged to stay in abusive relationships, are overlooked in their contributions, and who end up shouldering much of the lower-wage or unpaid work in the church and at home.

There is a real problem here—one built not just on deep injustice, but one that threatens our future viability. According to Barna, there is a generation exiting the church, with the majority of them being female.[4] The gender gap, that has seen women in the majority in churches for decades, is closing—*and not because we've seen an influx of men!* Women are exiting the church. And really, we shouldn't be surprised.

While some evangelical leaders are waking up to male and female equality, there is still little or no active recognition of female agency and voice within the prevailing systems of the church. Women have no place at the table. This, in itself, should serve as a warning because, if anything, this will further impact women leaving the church, particularly as in wider society women become more educated in contrast to the church continuing to unravel in the caustic condition of the last decade or so.

Before simply dismissing this as feminist nonsense, we suggest that men ask themselves if the situation was reversed, and they were the ones excluded from the equation, and that the best they could hope for in terms of vocational ministry was to perhaps be someone's personal assistant—would they even bother attending the standard evangelical church?! I (Alan) have to admit that I would likely not attend a church that operated under these conditions. I would feel neither safe nor respected. Honestly, I would rather stay at home and meet with a few others and follow Jesus in ways that celebrate the freedom of my God-given voice and agency.

I have sometimes wondered what might happen if women showcased the importance of their contributions by organizing a collective "strike." Imagine if, for several months, all women refrained from attending church and offering their usual assistance in running things. Perhaps they could gather separately during church hours to pray for the men who are supposedly running the church. What do you imagine would happen? I tend to think that our churches would come to a grinding halt.

And we ought to miss more than their service and contribution, because this formidable force of witnesses and workers is currently being left out of the discussion on movement leadership for the church in this era. Women's perspectives have been excluded from most leadership structures and systems, even in churches where they have been "allowed" to lead and sit at the decision tables. And what has been the result? A declining and failing church.

All of this leads us to consider two fundamental propositions: What do we lose by not having women at the table? And what will we gain by inviting them into the system, to help shape and change it?

What are we missing? Well, for one, consider that according to Scripture, men and women were made together in the image of God (Gen 1:26–27). This means that male and female *together* represent the image of God in human beings, and this concept is foundational to the equality and dignity of all human beings, regardless of gender. But with our limited number of female theologians, archetypes, and heroes, might we only be getting "half of God" in terms of theological expression? Do we have a rather serious case of exaggerated male-brain theology? If this is so, and we think it is, then we have to ask the question, "how much of God are we missing because of a faulty epistemology?" This question ought to shock us to the core. Needless to say, correction at this point will change everything—how we pray, how we perceive the world, how we resolve problems, and how we become the prefigurative community that stands in contrast to the patriarchy we see in the world. This calls for deep repentance—the process of *metanoia* that Jesus set out as his first principle as he began his ministry (Mark 1:15).

What do we gain by adding women to the equation? One of my (Alan's) favorite sayings is that we are perfectly designed to produce what we are currently producing. If we are flourishing, then it is likely because we have proactively created a system that has resulted in that outcome. If we are in decline, it is largely because of factors *internal* to the organization. It's all in the design. So, for instance, if you had a factory that wanted to produce V8 engines, but there are lightbulbs popping out at the end of the production line, you would rightly assume that there are problems in the production system that are producing these outcomes. You would have to look into the system and correct it—redesign it—to produce the desired outcomes. If we say we want the inclusion of women's equality, and yet women are still experiencing exclusion, oppression, and abuse, we must proactively examine the system we are in and fix it—not just share empty platitudes.

Examining the world in general and the church in particular, we can legitimately say that most of the problems of the world have been produced by a system overwhelmingly dominated by men. This is demonstrably true because there are very, very, few examples of women having the kind of power and influence being explored here. And where there *are* rare situations in which women have significant influence, the outcomes are much more holistic. In fact, studies have consistently shown that, all things being equal, women will excel over men in most categories of leadership.[5] If we want to change the outcomes of the male-dominated system, then we will have to redesign it to include female genius and contribution. And here's the wonderful thing—women, being the collaborative creatures that they are—don't want to take over. They simply want an equal place at the table!

Many men readily agree that the various women in their lives—from mothers, sisters, daughters, and wives—are amazing and remarkable people. We all know of men who readily admit to their friends that they "married up," hinting that their wives are, in some sense, better people than they are—women xviii | DANIELLE STRICKLAND AND ALAN HIRSCH

who bring a huge amount of goodness into the world. We can't imagine a world without women! So why, then, would we not want these wonderful expressions of the image of God to be included in the equation of leadership and ministry? Why would we want to exclude them? And what could we gain by having them around the table?

This book is written primarily to men to show them, like our young fish, some of the things that their male privilege has blinded them to. We asked some wonderful people to tell us about it. To challenge us. To point out the obvious so we don't miss it. To compel us and implore us and warn us and rebuke us. In these pages, you will find a diverse company of prophetic, apostolic, and predominately female voices to help us become aware of the culture that has excluded and harmed, limited and confined, and that threatens to undo the expansion of the church in the west without some kind of intervention. Many of these female voices are from Black and brown women, highlighting yet another level of exclusion many people experience in white patriarchal systems. The voices we've compiled here are ones we trust. Some of them are speaking out of their personal pain. Some are speaking out of their theological expertise. Some out of their practical experience. All are experts in the areas of assigned topics. Their willingness to share their experiences and hope for the future is a gift that we believe will keep giving to a future generation of church leaders, and speed the gospel prerogative for advancement in the world. Consider this book as something of an intervention and an invitation. Part of the invitation is to dream of a future church and what it might look like to shift the culture in a way that might make our dream of God's kingdom a reality sooner.

We are glad you are here, reading this book. We believe that the fact you are willing to read it means you are ready to become the change we need. This is an invitation for leaders just like you to listen and to learn. You don't have to agree. But we are asking you to be open to discover what seems so obvious to others but might have completely escaped you because of the culture you've been swimming in.

Consider this book a primer on topic. Our hope is that each section will invite you to further study. Many of the voices in this book have their own expertise, books, theological training schools, ministries, non-profits, businesses, and platforms. Their one piece of work in this book is not everything they have to say, but it does introduce you to them. And we believe it will spark your curiosity to uncover even more of what you need to know so we can grow together.

So, if you have questions about culture and how to change it; if you are concerned about the realities facing people who are not included in a system that privileges people because they are born male; if you wonder, as we do these days, how church got so toxic towards women, as pastor after pastor after pastor is exposed as abusive and disgraced publicly; if you question the practices that have excluded and wounded; if you genuinely want to know about a culture that needs to change for strategies to emerge that will advance the gospel—then this book is for you.

SECTION ONE

IT'S NOT US VS. YOU

Engaging in the conversation around female equality in the church can often feel combative. It can quickly become "Us vs. You."

It doesn't have to be like this.

In this section, we begin to look at how it might be possible for men and women to come together for human flourishing. As Dr. Oneya Fennell Okuwobi expertly unpacks, if we "other" those unlike ourselves, we miss out on the fullness of God's design. This fullness is what Dr. Natasha Sistrunk Robinson has termed "the blessed alliance"—the richness available when we work together.

In order to get to this place, we must find ways to listen to those who have been silenced for so long. As Mandy Smith shares, women can fear speaking out about their experiences and subsequently censor themselves in many of our spaces. And this censoring is not just evident today but also—as Anita Giardina Lee highlights—in the way some of the remarkable women of faith throughout history have been erased and forgotten.

How might raising women up to equal status and inclusion be beneficial for the fullness of the body of Christ? How can we leave behind our exclusions, othering, and rivalries? How will we pursue greater kingdom transformation by recapturing God's original intention—a blessed alliance?

1

WHAT I NEED YOU TO KNOW

Mandy Smith

is pastor of St. Lucia Uniting Church, Brisbane, Australia and the author of *The Vulnerable Pastor: How Human Limitations Empower Our Ministry* and *Unfettered: Imagining a Childlike Faith beyond the Baggage of Western Culture*. Her next book, *Confessions of an Amateur Saint: The Christian Leader's Journey from Self-Sufficiency to Reliance on God*, will be released by NavPress in October 2024. Mandy and her husband, a New Testament professor, live in a little house where the teapot is always warm. Learn more about Mandy's work at www.thewayistheway.org.

I don't want to write this.

I'll just email: "Sorry, I've changed my mind."

But what excuse can I give? Will they understand the decades I've spent carefully choosing my words? How can I explain my anxiety that, if I honestly share my pain, I'll be called an "angry woman?" Even if my chapter could find the perfect balance of honesty and grace, I can't control the tone of the other chapters or the marketing that will shape how my words are presented. Will my participation in this book limit my future ministry opportunities?

I hear myself. And I know it's a problem that I have to do all this extra work. If I heard someone else talk like this I'd say, "It's concerning that your first thought, in telling your story of mistreatment, is how it might make men feel. That, in itself, is often a sign of abuse."

So, I'm just going to write, with the most honesty and grace I can find, trusting in the graciousness of my readers.

I'm grateful to be able to say my life has not been filled with trauma. But, if there has been any trauma, it's mostly come from the ways I've been treated by men. Not all men. But men, nonetheless. (There it is again—I feel myself worrying about how such a statement might make men feel. Can I write it, trusting that if my story brings up negative feelings for men, they will know what to do with them?)

I don't need to dredge up my mistreatment to make anyone feel bad. But if I don't begin with the pain, how can I then share the good news? Unless I share the abuse, how can I share the salvation? If we don't sit with Good Friday, does Easter Sunday mean anything? Wherever the trauma has taken place in me is also the tomb where the miracle unfolded.

So let the story be told.

I looked like a woman by the time I was thirteen and had to grow up quickly, although I still saw myself as a girl. If I've had any trauma, it began in sixth grade when a band of older boys sought me out every lunch break to lift my skirt and to grab what were barely breasts. And the trauma was compounded when I complained and the boys said, "Who are you to think you're all that?" and the teacher chimed in, "Just boys being boys." My changing body was taking up more space, and in a different shape than before. It led people to mistreat me. It wasn't safe to say, "That's not okay." Survival instinct said, "Stay small."

That instinct was well-practiced by the time, as a young woman, I found myself in a Bible college which proudly defined itself as a place where women didn't learn to lead. (I had been too naive to even ask about such a thing before registering.) I was told my great grades in Greek and hermeneutics would allow me to give helpful feedback on my husband's sermons. I learned how to argue from Scripture against the growing threat of women's leadership. I heard the warnings that when a woman takes the role of preacher or elder, it's the end of absolute truth, a sign that Christians have sold out to the world's ways. I learned the stereotypes to use against Jezebels who take on roles only men should fill.

My developing gifts were taking up more space, and in a different shape than before. It seemed to threaten the foundations of our faith and disrupt the people around me. Survival instinct said, "Stay small."

But something was growing in me, which pressed me into ministry. By thirty-five, I was an associate pastor and by forty-two, lead pastor—as far as I know, the only female lead pastor in a fellowship of six thousand congregations. I had to confront the warring instincts in me. On the one hand, this thing stirred in me, expanding like the universe, threatening to burst me open if I held it in. And at the same time, I'd had decades of practice at surviving by staying small. That survival instinct is difficult to override! And when a peace-loving, people-pleasing introvert becomes a national denominational controversy—seen as a sign of godlessness and a threat to the future of the church—she's tempted to defer to that safe old habit of smallness.

My growing leadership calling was taking up more space, and in a different shape than before. It made powerful people around me publicly question my faith and my character. Once more, survival instinct said, "Stay small."

I often found myself the only woman in the room. I could feel the eyes on me, hear the whispers, feel the righteous indignation. Some assumed I was only in the room because I was someone's personal assistant (which is nothing to be ashamed of, by the way—and a role I'd previously filled—but not the role I was filling now). In the beginning, I was tempted to take the offer of Saul's armor. I wore my tallest heels and sharpest jackets. I rehearsed elevator pitches about my ministry. I faked self-sufficiency. But, like David, I knew I was small. To the person shaking inside over-sized armor, it's especially apparent just how small they are, how much they're pretending.

The healing in me did not come from making my small self larger, but instead from being released from my shame in my smallness.

My shame said something like this: "There are guys with quicker answers, bigger ideas, more impressive strategies and outcomes. Those are the people God calls to leadership. All the ways you pray and long and follow are nice, but that's not what leaders do. If you can make yourself more, maybe then you can lead, but until then, stay small."

If I was so small, what was this huge thing growing in me that strained for release?

The joy of Jesus could not be contained any longer.

If the trauma came from men, the breakthrough also came from men: Paul's honest confession of his smallness flipped my story. The task is not to feel ourselves small and work to overcome it; the task is to feel ourselves small, and to choose, like Paul, to say, "In our weakness, God is strong!" (see 2 Cor. 12:9–11).

I'm not small because I'm a woman. I'm small because I'm a human.

Instead of seeing my male counterparts as a judgment—a sign of my inadequacy—I began to feel a deep grief for them—a longing for them to be freed from the inhuman pressure to be big. These strong men with their quick answers and impressive programs were not my enemy. We had a joint enemy, the Lord of Darkness, who also taunted Jesus in the wilderness: You see how measly you are, little human? Take a shortcut to avoid the shame of living in one small body (see Luke 4:1–13). Jesus saw the massive divide between the scope of his mission and the size of his own little feet. But over and over Jesus refused to be ashamed. He knew that to step into this immense task, he would have to just keep coming back to the Father, day by ordinary day. Jesus was not ashamed to be human. And praise God that he wasn't! How could he save humans if he couldn't be one? He was more willing to be human than I usually am. How could I be saved by his work for humans if I'm desperately trying to avoid being human?

And here's where God used another man to heal my trauma—the ancient prophet, Jeremiah. A man who, unlike many of my contemporaries, was willing to confess his smallness. In the face of his huge calling (to be a prophet to the nations, no less!) Jeremiah cried, "But I'm only a child" (Jer. 1:6). God's response does not begin with the word "you" in the way Jeremiah may have preferred—"You're smart, you're gifted, you're qualified." No, God's response begins with "I"—"I send you, I appoint you, I have put my words in your mouth, I am with you to deliver you." Even though we all—men and women—feel our smallness, the God of all creation tells us, like Jeremiah, "Stand up and say to them whatever I command you ... I have made you a fortified city, an iron pillar, a bronze wall ... I am with you and will rescue you" (Jer. 1:17–19).

Alongside those men in Scripture, God brought into my daily life living, breathing brothers. Even in the trauma of men constraining my call, God knew it would be men who would also bring healing. One brother blessed me by letting me see behind the scenes of his leadership to the places where he was frail and had little but the Lord. Several brothers were willing to fight battles on behalf of my calling, able to say things to other men that would not have been heard if I'd said them. One brother saw gifts in me I didn't see in myself, and gave me grace to try and to fail. When I was ready, that brother also stepped out of leadership to make space for me, placing in my hands something he had created and releasing his hold on it. One brother expanded his capacity for my emotions, setting aside his need to fix me and learning the sacredness of tears. One brother blessed me by suspending his desire to fully understand my leadership, choosing to work in the discomfort of being led by someone very unlike himself, and confessing how it stretched him, but allowing himself to be stretched anyway. Another brother blessed me by taking on the less glorious tasks I'd been doing to give me space to teach and cast vision. Yet another brother blessed me by having more faith in my leadership than I did, stopping me when I felt the need to explain myself, and assuring me, "You don't need to defend it. Just do what God calls you to do, and I'll be right behind you."

This was not about gender dynamics—about proving ourselves and defending our territory. This was about pilgrims on a journey together, feeling the mystery of the path ahead and calling one another forward with faith. We had become fellow travelers, honest about the ways we get weary and the ways we need the Lord, and drawing out courage in one another.

The good news is this: God is not calling any of us—men or women—to puff ourselves up and pretend to be enough. God is calling us—like Paul, like Jeremiah, like David, like Jesus—to feel our frailty and to find in it one more invitation to depend on him. May the world not see us and say, "How impressive!" May the world see us and say, "How can something so remarkable come from such an ordinary being? It makes no earthly sense!" Even when we feel our smallness, may our lives give grace to every man and every woman still lost in the lie that their smallness is shameful. And may each day expand our capacity for the ridiculous miracle: the God of all creation birthing his joy through these small, human lives.

2

OTHERING

Dr. Oneya Fennell Okuwobi

is an assistant professor of sociology at the University of Cincinnati. Her research examines how processes in religious and secular organizations reproduce inequality. Together with her husband, Dele, Oneya planted 21st Century Church in Cincinnati, Ohio, where she also serves as a teaching pastor. She is co-author of *Multiethnic Conversations: An Eight-Week Journey toward Unity in Your Church* and *Multiethnic Conversations for Kids*.

In one of my favorite scenes from the American version of the sitcom *The Office*,[1] Pam tries to distract her coworker from destroying the company by handing him two pictures and telling him that corporate wants him to find the differences between them. He eagerly exclaims, "I already see five differences." A moment later, Pam, in a shot to the camera, informs the audience, "They're the same picture." The lesson of this scene is more than how easy it might be to distract our coworkers. What we learn is that when we are looking for differences, we will invariably find them.

When it comes to women and men, and girls and boys, we have been taught to search for differences since before we were born. At gender reveal parties, an expectant couple and happy revelers gather to see if pink or blue will rule the day. The stakes of that reveal are based on the underlying premise that having a boy or having a girl means divergent futures for the unborn child and the dynamics of the family. In childhood, Sunday school teachers eagerly separate the class into boys vs. girls, each working to show who has absorbed the lesson best. In school, girls are pushed toward nurturing professions and boys toward STEM professions, as if these would be the best expressions of their innate natures. And even in marriage, we are told "men are from Mars and women are from Venus." We are so distinct that only separate planetary origins are an apt analogy to explain our mutual incomprehension of each other.

What if these distinctions, like the differences between the pictures on *The Office*, only exist because we are looking for them?

Think for a moment about the premise that men are from Mars and women are from Venus. Imagine an actual being from Mars, Venus, or another galaxy showing up to examine men and women. Would their assumption be that two extraterrestrial species are living together on Earth in relative harmony? No! They would instantly see that men and women are more alike than they are not alike.

When we as leaders treat men and women as though they come from separate planets, this amounts to "othering." Othering consists of "viewing or treating (a person or group of people) as intrinsically different from and alien to oneself."[2] Identities are the meanings we are willing to assign to ourselves. They do not just help define who we are; they define who is not like us and cast them in opposition, calling them "other." Othering thereby creates an "us vs. them" dynamic that hinders human connection, assuming barriers between ourselves and others that do not need to exist. Othering also connects to stereotypes because others are often objectified in a way that ignores the individual qualities of people.[3] For example, this could include assuming that all women like to talk or that all men are stoic. We tend to simplify others and not allow for the complexity of traits in others that we recognize exist in ourselves and people like us.

The degree to which men and women "other" one another is neither obvious nor by design. It is the result of choices that we make on a day-to-day basis as we interact. Now, this is not to say that there are no differences between men and women. There are some well-established biological ones that we do not need to discuss here because we're all grown-ups; but, we often use those biological differences to explain things they have very little to do with. Biological differences don't make us gravitate toward pink or blue. They don't determine our brilliance or the vocations for which we are most suited. They don't determine if we are loud or quiet, assertive or compliant. *We* decide all of that through the assumptions we put on men and women. *We* are the ones who dress baby girls in pink and baby boys in blue. *We* are the ones who give little girls dolls and little boys building toys. *We* are the ones who listen to little boys who speak out of turn but chide little girls who fail to raise their hands, teaching them to act in ways consistent with the behavior for which they are rewarded.

Othering has been particularly disadvantageous for women. Men have been considered the default in many situations. As Simone de Beauvoir once wrote, "Humanity is male and man defines woman not in herself, but as relative to him; she is not regarded as an autonomous being ... He is the Subject, he is the Absolute—she is the Other."[4] When men are the default, women's needs and their stories are not taken into account; they end up being absent in many places where they should be present. Women are not properly represented in clinical trials of new drugs; women's stories are not equally represented in movies and television shows, except as accessories to male characters; and women are not proportionally elected to leadership roles in politics, business, and especially, Christian religious organizations.[5] This absence, this othering, has implications for the gospel as it limits women, whom God has gifted, from using their gifts to further the church and other organizations.

On the day I received the invitation to write a chapter for this book, I was doing research on women in the church. I was reading about women in a particularly conservative church and how they felt unworthy because they couldn't submit to their male leadership enough to feel accepted. No matter how low they were bent, there was something in their hearts that rebelled against their treatment. Instead of blaming the treatment, however, they blamed the sin nature within themselves, thinking they weren't good enough. I was furious at this violation of their humanity and tears sprang to my eyes. With guttural cries, I prayed to the Lord that these women would recognize themselves, not as second-class citizens, but of the same essence and same worth as these leaders to whom they were trying so hard to submit. Submission is a beautiful and necessary gift when it is mutual and for all. But forced submission by gender crushes and perverts that beautiful gift and robs the church of the full expression of humanity in their leadership.

This is why we must overcome the issues of othering and find ways to see the gifts of all, both women and men, flourish.

So, in this chapter, I would like to ground us in why our oneness matters, what is the best model for inclusion, and how we can lead together. By understanding what othering looks like and how to change it, we can end the "us vs.

them" dynamic and focus on becoming us—one fully functioning and complete body in Christ.

WHY OUR ONENESS MATTERS

The first reason why men and women must end othering is that our oneness is the greatest apologetic for the gospel. Jesus tells us this in John 17:20–23:

> My prayer is not for them alone. I pray also for those who will believe in me through their message, that all of them may be one, Father, just as you are in me and I am in you. May they also be in us so that the world may believe that you have sent me. I have given them the glory that you gave me, that they may be one as we are one—I in them and you in me—so that they may be brought to complete unity. Then the world will know that you sent me and have loved them even as you have loved me.

Jesus knew that it would be an uphill battle to convince not just his own Jewish people that he was the Messiah, but also the Gentiles, who were not even looking for him and did not know that they were part of God's story. The most powerful evidence that could be marshaled was needed—something so miraculous that it would literally be impossible without God's intervention. To supply that kind of evidence, Jesus didn't name healings, or mysterious weather events, or even exceptional preaching. Instead, the thing so compelling that it would convince every skeptic was *oneness*. Jesus tells us that when everyone who believes in him is one, the world will know that Jesus was sent by the Father.

When I first learned about John 17, I was dubious whether oneness could have such an effect. Since then, I have become a sociologist and have had the opportunity to study organizations of all sorts. From the church to schools and universities, to the military and corporations, no place is a place of oneness. If social scientists could find any place where male was not considered better than female, white was not considered better than Black, or rich was not considered better than poor, it would make more than a minor impression. Division among people is so endemic that an unusual display of oneness is just what could be surprising enough to convince people of God in the flesh. And I believe that we don't see it anywhere else because God chose his people to be the first to display it.

The oneness that God wanted was no ordinary oneness. Far from being a superficial coming together, the sort of oneness Jesus called convincing is the same kind of oneness that Jesus shares with his Father. As Augustine puts it, "The Father, therefore, is in the Son, and the Son in the Father, in such a way as to be one, because they are of one substance."[6] As affirmed by the Nicene creed, Father, Son, and Holy Spirit are co-substantial, but not the same person. There is no Mars and Venus here. One divine essence unites three distinct persons.

Interestingly, this sort of oneness most clearly harkens back to the story of creation, when God made God's very good intentions for men and women known. There was oneness in the creation of people.

> Who is *ha-adam*? It is neither a man (*ish*) nor the first man (*adam*). To identify *ha-adam*, we turn to Genesis 1:27. "And God created *ha-adam* in His image, in the image of God He created him (*oto*); male and female, He created them (*otam*)." The first part of the verse clearly indicates that *ha-adam* is a single being. The second half indicates that this single being is both male and female. Finally, this single being, at the conclusion of the creation process, becomes "*otam* (them)," two individuals. In other words, *ha-adam*, the first human being is a unique creation; both male and female, simultaneously. The first man and woman were created at the very same time; not, as is commonly assumed, that Adam was created first and Eve second, from Adam's "rib."[7]

This account of creation shows the mutuality and equality of man and woman. They are of the same essence, created simultaneously and for the same purposes. In that moment of creation, God gives a particular charge to *ha-adam*, "Be fruitful and increase in number; fill the earth and subdue it. Rule over the fish in the sea and the birds in the sky and over every living creature that moves on the ground" (Gen. 1:28). In the perfection of creation, God did not give the male part of *ha-adam* one set of commandments and the female part another. God does not turn to the female part of *ha-adam* and say, "And if you could make some sandwiches while he rules, that would be great." We see at the beginning the full range of humanity: male, female, intersex, and endosex. All there, all made in the image of God, and all given a common humanity and a common charge—one command they were to carry out together without an activity list or pecking order separating male from female.

This is not what many people outside of the church see today. At least half the students in my research methods class know little about the church. Based on their social media feeds, however, their key assumption is that women in the church exist to become "trad wives" (traditional wives) whose sole purpose is serving their husband and children with little leadership of their own. Far from attracting my students to Jesus, the gender dynamics they see repel them. People are looking for oneness. When they perceive the opposite in the church, they go looking elsewhere. This should not be. Men and women were created as one essence. Living in that way is what allows people to believe in Jesus.

The Gospel Expanding

Women and men working side by side with a common purpose was not just central at the beginning; it was repeated at the advent of Christ. Women were included among the disciples. It was not just the Twelve, but the Twelve and the women, who traveled with Jesus, bringing the good news of the kingdom (Luke 8:1–2). Mary sat at Jesus' feet and was affirmed as a disciple (Luke 10:39). Women stood and witnessed the crucifixion (Luke 23:49). Not only that, but women like Joanna and Susanna ministered to Jesus and funded his work (Luke 8:3). Because Jesus fully included women, the gospel spread faster than it would have otherwise.

Jesus reaffirmed this choice in the resurrection. All four Gospels record that Mary Magdalene was at the tomb that first Easter morning. Jesus sent her to tell the other disciples of his resurrection and she became the apostle to the apostles (Luke 24:1–10). There was no reason that Jesus needed to do this. We see him teleport himself places just a bit later to speak to the disciples himself. He absolutely could have popped back over to the disciples with no need to send a messenger. Jesus purposely sent Mary back to his brothers. Once again, we see a picture of male and female, both needed, both given equal roles and dignity in the new reality created by Jesus' return to life.

The centrality of women and men together in the New Testament narrative continues as the early church is born. In this narrative, women are not only in support positions but also in leadership alongside their brothers. Perhaps the clearest example of this is the last chapter of Romans. In his greetings to church leaders, Paul names half women and half men (Rom. 16:1–15). Even the medium was part of the message of gender inclusion in this letter. Paul, a man, wrote and sent the letter to the Romans. However, Phoebe, a woman, was responsible for reading it, interpreting it, and answering questions for the listening audience. Deacon Phoebe was the first person to preach the book of Romans. Men and women, working together with mutual respect, is what made this letter possible.

God seems to be emphatically joining men and women together in leadership; why should we separate what God has joined?

Women Achieving Their Potential

Seeing men and women work collaboratively remains incredibly important today. In 2018, a study examined what happened to girls who had a woman as their most influential religious leader growing up.[8] The researchers found a stunning effect. When these girls grew up, they had higher self-esteem, higher levels of self-efficacy, higher educational attainment, were more likely to work full time, and had more children. In almost every area of life—be it as a student, employee, or mom—women were more successful when they had experiences with influential clergywomen. Men grew up to do equally well whether or not they had this experience, showing that the representation of women in clergy positions helps girls but does not penalize boys.

But many girls will not ever experience these benefits because they won't have a woman as their religious leader. Christian women make up the majority of the church, and are more likely to pray, attend church, and identify as religious than Christian men.[9] Despite their overrepresentation in the pews, they are underrepresented in the pulpit; while 60 percent of church members are women, only 20 percent of clergy are.

The disproportionate number of clergy who are men is not just attributable to churches that have a theological objection to women serving in certain roles. In many denominations affirming women's equality, the disadvantages clergywomen face persist even when churches have neutral or supportive gender ideologies. Sociologist Katie Lauve-Moon, for example, investigates the experiences of women clergy in a denomination founded expressly to support women's ministerial leadership. Her study shows how gender inequality reveals itself in subtle ways that penalize women and their religious leadership. For example, many congregants picture the ideal pastor as a man, and are less likely to hire or to respect equally qualified women.[10] As a result, male clergy continue to predominate in their denominations. Likewise, Lisa Weaver Swartz finds theological support for women ministers among evangelical seminary students, but paradoxically little assistance to make changes remedying impediments to women's ministerial leadership.[11] Such changes could include helping women cope with the additional expectations of volunteer work and family duties that women bear in addition to their ministry work. In these cases, it is not just official theology but also church norms and practices that make women's leadership difficult.

Today, over two thousand years after Mary Magdalene delivered her message, I still have women coming up to me after a sermon saying that they have never seen a woman preach before, much less had an influential woman as their religious leader. Some have tears in their eyes, feeling that God represents them in a way they never knew—a God they, too, are created in the image of as women. Others remember times when they felt called but let that calling die because they didn't know it was possible to pursue it. Still others point me out to their babies or grandbabies and say to these girls, "You can do that someday." When women are represented—not instead of, but alongside men—it leads to better outcomes for all. We preach the gospel because we believe that it will lead to wholeness and freedom—not just in the life to come, but here and now as well. We have the research and the experience to show this is only true for women when they are fully included and not othered.

WHAT IS THE MODEL FOR INCLUSION?

Women and men working together confirms Jesus' message, expands the gospel, and helps all women achieve their potential. But what is this supposed to look like? We find some direction in the New Testament. The book of Ephesians is special to the local church as Paul outlines what our new multiethnic family— including Jewish and Gentile believers, and men and women—is supposed to look like. It does not just speak to conduct in the church; it has implications for our lives in community, at work, and in the home. In chapter 4, Paul lays out a five-fold framework for giftings, referencing apostles, prophets, evangelists, shepherds, and teachers. Here, we will refer to it as APEST for short.[12]

There is one body and one Spirit, just as you were called to one hope when you were called; one Lord, one faith, one baptism; one God and Father of all, who is over all and through all and in all. But to each one of us grace has been given as Christ apportioned it ... So Christ himself gave the apostles, the prophets, the evangelists, the pastors and teachers, to equip his people for works of service, so that the body of Christ may be built up until we all reach unity in the faith and in the knowledge of the Son of God and become mature, attaining to the whole measure of the fullness of Christ.

EPHESIANS 4:4–7; 11–13

I observe three takeaways from Paul's message about how we interact as the body of Christ. The first is to emphasize *oneness*. I will not belabor this point since I've already discussed how our oneness is the greatest apologetic for the gospel. But it is noteworthy that, before Paul talks about separate functions, he emphasizes that this is only possible if we already see ourselves as one.

The second is *inclusion*. Note verse 7. The emphasis is that "to each one of us grace has been given." The gifts Paul is about to name are an invitation to all and present in all. In other words, we're all on the field; no one is on the bench.

This is very different from the way I was first taught APEST. Traditionally, I was told that there are some special folks who are apostles, prophets, and the like, and they have these offices to teach the rest of us how to work. That the grace given to us is our *leaders*. Based on the context of oneness that precedes and the way that grace was used in other places, I no longer believe that is an accurate understanding of this Scripture. Grace throughout the New Testament references a gift of God and is used to talk about spiritual gifts. It is not used to talk about leaders being given as gifts. Once we know what this grace is, Paul is clear that it is given to each one of us, here again emphasizing the priesthood of all believers. We are each gifted through the generosity of Christ.

Finally, Christ, through the Spirit, determines how we are gifted. Some *as* apostles, some *as* prophets, some *as* evangelists, some *as* pastors and teachers. Nowhere here is the gender of the person being gifted named as a limitation to how this gift might function. With the foundation of oneness laid out before these gifts are described, we can understand that women are not the other within this framework. They are not alien but are also of the same baptism, Spirit, and God.

These APEST functions are designed to equip the body for works of service. With the understanding that all of us, not just leaders, are part of this equipping, the meaning here is revolutionary. This means we are equipping one another. If I am strong as a prophet—meaning I hear from God and share direction with the church—then I must give what I have to the whole body. I also receive equipping from people, such as teachers, who might be the best ones to help me formulate a message people understand and can act upon. This process is not to be stymied by gender. I share my grace with each person in the church and receive their gifts in return. This investment in one another is to occur until we reach maturity with the body fully reflecting the head.

So, what happens when we short-circuit this process? When we eliminate the full expression of gifts of some of the body, simply because of their sex, we all miss out. Women, gifted by Christ, are hindered from sharing what God has given them with the rest of the body—men, women, and children. As a result, the maturity of the body becomes impossible, and we fail to attain the full stature of Christ.

Unity, inclusion, and Spirit empowerment are marks of the New Testament model of working. And Ephesians is not the only place that we see this. Think about the day of Pentecost when the church received the gift of the Father. First of all, "they were all together in one place"—unity. Then, "tongues of fire ... came to rest on each of them"—inclusion. Finally, they "began to speak in other tongues as the Spirit enabled them"—Spirit empowerment (Acts 2:1–4). Explaining this event, Peter specifically highlights that men and women are equal partners. Sons *and* daughters, male *and* female servants. Everyone is meant to be in on what God is doing.

HOW DO WE LEAD TOGETHER?

We have operated from a model of othering and competition for far too long, but it is different from the model Scripture gives us. How might we turn the page from men vs. women to men and women leading together with equal respect and dignity?

Focus on Equity

Equity has become a dirty word in some circles, but it is nothing to be maligned. It simply means everyone has what they need to succeed. Equity is a profoundly simple and biblical principle. A good example of equity is the manna God gave the Jewish people in the wilderness. Each person was commanded to gather an omer of the thin wafers that covered the ground each morning. However, you can imagine that people had differing levels of ability to follow this command due to age, agility, or health. Despite this, when the manna was measured, something miraculous happened. We're told in Exodus 16:17–18, "The Israelites did as they were told; some gathered much, some little. And when they measured it by the omer, the one who gathered much did not have too much, and the one who gathered little did not have too little. Everyone had gathered just as much as they needed."

That everyone gathered as much as they needed could mean that God sovereignly multiplied the smaller portions and shrunk the too large ones. But given the explicit mention of measurement, perhaps it's a more obvious solution: that, after measurement, any excess was shared so that every family had as much as they needed. Some portions were large, some small, but what they were all able to gather was exactly enough for the community. In this situation, equality would say, "Hey, everyone had a chance to gather. If you don't have enough, that's too bad." This policy would leave the community fractured as some slowly starved while others became fat. Equity alone could keep the community whole by recognizing each person's situation and treating them accordingly.

Creating equity means treating people differently so that they have what they need to succeed. But isn't that othering? No. Correcting othering is not itself othering. As an illustration: Some women and men are working on team tasks together, and everyone in the group considers women to be of lower status. As a result, the women are not listened to as much as the men and the ideas that the women express are less influential (regardless of the quality of the idea). Seeing how they are treated, the women become less likely to speak up and expect less deference when they do.[13] If you've ever seen a brilliant woman start her thought with, "This may be a dumb idea, but ..." that's why. This situation is an example of women being othered. Their competence and ability to contribute is assumed different from and less than the men. Correcting othering means consciously realizing women as a group are not less competent than men as a group, so if the women in this task are not contributing at the same level, there must be a barrier hindering that contribution. Someone working to correct this othering could then perhaps amplify the words of the women at the table by repeating what they have said and giving them credit for having said it, so that the rest of the group can latch on to their ideas. This is treating women differently, but it is not othering. The othering happened beforehand. Equity serves to correct it.

Creating equity, I believe, reflects the truest meaning of 1 Peter 3:7: "Husbands, in the same way be considerate as you live with your wives, and treat them with respect as the weaker partner and as heirs with you of the gracious gift of life." Many have spent time on statistics about women's strength ratios and top deadlift weights to reinforce the idea of women as weaker—this is not the point here. Women need consideration because they are *sociologically* weaker. They are more at risk in society because they have been subjected to gross inequality, disproportionate levels of violence, and unfair treatment. Being considerate then, is emphasizing the "co-heirs" part of this verse. This results in respecting the humanity of women and correcting these areas of sociological weakness. Regarding women and men being together in leadership, that means recognizing that women experience deficits. Not due to their lack of skill or gifting, but due to societal constraints that put them on the outside relative to men. Men who value women's leadership cannot therefore just take a neutral stance toward women in their organizations, they must actively empower them.

To give you one small example: I went to preach in a new church for the first time. I was coming from another event, and I had forgotten to wear an outfit with pockets. (Yes, men, this is a thing!) I went into a momentary panic, thinking I was going to need to use a handheld mic, which is a problem because I talk with my hands. But I needn't have worried. The sound person at the church handed me a "preaching purse"—a small, cross-body bag just big enough to hold a microphone pack. They always kept it on hand for people without pockets. Ever since then, there has been a preaching purse at the ready at every church I have served at. This tiny act of accommodation let me know that this church knew enough about women's experience of leadership to know about the pocket problem, that they expected to have women in the pulpit, and that they wanted to be prepared for those women. Now, this step could also help men if they happened to be preaching in basketball shorts, but it wasn't neutral. It recognized a problem faced by a minority group of pastors and provided a solution.

Women graduate college at higher rates than men[14] and are entering seminary at the highest rates in recorded history, but they are a minority of leaders.[15] Women are already ready—they don't need another training. For them to be better represented in leadership, the barriers that stand in their way need to be erased. One such barrier within the church is acceptability with congregants. Congregants tend to hold male pastors as prototypical and may balk at hiring a woman. Some congregants may even leave the church as a result. When this happens, male leaders in the church must elevate the message that this is othering and inconsistent with Scripture. Instead, male leaders often side with congregants, blaming the new pastor for the congregants' departure and speeding her ouster. Another barrier that women in leadership face is the expectation of hospitality, home, and family that falls disproportionately on them. Studies have shown that male leaders benefit from the unpaid labor of their wives, and that the husbands of women leaders do not make similar contributions.[16] Creating flexible work policies, even in smaller organizations, relieves the additional load that women face and allows them to do the work they are capable of.

Most importantly, listening to women and what they need as individuals can help your church or organization take the right corrective actions. If we put in place policies and practices supporting women's leadership, we stop the othering by recognizing women are no less capable, but face different constraints than men.

Value Masculine and Feminine Qualities

I was once at a leadership meeting for women. A well-meaning woman leader gave us a presentation on how to prepare for meetings with men. We were to be careful to be extremely logical and not talk in circles because men hate that. If we felt we couldn't follow those directions, we were to script our talking points beforehand so we wouldn't waste men's time with our asides. Beyond being incredibly insulting, this presentation assumed that there are default ways of communication that are better than others. Valuing direct communication and a task vs. relational orientation is a fine choice to make as an organization, but it is not the only way to be effective. These orientations also do not follow strict sex divisions; many male leaders are incredibly relational. Instead of encouraging us to find what worked but was true to ourselves, this leader told us that being listened to depended on us becoming like the men that she had successfully worked with.

Our society associates certain traits with the masculine, such as assertiveness or independence, and others with the feminine, such as gentleness or warmth. The association of these traits with masculine and feminine are not fixed, but vary by time and cultural context; this is how we know these associations are a man-made assumption and not a God-ordained fact. Society tends to devalue traits associated with femininity, especially when present in men. Women receive mixed messages about their ideal traits; they have been told to exhibit more masculine qualities to be successful only to then be negatively sanctioned when they do so![17] Assigning "masculine" traits to men or "feminine" traits to women is a mistake that limits our full humanity. In this way, the terms "masculine" and "feminine" are misnomers; there is no human trait that belongs to one sex. Assertiveness, independence, gentleness, and warmth each can be found in both men and women. For example, gentleness is part of the fruit of the Spirit. We certainly don't want to imply men can't be filled with the Spirit!

Assuming that being analytical belongs to men or that being understanding belongs to women, others women because it assumes they are less capable of the traits that are most highly valued in our society. It also others and stifles men who may not fit the stereotypical mold that is being placed on them. Both men and women are free when they can express the full range of human traits without being any less a man or a woman. This sensibility allows teams to figure out who the people on their team are and how they function best (this could involve drawing on APEST as mentioned above). It also permits everyone to lean into the gifts that God has given them instead of crude stereotypes.

Freeing men and women to express their full humanity starts early. That's why at our church, we have a training for children's workers as to how to avoid othering in kid's ministry. Here's an excerpt:

> At 21st Century Church, we avoid grouping expected behaviors by gender so that we don't miss the uniqueness of each kid.
>
> We avoid phrases like:
> - Boys are so much harder than girls.
> - Girls like to do this; boys like to do that.
> - Let's do a competition, boys vs. girls!
>
> Instead, we practice respecting the full image of God in each child by:
> - Asking boys about their feelings and girls about their strength.
> - Having consistent expectations for behavior across gender.
> - Encouraging boys and girls to view each other as partners, not opponents.

Nothing about Us without Us

One of the few things that stuck in my head from middle school social studies was the US Supreme Court case of *McCulloch v. Maryland*. Its key conclusion was that the power to tax means the power to destroy. Every non-profit and church leader should love this case. We maintain our tax-free status because giving the government the power to tax the church would imply the power to destroy it—a violation of the separation of church and state. When it comes to othering, I want to try out a corollary to this logic: The power to define means the power to destroy. Othering objectifies people, and, as bell hooks put it, "as objects, one's reality is defined by others, one's identity is created by others."[18] To the extent that rooms of men have taken the role of determining what they believe women can or cannot do per Scripture, they are taking the power to define them and the limits of their leadership. Some call this complementarity. They claim that this distinction can coexist with equality. This is not the case. As soon as women become objects to be defined by others, the definers gain power over women and can destroy the expression of women's spirit-empowered gifts. When men claim this sort of power over women, it is inequality by any definition.

Furthermore, say what you will about Paul's words and our interpretation of them, but Paul never wrote epistles from the perspective of sitting in a room full of men. He labored alongside women, met in their houses, trusted them with the mission he was graced with, and called out their leadership. If leadership teams full of men and women worked then, they will work now. I've become fond of the saying, "Nothing about us, without us." This means that if decisions are made that affect any group of persons, those persons should be at the table for the decision-making. When we violate this rule with respect to decisions that affect half of humanity, our decisions cannot but be suboptimal and we replace joint dominion with power of one group over another.

Voice, Exit, Loyalty

Finally, moving the needle on othering means knowing when it is time to leave a place that insists on it. When someone is unsatisfied with an organization, economist Albert Hirschman theorizes three different options: voice, exit, and loyalty.[19] People can either give voice in protest of their treatment, exit to another organization, or stay loyal when experiencing a decline in benefits. As mentioned, women are 60 percent of the church. It is only because they assent to their othering by giving their time and resources that these organizations still exist. Men are the other 40 percent of the church. This means they are currently ignorant to, willfully ignoring, or actively benefiting from this othering. Either way, othering continues because we all allow it to. This is not what Jesus meant by being one. Change requires that we collectively, women and men, begin to raise our voices against the absence of women when they should be present. If voice doesn't create change, it means that we must vote with our feet, exiting to or creating organizations that fully support equity for women in their ranks. Loyalty to the status quo is a betrayal of the unity that Jesus died for.

Women have been bent low for entirely too long through treatment as alien and other. The consequences of this othering are diminished belief for those outside the church, diminished potential for women in the church, and a diminished faithfulness to Jesus' call for oneness. In the garden, male and female turned against each other in finger-pointing and accusation for the fall. We don't have to live like that anymore. When we recognize that we are more alike than not alike, and join together in unity, there will no longer be us vs. them. There will only be us.

3

THE BLESSED ALLIANCE

Dr. Natasha Sistrunk Robinson

is president and CEO of T3 Leadership Solutions, Inc. and visionary founder and chairperson of Leadership LINKS, Inc. Dr. Robinson is a graduate of the US Naval Academy, Gordon-Conwell Theological Seminary (*cum laude*), and earned her doctorate degree from North Park Theological Seminary. She is a sought-after thought leader, international speaker, certified executive leadership coach, and consultant with more than twenty years of leadership experience in the military, federal government, academic, and nonprofit sectors. Dr. Robinson is the author of several books including *Voices of Lament, Journey to Freedom, A Sojourner's Truth, Hope for Us: Knowing God through the Nicene Creed*, and *Mentor for Life* and its accompanying leader's training manual. She hosts *A Sojourner's Truth* podcast. She has honorably served her country as a Marine Corps officer, obtaining the rank of captain, and she is also a former federal government employee at the Department of Homeland Security.

Let me tell you a story of a Black girl from the small town of Orangeburg, South Carolina. She was born the eldest of what would become a family of three children. Whenever she played with her cousins—whether "cooking" mud pies in the backyard or mimicking school in her bedroom—she was dreaming about making a life and a living for herself, her family, and her community. She loved to read, was a stellar student, and became a competitive athlete. Whether at home, school, or within her local community, people listened to what she had to say. Adults encouraged her and peers voted for her. She was born to lead.

So, it was no surprise when she graduated high school and had her choice of attending numerous colleges with full scholarships. She chose to attend the United States Naval Academy (USNA), where she was commissioned as an officer in the United States Marine Corps. After attending USNA and serving in the military, she began her professional career at the Department of Homeland Security—a career where she was often the only Black woman, or among the few women or few Black people in the room. She continued to lead, nonetheless. While there were both spoken and unspoken biases, she grew in character and in faith. She continued to learn what it meant to fulfill the purpose for which she was created: becoming a Black Christian leader who partners with God to advance his kingdom on earth. This was and is her life's commitment and redemptive work.

That little Black girl grew up to obtain her doctor of ministry degree and become a social entrepreneur and philanthropist. She now has more than twenty years of leadership and mentorship experience in co-ed, intergenerational, and multiethnic professional and ministry workspaces. She is the one writing to you about a new view for women and men engaging in the workplace, and how we can leverage the leadership of women.

THE ISSUE: WOMEN CANNOT BE TRUSTED

Recently, I was having a conversation with one of my classmates from the Naval Academy. He is a Black man whom I trust, so I lamented to him about the restrictions, the closed doors, and lack of equity there is for Black women. He owns two successful franchises, so there is a certain caliber of people in his professional circle. As we discussed the opportunities he has to use his power as a man to sponsor and share information with the sistas, I communicated my wish for a formal way for us to practice this behavior among our peers. He replied that the brothas have informal get-togethers for this very purpose (you know, the "good ole boys" club): They go to the cigar lounge to have drinks and talk it up. I commented "I have no desire to respond like a man. I don't drink or smoke, and being in a cigar lounge would stink up my clothes and linger in my natural hair!"

As we continued our conversation, my male friend acknowledged another barrier that women face. He confessed that many of the men on his professional level don't mentor or sponsor women because their wives would not allow it. Too often, wives assume that professional women leaders are seeking a personal or romantic relationship with their spouse. While it is true that we need to exercise wisdom and discernment in our dealings with each other, it is *not* true that all women should be met with suspicion. This thought process only feeds into the fallen narrative of women being harlots, temptresses, or Jezebels. As Christian leaders, we must reject the metaphors and tropes that women are conniving and deceptive humans who use their minds and bodies to abuse their God-given power to get what they want from men. While abuse of power is a result of sin, it is not due to actions women exclusively take. This conversation reminded me of the ongoing relational and professional gaps between men and women, and the challenges that women face due to our lack of access to critical information, which restricts the abilities of women to fulfill our calling or pursue our work.

According to the latest "Women in the Workplace" report by McKinsey, "Women are more ambitious than ever, and workplace flexibility is fueling them." But, despite this drive and desire, women continue to be less likely to be promoted than men, more likely to be mistaken for someone junior, more likely to receive comments about the state of their emotions, and, in terms of their representation in the workplace, only seeing modest gains in positions across all sectors, with women of color remaining underrepresented.[1]

THE QUESTION: CAN WOMEN LEAD?

Whether we acknowledge them or not, we can hold biased views about womanhood, manhood, and leadership. Humans have been socially conditioned to approach women with suspicion regarding their sexual ethics or ambitious motivations. If women have a scarcity mindset in a patriarchal culture, they can approach other women with envy or as enemies. If men have an entitled posture, then pride or their egos will not allow them to partner with women. These unconfronted biases continue to impact the ways we relate to one another. So, we continually pedal questions like: *Who has the authority or power to lead? What does leadership look like in a particular space? How do we exercise leadership in the church and/or within a Christian community? How do people experience our leadership? How do we train or prepare people for leadership, and how do we respond when people have varying leadership skills?* These are fundamental questions about practices, and the appropriate responses to these questions can differ significantly based on our work environments, church history, traditions, or theology; but none of these questions acknowledge God's original intent or offer a restored view of women and men working together. Therefore, we must ask the right question: *Do we agree with God's view of and purpose for women?*

I am not interested in rehashing stalemates of the gender debate; asking the same theological, traditional, or cultural questions; or presenting practical tips that might work for some but not for all. Instead, we must elevate the conversation by centering our focus on God—taking note of God's revelation in the Scriptures, God's authority, and the authority that God bestows on *all* human creation. As men and women in God's kingdom, we need to know that effective leadership requires us to remember God and his intention for all humans before our sinful revolt, to repent or "put off" our thoughts and actions of old, and to become renewed in our thinking and redemptive in our actions to the glory of God.

THE NEED: REMEMBER GOD'S INTENT

When considering the leadership of men and women, we must remember God's original intent. Let us, therefore, revisit the beauty of the garden with fresh eyes. Let us consider creation—including the purpose of work and human relationships, the authority bestowed upon humans, the shared leadership of man and woman, and the unique call of the *ezer* (Gen. 2:18). Let us remember what God did and what God said.

God first reveals himself to us as Creator. God has the authority to create and the authority to define purpose for whatever he creates. "In the beginning God created the heavens and the earth" (Gen. 1:1). Day after day in his creation, God declared that everything he made was good. Whenever creation is in alignment with the purpose and intentions of God, God is pleased with the reflection, glory, and goodness of his work. As the grand finale, on the sixth day, God reveals that he does not and has not created alone: "Then God said, 'Let us make humankind in our image, according to our likeness; and let them have dominion ...'" (Gen. 1:26 NRSV). Some theologians argue that this declaration reflects the presence and work of angels or heavenly hosts in creation. We must acknowledge, however, what Scripture reveals in Genesis 1:2, what the psalmist professes in Psalm 100:3, and what John declares in John 1:1–2 and 1:14: the triune God is the ultimate creator of the universe and everything in it.

The Second Ecumenical Council (Constantinople I) and the Nicene Creed affirm "there are three *eternal hypostaseis* [persons], all on the same level of *divine* being distinct yet indivisible … 'Not only [are] the Son and Spirit coequal with the Father; all three were together declared to be one God.'"[2] To see and understand ourselves rightly as women and men of God who are called to leadership, we must first remember and see God rightly. When three *hypostaseis* [persons] are presented as God—the Father, the Son, and the Holy Spirit—without hierarchy and with "distinct yet indivisible" characteristics to reflect unity and oneness in diversity, that revelation communicates a truth about what it means for men and women to bear God's image and to rule or exercise shared leadership in God's universe.

"So God created humankind in his own image, in the image of God he created them; male and female he created them. God blessed them and said to them, 'Be fruitful and multiply, and fill the earth and subdue it, and have dominion over … every living thing that moves upon the earth'" (Gen. 1:27–28 NRSV). This text is what theologians refer to as the Cultural Mandate. It reveals the authority God bestows upon man and woman to exercise dominion or leadership together, to steward everything that God created, and to work so that God's creation flourishes, continues to produce as God intended, and remains beautiful and good to the glory of God. I love how theologian Carolyn Custis James writes about this:

> According to the biblical record, the history of men and women working together is *longer* than men working with men and women working with women. This has profound implications for husbands and wives, but goes well beyond marriage to encompass *every* relationship between men and women in the family, the church, the workplace, and the wider world community. The clear message of the Bible is that God intended for men and women to work together. God put an exclamation point beside his choice of male and female. He blessed them before presenting them with their global mandate. They are a *Blessed Alliance.*[3]

We must remember that women and men working together and sharing leadership was God's original intent. The *Blessed Alliance* is the epitome of God's creation, reflecting the unity and oneness that God has within God's self, and becoming a physical manifestation of the spiritual reality of the Trinity. It is only after human creation that we read, "God saw all that he had made, and it was *very* good" (Gen. 1:31, emphasis added).

God's Vision: Humans Created to Lead Together

Whenever the issue of male and female relationships and leadership is addressed within white, Western evangelical churches, the conversation goes back to the garden with questions like: *Who was created first? What is the importance of the headship or leadership of Adam? What role or responsibility does Eve have "to help" Adam?* If we ask the wrong questions, then the answers matter little in the end, especially when we consider what gets lost in translation. We must remember to ask the right questions of God and of the sacred text. The question to ask in this context is, "What did God create?"

The triune God had a council to create humans and was intentional in informing readers that these humans are unlike anything else that was created on the previous days. When we read the English word "man," it is not referring to the male gender or sex. Theologian Anthony A. Hoekema explains, the Hebrew word translated as "man" is *'ādām*, and is presented in the generic sense, in the same way that we use the proper name, Adam, to refer to the first representative of the entire human species before God.[4] Hoekema also notes:

> The word has the same meaning as the German word *Mensch*: not man in distinction from woman, but man in distinction from nonhuman creatures, that is man, as either male *or* female, or man as both male *and* female. It is in this sense that the word is used in Genesis 1:26 and 27. The word *'ādām* may also occasionally mean humankind (see, e.g. Gen. 6:5).[5]

When the triune God creates *'ādām* in "our *tselem* (image), after our *demûth* (likeness)," God is "carving out" or "cutting" so *'ādām* can "be like" or represent God on the earth.[6] Humans are created to represent God, yet humans are *not* God. Hoekema notes three ways in which humans are like God. First, humans reflect God's image by exercising their leadership or dominion over God's creation.[7] God is a spirit, therefore, human gender or sex, while important, does not determine human ability to bear God's image or exercise dominion. The Creed of Nicaea, a product of the First Ecumenical Council (Nicaea I), "took care to emphasize *homoousios*, a word that expressed that the Father and Son shared the same essence or being."[8] Likewise, it is important to remember that, regardless of their gender or sex, all humans are of the same essence or being. While the roles of men and women are socially and cultur-ally constructed, their joint responsibilities to reflect the unity in diversity of the Holy Trinity is a humbling and unique calling that only humans bear. This representation is what God had in mind when creating this very good and beautiful world.

The second human resemblance of God "must be found in the fact that man needs the companionship of woman, that the human person is a social being, that woman complements man and that man complements woman."[9] In the same way that the Father, Son, and Holy Spirit love, need, and counsel with each other, women and men need, are called to love, and must regularly counsel with each other for their relationships, society, worship, and work to flourish. This is the way that "human beings reflect God, who exists not as a solitary being but as a being in fellowship."[10]

Third, "from the fact that God blessed human beings and gave them a mandate (c. 28), we may infer that humans also resemble God in that they are persons, responsible beings, who can be addressed by God and who are ultimately responsible to God as their Creator and Ruler."[11] Therefore, we must contemplate the work and partnership of women and men as fellowship, an exercise in worship to our Creator, and a spiritual rhythm and practice of belonging to each other. Denying the importance of this partnership misses God's vision and the mandate God originally gave women and men to lead and partner together from the beginning.

Theologian Kat Armas writes, "Our world and everything in it tell a story of belonging—a belonging established at the very beginning, in accordance with God's desire for all of creation to be in concert together."[12] Together, we belong to God. We belong to each other. This sense of belonging affirms God's statement that, "It is not good for 'ādām to be alone" (Gen. 2:18). We will come to this vital point in a moment. Our need for belonging means that God places humans in families; makes us brothers and sisters, wives and husbands, fathers and mothers. We dwell together in community as neighbors and friends in love with God and each other, and this equips us to fulfill the two greatest commandments.

Human Nature: Created Together to Work

One of the ways humans exercise dominion or leadership is through our work. The creation account, as presented in Genesis chapter 2, communicates the interconnectedness of who God is, what God does, and how 'ādām bears God's image through work and creation. Verse 2 begins by informing the reader that God has set his creation in motion, yet nothing is producing as

God intended: "… no shrub had yet appeared on the earth and no plant had yet sprung up" (v. 5). The author also informs us that "there was no one to work the ground" (v. 5). In the next sentence, *'ādām* was formed from the ground as the only creature into whom God breathes life, and "man became a living being" (v. 7). Verse 15 reads, "The Lord God took the man and put him in the Garden of Eden to work it and take care of it." Therefore, "the concept of man as the *image* or *likeness* of God tells us that man as he was created was to *mirror* God and to *represent* God."[13] Image-bearing is both form and function. We don't just carry God's image in our physical beings, we also enact God's image by working, nurturing, and stewarding what God has created; these are the unique functions and responsibilities of humankind.

GOD'S TRUTH: MEN NEED FEMALE LEADERSHIP

After creating the heavens, the earth, and Adam, the only thing that displeases God is Adam's aloneness: "The Lord God said, 'It is not good for the man to be alone …'" (Gen. 2:18). God has set the conditions for creation and then God, not Adam, states a problem. Before we can continue the discussion, we must agree with God on this matter: Men need women, not just for marriage or sex; men need women to share in the work that God has assigned to them.

We see how God doesn't just state the problem of man's loneliness; he provides the solution (although much of God's intent has gotten lost in translation). The NIV records God as saying, "I will make a helper suitable for him" (Gen. 2:18). In white, Western theological thought, "helper" has mostly been narrowed to the woman's role and function as wife, mother, and housekeeper. The problem with this line of thinking is that it ignores God's original intent, and it confines women. It doesn't even work within the context of the biblical text because there was no laundry to wash (for Adam and Eve were naked), there was no food to cook (for Adam and Eve were vegetarians, likely raw vegans), there was no house to clean (for the perfect garden was their home), and they had not yet had children.

The Hebrew word that is often translated as "helper" is *ezer*.

Theologian Carolyn Custis James elevates our interpretation here: "*Ezer* appears twenty-one times in the Old Testament. Twice, in Genesis, it describes the woman (Gen. 2:18, 20). But the majority of references (sixteen to be exact) refer to God, or Yahweh, as the helper of his people. The remaining three references appear in the books of the prophets, who use it to refer to military aid."[14]

In her being and function, Eve mirrors God as an *ezer*—a strong defense and warrior of Adam, the one she was born to partner with and to love.

One of the ways that I celebrate the goodness, beauty, and creation of God is through my collection of Thomas Blackshear's *Ebony Visions* figurines. With artistry inspired by his faith, Blackshear uses skill to blend "Art Nouveau and African culture," and to evoke "emotions like hope, love, tenderness, faith, and serenity" which has no boundaries.[15] Each of my collected pieces has special meaning. I purchased "The Protectors of Freedom" piece while I was serving as an officer in the Marine Corps. My husband and I are both veterans and former Marines, so this piece is aptly named in our home, and serves as a fitting reminder of our identity in God and affirms our commitment to each other. This three-dimensional masterpiece features a strong, bare-chested and bald-headed Black man wearing what resembles Ibheshu, the traditional leopard Zulu warrior attire, covering his bottom. He proudly holds a spear in one hand and a shield in the other. He is looking off into the horizon in one direction. To his rear, facing in the opposite direction, is a sista—whether a wife, biological sister, relative, or friend, we do not know; but we do know that she is also a warrior. She is dressed in Ibheshu and draped in gold and beaded jewelry. She, too, holds a sword in one hand and a spear in the other as she stares off in the opposite direction. Her left leg is elevated with her foot arched ever so slightly and solidly planted on a rock. The beauty, power, and assurance of these figures, their connectedness, and united purpose preaches a message all by itself. It is a magnificent display of what God originally intended in the garden.

For me, Eve is the sista in "The Protectors of Freedom" figurine. As a human, she was created to do and be for Adam what no other in God's creation could be or do. When Eve and Adam are working and leading together, they are a physical mirror of the Holy Trinity at work.

HUMAN FALLENNESS: WHERE IT ALL WENT WRONG

It is not until the human revolt—the "original sin" or "fall"—is recorded in Genesis 3 that we see a disruption of God's original intent. The human revolt produced an awakening of sorts, meaning Adam and Eve had revelations and awareness about things that were unknown to them previously (Gen. 3:7). The revolt produced shame, so they began to hide, cover themselves, and attempt to isolate from each other and God (v. 7–8, 10). The revolt caused humans to blame others and God for the problems they created because of their own sin

(v. 12–13). God "The Just" provided consequences, and for the first time in Scripture we see that each human is required to give an account for their own sin, and how the consequence of our sin causes self-harm and negatively impacts our relationships with other humans and all of creation.

The human revolt was a cosmic shift. While Eve was always intended to "be fruitful and multiply," childbearing would now be severe (Gen. 3:16). The Bible records, "Your desire will be for your husband, and he will rule over you" (v. 16). The human revolt resulted in the brokenness of unity in diversity within the human relationship. The oneness between Adam and Eve was severed. Verse 16 is the first indicator of hierarchy within human relationships, and it is a consequence of the human revolt.

Adam, like Eve, was always created to work, but because of the human revolt, human work would now be difficult (Gen. 3:17–19). The human revolt has made creation sick, so the earth does not respond as it should. The human revolt means that Adam's effort does not always produce results. The function of Adam's hands does not always steward the earth or cause it to flourish as God originally intended. Because of the human revolt, eventually all things, including humans, will die. That's the bad news, and if there was nothing else to report, that would be the end of the story and the end for us.

However, I am writing to New Testament believers, and there is hope for us! There is a person and a power that we too often forget in our theological, intellectual, and social exercises. Instead of focusing on the redemptive hope available to us through Jesus, we have elected repeatedly to respond like Adam and Eve by replying poorly to revealed knowledge, by isolating ourselves from God and each other, by blaming others for our problems instead of taking ownership for our actions, and by choosing death instead of life. Adam and Eve sinned through the human revolt and reaped the negative consequences of their sin. But how much do we see similar consequences in the way we relate to one another today?

As leaders in the church and the world, we have accepted the human revolt as the status quo and have adapted our theology on the ways humans should function around the fall, instead of focusing on God's original intent and the redemptive hope that we have in Jesus. I've referred to this Christian practice as "curse modification." As I shared with my friend Suzanne Burden (and as she recorded in her book *Reclaiming Eve*), "rather than view this tragedy [of the human revolt] as a temporary state overruled by Jesus when he ushered in his new kingdom, much of the Christian church has used the curse as a rigid code of conduct for women."[16] The result is a warped human identity for both men and women. Too often men are placed in positions of power and domination, to play god in the lives of women; and women are often confused about whether they have any right or responsibility to lead or speak. "When we take a closer look at the claims of the gospel, we see that Jesus didn't come to uphold or modify the curse, but to *reverse* it ... Rather than upholding the world's model of sexism and discrimination, through Jesus we are to restore the alliance he intended for human beings in the first place."[17]

NEW HOPE: A REDEEMED VIEW OF WOMEN

We can choose to shift our thoughts and actions in regard to women. In fact, the introduction to Matthew's Gospel subtly invites us to consider another perspective. When presenting the lineage of the God-man, Jesus, Matthew includes the names of four women: Tamar, Rahab, Ruth, and Mary, the virgin mother of Jesus. He also lists another woman as "Uriah's wife." Four of these women could fall into the category of harlot, temptress, Jezebel, or what Timothy S. Laniak refers to as "tricksters." When presenting the role of tricksters in Israel's history, Laniak reveals that these women resort to using their sexuality, immodest dress, deception, or clever words as part of a ruse: "The reader is endeared to these characters because of their courage and cunning in that crisis moment we have called *kairos* ... They also very clearly serve the higher purposes of God's promises to Israel."[18]

When Matthew features these women in Jesus's lineage, he is turning our gaze to systemic issues, not individual actions. Tamar tricked her father-in-law into having sex with her to preserve *his* lineage (Gen. 38). Rahab was a harlot who helped the Israelite spies and saved her entire family (Josh. 2). Ruth was a widowed foreigner (coming from a people birthed out of an incestuous heritage; see Gen. 19:30–37), who was perceived as barren and was living her life as a poor beggar. She likely exposed her body as a sign of her vulnerable social condition to a righteous man who had the power to redeem her father-in-law's name (Ruth 3). Matthew does *not* characterize Bathsheba as the temptress or adulteress, as do too many sermons and commentaries authored by men. Instead, Matthew presents her as a person of honor; she is Uriah's wife, a victim of the king's abuse, power, lust, and possible rape. In providing this historical account of Jesus, it's as if Matthew is elevating our thoughts and inviting us to look at how Jesus redeems all things—including broken relationships and broken systems.

As a result of the human revolt, all these women lived in a broken, fallen, and patriarchal world. Because society is not equitable, "the trickster wins by using the informal, nonconventional strategies common to the disadvantaged. Theirs are guerrilla tactics."[19] This is not a justification, it is simply an acknowledgement that we must consider women's actions alongside the injustice, inequity, and systemic realities that put their backs against the wall. Ruth's actions led Boaz to praise her kindness (Ruth 3:10) and her new community, even in a culture of patriarchy, said that she was better to Naomi than seven sons (4:15); Judah said that Tamar was more righteous than he (Gen. 38:26); Rahab saved her entire family including her father and brothers (Josh. 6:17, 22–23); and Bathsheba became the mother of Israel's wisest king (1 Kings 1:11–48). So, we can acknowledge that, as a result of the human revolt, "the Bible's narratives are messy and multilayered, its pages replete with characters who trick men into sleeping with them, who disobey authority, who lie, and even who steal and yet are still called 'blessed' by God."[20] While it is easy to judge or blame,[21] it is harder for men to exercise their privilege by truly living as redeemed humans to right the wrongs of society. This is what Boaz does when he redeems Ruth and what Judah finally sees when he pardons Tamar. Throughout her book *Abuelita Faith*, theologian Kat Armas acknowledges the guerilla warfare tactics that women in a patriarchal society must adopt just to survive, and, like the Hebrew midwives and the women named in Jesus' lineage, they are often blessed by God for doing so. Armas writes, "Perhaps recognizing the complexity of the human experience within the stories of Scripture can shift how we see and engage with the other."[22]

Considering the systems that the human revolt has produced means confessing that "we all play a part in upholding it and are thus accountable."[23] Jesus' lineage, as presented by Matthew, reveals that even with the fallout and brokenness of our human revolt, there is an opportunity for male and female leadership and partnership when we consider the hope and redemption that Jesus offers. The single, childless, Son of God represents the epitome of manhood and leadership for all men, but how was it that this God-man came into the world?

When God invited Mary to participate in his redemptive story by birthing the Savior, her response was, "I am the Lord's servant ... May your word to me be fulfilled" (Luke 1:38). Mary chose to look ahead in hope for what God promised, even when her "yes" meant being considered a harlot or adulteress who committed a communal sin punishable by death. Yet, she swallowed her fears, and stood against the prevailing societal and religious standards. She practiced self-leadership and courageously said "yes" to God. Upon receiving God's revelation, her fiancé, Joseph, stood with her.

What might it look like today for women and men to respond to God's call and lead together?

REDEMPTION: THE SIGNIFICANCE OF JESUS' PERSONHOOD AND PRAYER

In a presentation to the Ohio Women's Rights Convention on May 28, 1851, Sojourner Truth invited the audience to change their thoughts about women: "Well, if a woman upset the world, do give her a chance to set it right side up again."[24] She continued, "And how came Jesus into the world? Through God who created him and woman who bore him. Man, where is your part? But the women are coming up blessed by God and a few of the men are coming up with them."[25]

Men must consider their part. Women are ready to come up. As I highlighted earlier, women are capable and looking for leadership opportunities. Furthermore, families and communities thrive when women around the world are provided with educational advantages, leadership roles, and entrepreneurial opportunities.[26] But unfortunately, in too many cases, men still hold the privilege that restricts the flourishing of women. "Man, where is your part?" This is my rallying call for men to come up with us.

While Jesus came through a sinful bloodline, he was not born of it. The only perfect and sinless human was born of the Spirit (Luke 1:35) for the purpose of redeeming all things God created (John 3:16). Redemption is "the process by which sinful humans are 'bought back' from the bondage of sin into relationship with God through grace by the 'payment' of Jesus' death."[27] Because of Christ's finished work, humans are no longer under the sinful bondage of their human revolt. We can live into Jesus' prayer and hopeful expectation for all believers:

> My prayer is not for them alone. I pray also for those who will believe in me through their message, that all of them may be one, Father, just as you are in me and I am in you. May they also be in us so that the world may believe that you have sent me. I have given them the glory that you gave me, that they may be one as we are one—I in them and you in me—so that they may be brought to complete unity. Then the world will know that you sent me and have loved them even as you have loved me.
>
> John 17:20–23

Jesus' prayer communicates his desire for humans: to become hopeful witnesses and proof of God's vision for shared leadership and unity, ministering to a world that is consumed by the human revolt, demonstrating the love that motivates us in this pursuit. Remembering God's original intent for humans, Jesus "compares his union with us to the perfect oneness that exists among the members of the Trinity ... his prayer here is that we might come to understand our unity with one another through our unity in him and he in us."[28] The impact of this commitment to oneness is spiritual and physical, forming our practices of leadership and human connection.

Professor and researcher Dr. Patricia S. Parker writes of two meaning-centered views of leadership: "The view that focuses on leadership as the management of meaning" and "the view that focuses on leadership as socially critical and focused on emancipation and change."[29] Redemptive leadership requires that humans stand firm in God's original intent as the *Blessed Alliance*—witnesses to the world for the glory of God. Redeemed women and men collaborate. As Author Sandra Maria Van Opstal says, "Collaboration requires sharing power, real power. It requires co-creation and co-decision making. Shared leadership invites us to empty ourselves of complete power or control. With words and actions it expresses 'I need you.' This is most clearly modeled in Christ's emptying himself of power and going to the cross (Phil 2:5–8)."[30]

Jesus' invitation is for women today. As an *ezer* and protector of this freedom that we have in Christ, my commitment to the brethren is that "I got your back. I will keep a lookout; stand watch. I will go to war. I will not cause friendly fire. I will fully commit to the mission that God has given us." Jesus' invitation for men is to consider "Where is your part?" and his challenge is for you to do your part. Be bold and courageous enough to go to war with me and our sisters until God's kingdom mission is complete. Women need you to mentor and sponsor. We need your trust and support. We need you to become partners who cultivate healthy, loving relationships as we lead together. We need you to have fierce conversations with male counterparts and hold each other accountable. We need you to listen to and learn from, preach and teach about, and read more women! We need you to remember God and our human revolt. We need you to repent and reverse your thoughts and actions, and to redeem all for the glory of God. We need you to do this, by the grace of God, because Jesus has made it possible and desires this work and faithful response from us all.

4

IN MEMORY OF HER

Anita Giardina Lee

is passionate to amplify and celebrate the voices of women in the church: past, present, and future. When she's not tending to her young family or working with the team at Boundless Enterprise, she is excitedly researching the legacy of discipleship women have in the history of Christianity and dreaming up ways we can be the church Jesus intended us to be.

"What women these Christians have!"[1] These words are attributed to fourth-century pagan philosopher Libanius. I agree.

Yet when we turn to the index section of a history of Christianity textbook, we may not find many women's names. This oversight misrepresents both their presence and influence. The passing on of the Christian faith is not limited to what has been recorded in textbooks; it is much broader, and women have played an important role.

What did Libanius know that somehow failed to adequately make it into our history textbooks, seminary classes, and Sunday morning dialogue some two thousand years later?

In her book *Cassandra Speaks: When Women Are the Storytellers, the Human Story Changes*, Elizabeth Lesser cites historian Sally Roesch Wagner's view that "History isn't what happened. It's who tells the story."[2] It is alarming to consider the extent to which Christian history has favored some types of storytellers over others and what we lack in not hearing from the rest. Perhaps the old adage that history favors the winner is telling of this reality: The "winners"—whether bound by a limited world view, ill intent, or anything in between—have written out the influence of women, in favor of centering their own influence, authority, and power. This is a sad but telling tale of how Christian history parallels the secular world where women's contributions have often been downplayed and overlooked. In the words of religion scholar Bernadette Brooten, "The lack of sources on women is part of the history of women."[3] As we piece together the lives and legacies of women disciples who have been influential in our history, yet are little known, we must consider why their stories have been lost and how we might learn from them today—learning both from their example and that we all benefit when women's stories are told.

WOMEN IN CHRISTIAN HISTORY

Despite what may be assumed from Jesus choosing twelve male disciples, women have been central to Christianity from its very beginning. The gospels give witness that women followed Jesus, traveled with him, and financed the ministries of Jesus and his disciples (Luke 8:1–3). In fact, women were the closest witnesses to the life, death, and resurrection of Jesus. The traditional accounts of Jesus' death often focus on Jesus' abandonment by his disciples the night of his crucifixion and fail to call attention to the fact that, as the four gospel accounts suggest, several of his female disciples stayed (Matt. 27:55–56, Mark 15:40–41, Luke 23:49, John 19:25–27). Not only did the women remain watching from a distance but, when three days had passed and the Sabbath was over, in their devotion, Mary Magdalene and other women returned to the tomb with spices to perform the sacred act of treating his body for burial (Matt. 28:1, Mark 16:1, Luke 24:1, John 20:1). As such, women were the first to whom Jesus appeared after his resurrection; and a woman (Mary Magdalene) was commissioned by Jesus to be the first to declare the good news of his resurrection, even sending her to go and tell the disciples (Matt. 28:7–8, Mark 16:7–8, Luke 24:9–12, John 20:17). Laboring alongside women in the ushering in of the kingdom of God did not seem to be a problem for Jesus—nor Paul, for that matter.[4]

In the early church, wherever Christianity spread, women were leaders of house churches.[5] Women listened to Jesus and applied his teaching, and though they may not have been present in the text when Jesus gave the instructions, "go and make disciples" (Matt. 28:18–20), they give us beautiful examples of what it can look like to follow Jesus and his teachings.

Second-century Greek philosopher Celsus (175–177) commented that Christianity was a religion of women, children, and slaves, attesting to the numbers of early Christian women.[6] In fact, women have historically made up most of the church.[7] In his *Testimonia*, Bishop Cyprian of Carthage (c.210–258) commented that "Christian maidens were very numerous," so much so that it was difficult to find Christian husbands for them all, which indicates a church disproportionately populated by women.[8] Many of our churches still share this reality today, although the alternatives to marriage are thankfully more plentiful.[9] Given the prominence of women in the early church, it seems strange that they have received less acclaim in our history books than men. And when we consider Jesus' interactions with women along with his breaking of gender stereotypes to promote the liberation and agency of women, this omission from history seems contrary to Jesus' mission.

In each of the four gospels, there is a report of a woman who anoints Jesus with expensive perfume (Matt. 26:6–13, Mark 14:3–9, Luke 7:36–50, John 12:1–8), with each account saying Jesus praises this woman. In Matthew and Mark, Jesus is reported to have said, "Truly I tell you, wherever the gospel is preached throughout the world, what she has done will also be told, in memory of her" (Matt. 26:13, Mark 14:9). This declaration from Jesus—that a woman's actions be remembered—is arguably the only example we have of Jesus specifying what is significant in our history of the faith. Perhaps we are missing the importance of women's stories being told when we fail to remember both this woman and the many women throughout history who have played vital roles in the furthering of the gospel.

FROM PRIVATE TO PUBLIC DOMAINS

A societal stereotype of the woman as the ruler of the household may have contributed to the legitimacy of women's leadership within early Christianity.[10] Culturally, female leadership made sense when women led in the home because it was their sphere of influence: the private domain. It was not until the mid-third century that conflict really began between the social structures surrounding women's roles and the freedom women found in Christianity.[11]

As scholar Karen Jo Torjesen explains:

> Greco-Roman society defined proper roles for men and women according to whether they were household (and thus private) functions or public functions. This system gave a great deal of power to women in the household but segregated them for public political life, since public space was male space. The role of teacher, for instance, was not restricted to one gender, but the social space in which teaching occurred was. A woman could teach in the privacy of her household but not in the public.[12]

As the formation of the early church took place within the private sphere, its authority structures followed suit.[13] This meant that women could play significant leadership roles within the early church. However, as the church relocated to more public spaces, some of the leadership roles of women in the church began to be restricted because they moved outside of the women's domain.

Paul recognized women's contributions in his letters—highlighting, addressing, and praising women whom he sometimes called his co-laborers in Christ (Rom. 16:1–7). We might ponder Paul's letters to Timothy and how they instruct men and women in the church today, but fail to broadly share in his exaltation of Lois and Eunice, Timothy's mother and grandmother who taught Timothy their sincere faith (2 Tim. 1:5). There is a significant disconnect between the use of Paul's teaching to silence women and the evidence found in his letters which mention women who are part of his ministry team. The most prominent of these women are Junia, Priscilla, Phoebe, and Lydia.

Junia

Paul hailed Junia as "foremost among the apostles" (Rom. 16:7). She traveled with her husband, Andronicus, teaching and preaching. The turmoil and riots that sometimes arose from Christian preaching resulted in the couple's imprisonment, which is where they met Paul.[14] His words of greetings in his letter to the Romans reflect his esteem for them: "Greet Andronicus and Junia, my fellow Jews who have been in prison with me. They are outstanding among the apostles, and they were in Christ before I was" (Rom. 16:7).

Junia was recognized as a church leader by church father John Chrysostom (c.347–407) who noted, "How great the wisdom of this woman must have been that she was even deemed worthy of the title of apostle."[15] Chrysostom's sermons encouraged the Christian women of Constantinople to imitate Junia and point to Junia's ongoing legacy of discipleship in the early church.[16]

Junia also became a controversial figure in the church. At some point in history, Junia's name was translated as a male name instead of female. Investigative journalist Rena Pederson spent months in Italy researching how Junia got "lost." She eventually discovered that a thirteenth-century archbishop, Giles of Bourges (1243–1316), appears to have been the culprit.[17] In Pederson's words on her discovery:

> Giles was the first scholar that can be found who referred to Andronicus and Junia in his commentaries on Romans as "honorable men." According to Bernadette Brooten, Giles noted that there were two variant readings of the second name in Romans 16:7: Juniam and Juliam. He preferred the reading "Juliam" and assumed it to be a male name since it referred to an apostle. Everyone before Giles had referred to the name as belonging to a woman. For centuries after Giles, the same person was referred to as a man. Then there was a period of confusion over the gender of the name that has continued until now.[18]

Giles may have been influenced by his contemporary, Pope Boniface VIII (1235–1303), who wanted nuns to be limited to their convents and believed that a woman could not rank as an apostle.[19] This sort of movement to limit women's roles in ministry contrasts what we see in Jesus' ministry.

Priscilla

Priscilla is mentioned in four books in the New Testament (Rom. 16:3; Acts 18:2, 18, 26; 1 Cor. 16:19; 2 Tim. 4:19). Priscilla was a well-educated woman who had been a member of a synagogue in Rome and was skilled in the interpretation of the Law.[20] She was a leader in the early Christian movement and was instrumental in having Paul's letters copied and dispersed.[21] Priscilla is a woman Paul celebrates as his co-worker (Rom. 16:3), a distinction she shares with men such as Timothy, Titus, Epaphroditus, and Philemon.[22] In the words of Paul:

> Greet Priscilla and Aquila, my co-workers in Christ Jesus. They risked their lives for me. Not only I but all the churches of the Gentiles are grateful to them. Greet also the church that meets at their house.
>
> ROM. 16:3–5

Priscilla helped start three house churches from scratch in three cities (Rome, Corinth, and Ephesus) at a time when a person could be flogged, stoned, expelled, or imprisoned for doing so.[23] Elsewhere in the Bible, Paul refers to Priscilla as someone who had earned his respect as a house church leader (1 Cor. 16:19) and as a teacher of men in her correction of Apollos (Acts 18:26).[24]

Phoebe

Phoebe is known to have been wealthy and generous in service. She delivered Paul's letter to the Romans, where Paul writes, "I commend to you our sister Phoebe, a deacon of the church in Cenchreae. I ask you to receive her in the Lord in a way worthy of his people and to give her any help she may need from you, for she has been the benefactor of many people, including me" (Rom. 16:1–2). Paul speaks highly of her as a leader and asks the Roman Christians to give her any help she needs; presumably to continue her work of sharing the gospel of Jesus Christ. It is possible that Phoebe was the bishop of the church in Cenchrea.[25]

Origen of Alexandria (c.184–253) makes a significant comment on Paul's words about Phoebe: "Women are to be considered ministers in the Church and … ought to be received in the ministry."[26] Despite often being demeaning in his assessment of women, Origen believed Phoebe had been officially ordained.[27] Origen's contemporary, Chrysostom, wrote: "You see that these were noble women [Junia and Phoebe], hindered in no way by their sex in the course of virtue, and this is as might be expected for in Christ Jesus, there is neither male nor female."[28] In this description, Chrysostom pushes the boundaries of tradition and describes these women in ways that move them outside of the cultural limitations of their gender in order to attribute virtue to them.

Scholar Elizabeth Gillan Muir depicts the difficulties the church has had in accurately presenting Phoebe's legacy as a witness to Christ:

> Phoebe was called a *diakonos* by Paul, a word which can be translated from the Greek as servant, helper, deacon, or minister. Often, Paul used it interchangeably with missionary or coworker for the same people. Generally when it referred to men, it was translated in Bibles as "minister," but when it referred to a woman such as Phoebe, it became downgraded to servant or helper.[29]

The history of the translation of Phoebe's descriptors reminds us that we are all biased interpreters and are often blinded to historical realities because of our preconceptions. Sadly, our blindness has meant that the legacy of these early women disciples has been less accessible to us for centuries.

Lydia of Thyatira

Many are familiar with Lydia. She is perhaps best known as the woman who sold purple cloth and supported Paul's ministry, but few would recognize her as the founder of the church in Europe.

We learn of Lydia in Acts 16. She was a businesswoman and networker originally from Thyatira, but her business selling purple cloth took her far and wide. When Lydia became a Christian, her household converted with her, which demonstrates her authority (Acts 16:15). Paul engaged women on questions of the interpretation of Scripture and spoke to them of the Messiah (Acts 16:11–15).[30] Lydia was the first woman to respond to his message.

Muir provides some helpful context in *A Women's History of the Christian Church*:

> Although she was one of the women participating in the reading and prayers, she was not a Jewish convert but a so called God-fearer—someone who worshiped in the Jewish community but had not taken on the full observance of the Law. Paul's teaching about a Jewish-Christian piety that reverenced Scripture but did not require an exact observance of the Law found in Lydia a ready convert.[31]

Lydia's prosperity made it possible for her to contribute to Paul's ministry by extending hospitality to him; he stayed in her home for some time.[32] From there, he carried out his ministry of teaching and preaching as newly converted Christians gathered to hear and discuss the new doctrines (Acts 16:40).[33] Since homes were the women's domain, Lydia would have been the leader. She and other women could legitimately teach and preach in that context. By starting the church in Philippi in her home and being Paul's first convert in Europe, Lydia could reasonably be called the mother of the church in Europe.[34]

OTHER MOTHERS

While some of the women of the early church, listed above, are at least enshrined in our history due to their mention in the New Testament, many other women who have had significant influence in the spread of the gospel have been forgotten. These women were often not only co-laborers for Christ but discipled the men we have remembered and call church fathers today.

Macrina (c.327-379)

The Cappadocian Mothers were lost within the pages of ancient manuscripts for generations until the last century when scholars began to uncover them.[35] While there are seven of the Cappadocian Mothers, Macrina the Younger is one of the better-known because of the writings of her brothers—church fathers Basil of Caesarea and Gregory of Nyssen.

While the Cappadocian "Fathers" have experienced notoriety and fame, it was often the "Mothers" who shaped their character.[36] This is especially evident in Macrina's case. Macrina encouraged her brothers to pursue a higher calling in how they lived their faith. Her brother Gregory of Nyssen writes about her influence on her brother Basil ("the Great"), who became the bishop of Caesarea Mazaca:

> Macrina's brother, the great Basil, returned after his long period of education, already a practiced rhetorician. He was puffed up beyond measure with the pride of oratory and looked down on the local dignitaries, excelling in his own estimation all the men of leading and position. Nevertheless Macrina took him in hand, and with such speed did she draw him also toward the mark of philosophy that he forsook the glories of this world and despised fame gained by speaking, and deserted it for this busy life where one toils with one's hands. His renunciation of property was complete, lest anything should impede the life of virtue. But, indeed, his life and the subsequent acts, by which he became renowned throughout the world and put into the shade all those who have won renown for their virtue, would need a long description and much time.[37]

Gregory presents Macrina as the teacher who helped Basil become the virtuous person he developed a reputation for being. He also describes Macrina as the model of *theosis*, as she spent her life preparing for the moment when she would become the bride of Christ.[38] Gregory of Nyssa is remembered as a figure of great importance in the history of Christian doctrine and the Nicene orthodoxy,[39] yet Macrina's life and legacy, for which her brother praised her so highly, was for the most part passed over in Christian history.

As a translator of *The Life of Saint Macrina* observes, "It is surprising that a story of antiquity, so charmingly told and full of human interest, should have attracted so little attention.[40] Macrina's legacy of discipleship was recognized and celebrated by her brothers and is valuable to the church today.

Monica (c.332-387)

Despite Augustine of Hippo (354–430) making some controversial comments on women, Monica, his mother, was commended by her son for her tireless commitment to prayer for his salvation, her bright mind for philosophical dialogue, and her maturity in faith.[41] Monica demonstrated a commitment to practical Christian living and directed her son through an informal Christian education at home.[42] Speaking of his conversion, Augustine wrote that he "believed with his mother"—suggesting her influence. He wrote, "Thus I at that time believed with my mother and the whole house, except my father; yet he did not overcome the influence of my mother's piety in me so as to prevent my believing in Christ, as he had not yet believed in Him."[43] Augustine's father was a pagan throughout his life, but he too converted to Christianity on his deathbed, which Augustine accounted to his mother's pious behavior, prayer, and relentless hope for his conversion.[44] Augustine's famous work, *Confessions*, which is often celebrated by the church, was written to help him deal with his grief over the death of his mother.

Furthermore, Augustine corresponded with a number of women, pastorally discipling them and encouraging them, showing that he believed women were spiritually capable and could respond to Christ, just as men could and just as his mother Monica had.[45] Monica's example of persistence in her faith for her child continues to bless the church today, both through the reach of her son's ministry, and as an example of a Christian mother prayerfully raising a wayward child.

This small sample of women is far from exhaustive. In the early church and beyond, women were living out their faith and discipling those around them, and their lives of devotion were recognized and admired by their peers and other witnesses. From Susanna Wesley to Sojourner Truth, Teresa of Ávila to Frances Joseph Gaudet, it is to the detriment of the church when we fail to accurately label and celebrate women in their equitable place in Christian history. These women are not significant only because of their influence on men; they were significant because of their response to Jesus, the way they witnessed to Jesus and their faith, and the way they inspired others to do the same.

CONCLUSION

To speak of the history of the church is to speak of women's contributions. Women who have served as witnesses pointing us to Jesus also point us to a history that is incomplete. From the foot of the cross to the declarations of the gospel that are still being made today, women have been willing participants in Jesus' call to go and make disciples of all nations (Matt. 28:18–20). While women's legacy of discipleship in church history continues to be uncovered, there remains much that is lost. It is appropriate to pause to consider how things may have been different had our Mothers' voices been listened to and remembered alongside the voices of the Fathers throughout history. Imagine the exponential impact it could have on our communities of faith to have a fuller range of voices speaking into the present—not just women, but minorities and marginalized voices, the full spectrum of people made in the image of God. Without examples to emulate and a shared history, women have had fewer opportunities to see themselves in the life and history of the church. The church can only benefit from women continuing to step forward and offer all of themselves in service to God as so many women in our faith history have demonstrated. Both men and women will benefit from knowing our fuller history and drawing upon the wisdom of our Mothers as well as our Fathers. Equity in this will require committed work on both sides.

We must now look to the future of Christianity to expand and delight in what is increasingly being uncovered: the history of our Mothers and the telling of women's stories.

ALL ARE MADE IN THE *IMAGO DEI*

For several hundred years, our English Bibles have translated terms for God with masculine pronouns where none were present in the original text. The terms "men" and "man" appear more than a thousand times in both the King James Version and pre-2011 versions of the New International Version translation of the New Testament where no such terms were used in the original Greek.[1]

And what are the consequences of this mistranslation? When we only refer to God as a man, it can be harder to perceive women as made in the image of God. As a result, we can devalue the contribution that women make, viewing them as "less than" the fullness of who God has made them to be. When our interpretation of Scripture misrepresents women, we can fail to include them in our view of leadership, acknowledge their contributions, or encourage them in their potential.

The authors in this section draw our attention to the biblical equality of males and females. Jo Saxton considers the significance of the term *ezer* (helper) and its implications for how today's women perceive their leadership roles. Bob Ekblad delves into our theological understanding of being made in God's image, unpacking the importance of how we view Genesis 1 and 2. Scot McKnight expounds the role of Mary, Jesus' mother, illuminating how The Magnificat is a prophetic foretelling of how she nurtured the Son of God and served his church. Addressing some of the difficult passages written by the apostle Paul, Aaron White draws on learnings from his colleague, theologian Lucy Peppiatt. And Mimi Haddad helpfully unpacks the conflicting positions of complementarians and egalitarians, considering the impact these views have on how women have been treated historically and how this has affected our Christian spaces today.

In order to reconcile a way forward together, we must realign our biblical understanding of who we are made to be. As Inés Velásquez-McBryde shares in her letter, in order to be reconciled, we must first remember the divine design in God's creation—to remember the true *imago Dei*.

5

WHAT I NEED YOU TO KNOW

Inés Velásquez-McBryde

is a pastor, preacher, reconciler, and speaker. She is co-lead pastor of The Church We Hope For, a multiethnic church planted in Pasadena, California during the 2020 pandemic. She is originally from Nicaragua. Inés earned her MDiv at Fuller Theological Seminary. Inés has been married to Rob for nineteen years and loves being a soccer mom to their son, Nash.

Re. Conciled.

Despite my work, reconciliation is a word I find hard to use. What do we mean by reconciliation? Is it possible? When were we ever *conciled*? To what are we trying to be reconciled? To whom? Female and male? Gentile and Jew? Slave and free? Poor and rich? Immigrant and citizen?

What we need is an honest and robust reconciliation, neither performative nor cheap.

Reconciliation for me is a return. We return to remember, repent, repair, and reimagine.

We must return to remember.

To remember the divine design in God's creation before un-creation. Before women and men started talking to serpents.

To remember when female and male were created equal before God and before each other.

To remember the female being an *ezer*—one equal in power and authority over all creation.

To remember the One who named the female an *ezer*, because who names and for what purpose is important. The male was neither consultant, creator, nor architect in her creation, for he was asleep. God mysteriously names her as God's own self. Seventeen times in the Old Testament God is referred to as *ezer*. God as *ezer* implies nothing weak nor inferior.

Psalm 121:1–2 says, "I lift up my eyes to the hills—from where will my *ezer* [help, rescue] come? My *ezer* comes from the LORD, who made heaven and earth" (NRSV). So it is with women—there is nothing weak or inferior about our sisters being *ezer*.

I say to my *hermanos* (brothers), *I'm not trying to take anything away from you. I simply come to reclaim what has been for me from the beginning.*

We must return to repent.

We must repent of the belief that the curse was a blessing. It was costly. It seeded a demon of domination of male over female. It birthed hostility, jealousy, violence, aggression, scarcity, subjugation, and dehumanization.

Under the curse, the ground and the serpent were cursed, but we act as if females were cursed. This was never God's intent for her.

The curse birthed even further death.

We must return to when Cain was his brother's keeper, not the first murderer among brothers. Now the blood of brothers and sisters cries out from the ground of boarding schools and borderlands.

We must return to repent of ways systemic racism has killed our indigenous sisters and brothers, our African-American sisters and brothers, our brown sisters and brothers, our Asian-American sisters and brothers ... I could go on and on about the curse having birthed un-creation, hostility, and hatred among and toward other marginalized groups cut by the -isms of empire.

The lie that justifies any injustice is that some bodies are worth less than others.

We must return to repair.

There is no honest reconciliation without repair and making amends. And before repair and trust can be actualized, forgiveness and repentance are required. In Christ, we are re-membered back together as he repairs that which has been dis-membered from God's own divine design.

Repair is possible because Christ came to heal the hostilities among enemies. Repair requires humility, vulnerability, and the willingness to put in the work. Repair requires a Zacchaeus mindset of returning that which was violently taken from individuals and communities. Jesus invites himself to dinner in your home as an invitation to consider repair.

And finally, we must return to reimagine.

Genesis 3 taught us that if you leave any of us alone for long, we are capable of talking to and entertaining the lies of serpents. Returning to a Genesis 1 creation narrative may be idealistic at best and naive at worst.

Instead of simply returning to what was and remaining, we must return in order to reimagine a new way forward for an honest and robust reconciliation. One that centers the margins and disrupts the narrative. One that is led by vital voices long-silenced. One that invites the poets, creatives, and artists to craft a new table of reconciliation—a table built with the wood from a blood-stained cross.

I refuse breadcrumb reconciliation. Christ has provided an abundant and bold reconciliation. The table he sets is a feast and all are invited. The last, the lost, the least, the lonely, and the left out have prime seats.

The church in North America is broken and divided, but the blood of Christ has not lost its power to heal and reconcile God's own people. Christ bears the scars of our broken bodies and has paid the price for an honest reconciliation. If it took his sacrifice on the cross for us to be reconciled to God, it's going to take our sacrifice to be reconciled to each other. May we hear the invitation to be reconciled to God, to be reconciled ourselves in our tender humanity, and to be reconciled to each other as we honor everyone's dignity.

6

WOMEN WERE MADE STRONG

Jo Saxton

is a speaker, podcaster, leadership coach, and author of numerous books. She is the founder of Ezer Collective—an initiative dedicated to investing in women leaders and equipping them to own their voice and boldly step into their calling. She also serves at Bethel University as the executive director of The 25, which focuses on emerging women leaders across industries as they launch their careers.

Born to Nigerian parents and raised in London, England, Jo now lives in Minneapolis with her husband and two daughters.

This chapter is adapted from a conversation between Jo Saxton, Danielle Strickland, and James Scholl on the *Right Side Up* podcast with Danielle Strickland and James Scholl, titled, "Women Were Made Strong w/ Jo Saxton."[1]

One theological insight has had a most profound impact on me in the last few years: God's description of women. And particularly, its contrast to the description of women I encountered in parts of contemporary Western Christian culture. This mind-blowing truth has somehow gotten lost in translation over the years and yet it has so many implications for a woman's potential, her purpose, and the negative reality of how the church hasn't received women in so many ways. For me, this has been a game-changing revelation. Once seen, things cannot be the same.

I've always believed in women in leadership. When I've looked at the Bible, I've always seen the Deborahs, the Priscillas, the Phoebes, and the Junias—the whole range. So, my understanding of God's description of women wasn't ever solely an equity thing. For me, it was also a theological thing.

When I went to university, I studied biblical languages. I was committed to looking at the Timothy and Corinthian passages to understand key verses in their context, to examine the syntax, and to explore what words like "authority" meant. So much can be lost in translation; I genuinely wanted to understand so I could accept the scriptural invitation to follow God's way. But I didn't study the Bible to work out what to say to people who disagreed with me! I mean, I figured we were human beings and we weren't all going to agree. "Proving something" wasn't on my mind.

It was years later, by which point I'd been leading and speaking for quite some time, when I gained a fresh perspective on what God was saying about women. It had been a long time since I had studied Hebrew actively, but I was reading Genesis and the creation accounts again. I was looking at how God created and everything's good: like the sun, moon, stars ... good, good, good, good. Wonderful. And then I got to Genesis 2:18 where it says, "I will make a helper suitable for him." As I looked at it in the Hebrew and saw the word "helper" translated as *ezer*, I thought, *Well, look at that!*

I emailed one of my Hebrew professors, and asked, "Hey, can we just talk about this word for a second? I know it's been years since we last talked, but can we just have a chat about the word *ezer* and what it actually meant in its original context?" This was because I knew the word "helper" usually carries connotations of "assisting." It's a common association that isn't even always pejorative—sometimes it's assisting in the sense of "you need some help"—but when I looked at the word *ezer* and realized it meant so many other things, I knew I had to share what I was learning.

Ezer means "to rescue, to save, and to be strong."[2] And talking with my Hebrew professor, he mentioned how there are one hundred references to the root of this word in the Old Testament and twenty-one instances of the identical word that we see in Genesis 2:18. Two times it's describing the woman, three times it refers to military aid, and sixteen times it's describing

God when he's helping his people in the context of delivering them from their enemies.

It often appears in parallel with words denoting strength and power. It was referring to one who had the resources to help. And then I remembered something else I'd read by author and theologian of Jewish heritage, Michele Guinness, who said that *ezer* is coupled with *kenegdo* as a verb as well as a noun, meaning to protect, surround, defend, and cherish.[3] She added *kenegdo* can be translated as "equal to stand boldly opposite."

I sat with that for about a month, thinking, *Hmm, that has implications, doesn't it?*

This newfound understanding of the word *ezer* enriched my understanding of being a woman made in God's image. In Genesis chapter one, it says, "Let us make humankind in our image, according to our likeness" (v. 26 NRSV). That's a powerful statement to all women about our worth and purpose: *You're made in God's image and likeness.* Then in Genesis 2, God specifically describes women with this amazing word *ezer*—a word that we see appear again and again in the Bible, often describing God himself.

We see how God—the helper God—is our refuge and our strength and our ever-present *help* in times of trouble (Psalm 46). When I look at the psalm that says, "where does my help [*ezer*] come from" (121:1) and other passages of Scripture that use the word *ezer*, I'm able to read that word understanding that this *helper* has the power and resources to help. They are a deliverer, mighty, loving, strong, powerful, engaged.

So, when God names women *ezer*, it's an exciting word to his image-bearers.

Danielle: How does this new understanding about women being an "ezer" change how women should see themselves in God's kingdom and in the world?

The reality is we don't rise beyond what we believe to be true about ourselves. One option we've purported as scriptural is to define women as made in the image of man, an option that is presented to people around the world as "biblical." But it's not. The biblical option that is faithful to the text is to see a woman as an *ezer*—someone who is designed "to rescue, to be strong, and to save." The fact is, we completely misdefine and redefine women in a way that isn't true to God's original design. Our belief is that humanity has a two-fold purpose: to know God, and to represent him in the world. We see this in Genesis 1, where Adam and Eve are commissioned to represent God (v. 28). What we don't see is a hierarchical view in this commission. In the following chapter, we see a definition of woman as *ezer*, but despite this term's full meaning, we've come to see her as the one who helps out, as a "could you just do the jobs I don't like doing" or "the things that your nature can cope with," rather than "all you have God-given potential and have been gifted to do."

The reality is that over the years I have seen women repackage themselves and take off the things that God put on them or apologize for being strong, as though their strength isn't feminine. I remember someone saying to me, "But aren't the women just more fragile than the guys?" That person clearly hasn't met any of the women in my family! But that question in itself is concerning when we think about how we can skew our understanding of God's intentions based on our cultural lens. When someone questions whether women can be strong, which women are they thinking of? Are they talking about a particular socioeconomic group? Are they talking about a particular ethnicity? Who *are* they talking about!? Because I'm left wondering, *Since when was strength a personality type anyway? Since when was it like extroversion or introversion?* We've added all these extracurriculars to the concept of strength and applied it to half the population.

In my own experience of dealing with this question, I remember wrestling and thinking, *God, you made me like this, right? I'm not pretending?* And yet, there was this feeling that if you want to settle down, you better "settle down"! You couldn't be an outspoken, strong woman and expect to find a husband or be accepted in a leadership role. And as a result, I would spend time trying to craft myself or morph into different ways that were more palatable. It was such a waste of my time and energy.

Our understanding of how God created women has implications for all of our lives. It comes in how we perpetuate the idea of marriage, or relationships, and in how we utilize (or don't utilize) our gifts and talents, our voice, and our place in society. It changes the kind of contribution we believe we can make. Do you get to be a leader if you're a "helper"? Do you get to dream? Do you get to have visionary thoughts or disruptive ideas that change the status quo?

And let me say this one more time: I'm happy to help and serve somebody else's vision. We're better together and we're designed for community! But that's not the point of what I'm saying. When we accept a limited interpretation of a woman as a helper instead of God's definition of *ezer*, it has many real-life implications.

When you're unable to be true to who you are, you end up trying to distort yourself into a package that is more palatable to your context. That even impacts the way you walk into conversations. Even more so, think about how that distortion affects the way you deal with threatening situations like a sexual predator, or how you deal with being manipulated in relationships, or how you negotiate pay at work—there are so many implications that impact women's lives.

Conversely, if you believe that you are made in the image of God and you are an *ezer* and that God designed you this way, you can believe that your gifts and your wiring are not a concession or an accident. They're not an aberration, but God's actual intention. God made you like this. That is incredibly liberating at the core, because you no longer have to approach every situation with a strategy—you've got nothing to prove and nothing to defend.

So much has been stolen. Because somewhere along the line, it became a battle that people had to fight. But maybe it's a fight that God never set us up to have because he knew we were insecure about it. Maybe God thought, *Let me be super clear about the design of women from the very beginning!* And then we simply missed it?

The result is everybody suffers. Everybody suffers. The ramifications are not just about women belittling themselves and settling for less. It's also about our culture. It's our limited understanding of what's feminine, and about the way we value what we perceive as masculine, in terms of giftings and talents.

Maybe much of what we're seeing as a crisis of current church leadership isn't just about leaders' behavior but about their deeply rooted beliefs. About all of our deeply rooted beliefs.

Danielle: How did this discovery impact you personally?

I think *ezer* has settled a few things in my character. Sometimes people would say I had more masculine traits because of being strong. And I thought, *No, this is just what femininity looks like. Right?* It was weird, because the initial response from me when I discovered the meaning of *ezer* was peace. Perhaps because naming truth is powerful in its effect on our spirits. I'm Nigerian by heritage and naming is a powerful part of not just Nigerian culture, but many cultures. When you give a name, you are telling someone about their story, their history, their potential, their purpose. We see this throughout Scripture—when God is giving names to people, their naming is definitive. Discovering God's naming of me as an *ezer* felt very definitive. I thought, *Wow, this is actually who I am. And this is good.*

There have been years of people hoping ..., "Could you just be a little less Black? Could you just be a little less woman, a little less emotional ... a little less of this, a little more that. And oh, we love you. But if you could just do this ...."

Now I realize that when I do all of those things, when I try to be what others want and expect, I'm being made in their image. *I'm not living as God's creation anymore; I'm your creation now. A creation that makes me feel palatable to you.* And so, this initial revelation of the word *ezer* and its implications in my life and heart and mind was peace.

I just sat with it by myself for a little while and thought "Maybe I could just be me." My husband said, "That sounds good to me. This sounds awesome. Do I get my wife back? That sounds brilliant." Each of us wins when we fully embrace who God made us to be.

Danielle: You ended up starting the Ezer Collective and calling women to be part of rising up to their true identity—living out their callings and giftings. How did that come about?

I think I probably saw the first ramifications outside of my own experience when I began to share it with other women, and say, "This is who God says we are!" And the amount of people who would just break down into tears. Or the number of women who would say, "I have been told I am too much. I have been told I am not enough."

What I saw when I spoke about these things to women was liberation. And it wasn't just the liberation of the women who were seen as strong—it was also the liberation of the women who were seen as gentle and tender. It was liberation for everybody because they were made in God's image. And that meant there was room for all of them to be themselves. They didn't have to hide anymore.

It was disruptive in the best way and it led to women responding to that liberation. It was like this army rising. Finally, after years of women being named in so many other ways, they were experiencing those chains breaking.

And I think the reason why I wanted to gather those women together was because of what I'd noticed during most of my life, for much of my leadership, working with men. When I've been speaking, leading in nonprofits and churches, what I noticed was even in the most welcoming spaces, women would edit themselves. They would shrink a little and apologize a lot.

I also saw the habitual things: the guy recommending another guy because that's who he knows, because it's all about relationship (but not having dealt with the things that actually prevent them knowing any women). You see the perpetual things.

So, I started Ezer Collective. I knew there were *ezers* out there doing stuff and I wanted to go and find out who they were, what they were doing, what they weren't doing, and what they were called to do in every context. So, I started. When I attended conferences I'd have conversations with women during the break (in bathrooms!). They'd be in tears, breaking down because of something they've been named, or how a set of circumstances had named them. Whether it was abuse or sexual harassment (including in church) or "advice" like, "You'd be really gifted and you'd be able to do more if you lost weight," and so many other things we don't have time to say. But in my conversations I began to see these women throwing off those old labels and instead say, "You mean, I'm okay? You mean, if God calls me *ezer*, I'm okay? Wow. If that word appears again and again through Scripture, and he's doing all these things, I'm okay."

You're more than okay. We don't have to tolerate this. You don't have to minimize yourself to walk into a room, because you are fearfully and wonderfully made. And that must count for something.

When I started the Ezer Collective, I wanted to get those women in a space. One of the things we do at the beginning of every gathering is to get everybody (rather than me) to introduce themselves. I mean, if you're the host of something—they know you. But I get every woman (maybe sixty to eighty) to stand up, say their name, and what they do.

The feedback is always overwhelming. Women share how just being in a room and hearing other women call themselves leaders just wrecks them. They see women of every ethnicity call themselves a leader—to see Asian women, Latina women, indigenous women, Black women, immigrant women stand up and say, "This is my name, this is where I'm from, this is what I lead," is a chain-breaking moment. It is so powerful to see.

Then we commission them back into their spaces where they're working with an understanding that they don't have to edit themselves because they are not the only one. There are entire movements, all around the world, of women who are doing what they're doing. Yes. Building businesses, leading corporations, launching non-profits, leading churches, sparking movements, investing in people. And we do it from a place of God-given identity and commission, not from or for anything else.

This is just the beginning of what *ezer* means. And it's liberating for all.

7

GOD IS NOT A MAN

Bob Ekblad

is co-founder, along with his wife Gracie, of Tierra Nueva and The People's Seminary in Burlington, Washington. He holds a ThD in Old Testament from the Institut Protestant de Théologie in Montpellier, France. He pastors at Tierra Nueva, offering training around the world and online through The People's Seminary (www.peoplesseminary.org). He is the author of *Reading the Bible with the Damned, A New Christian Manifesto: Pledging Allegiance to the Kingdom of God, The Beautiful Gate: Enter Jesus' Global Liberation Movement, Guerrilla Gospel: Reading the Bible for Liberation in the Power of the Spirit*, and the *Guerrilla Bible Studies* series.

The assumption that God is a man—specifically a cis-gendered, white male—has been pervasive in Western society and around the world. However, Scripture offers a far more complex picture, presenting God using language that includes both male and female, while also transcending biological sex or gender stereotypes.

Western society's depiction of God as a European male is present everywhere in European Renaissance art. Michelangelo's famous painting on the Sistine Chapel ceiling (1508–1512) portrays God the Father as a gray-bearded white man, lying on his side, arm and index finger extended, touching a white

European Adam.[1] God's widespread depiction as a regal, male, white, European sovereign during the centuries of European colonialism and Western imperialism has caused extreme harm, associating God with the dominant gender, race, and systems of oppression.

Western theology's presentation of God as hyper-sovereign, governing the world's affairs like a micromanager, has further contributed to the mistaken association of God's will and the status quo. God's will has in this way been associated with systems of domination, including male domination over female.

Ordinary readers can easily get the mistaken impression that God is male and prefers males because most Scripture translations use masculine pronouns for God and human beings, Jesus is male, and Jesus called twelve male disciples.

To correct our mistaken view that God is a man, we need to look first at Genesis 1:26–27 and Genesis 2, to put divine and human identity in biblical perspective. Then we need to examine God's invisibility and the prohibition of images and idols, the use of diverse anthropomorphisms for God, and God as a father distinct from a biological mother or father. Finally, we need to see how Jesus is the visible image of the invisible God and examine Jesus' special commissioning of women to direct disciples to the maternal Father.

RECONSIDERING GENESIS 1–2

Genesis 1:26–27 reads: "Then God said, 'Let Us make mankind [*humankind*] in Our image, according to Our likeness; and let them rule over the fish of the sea and over the birds of the sky and over the livestock and over all the earth, and over every crawling thing that crawls on the earth.' So God created man in His own image, in the image of God He created him; male and female He created them."†

Scripture identifies God using the Hebrew word *Elohim*, the common term for God which is the plural of the masculine Hebrew noun *El*. God speaks using the first-person plural: "Let Us make ... in Our image, according to Our likeness." Even the briefest summary of the diverse interpretations of this expression is beyond the scope of this chapter. Suffice it to say that God is first presented in Genesis 1:26 as plural[2] and humans are referred to as made in God's "image" and "likeness." Then, in Genesis 1:27, God is referred to as One, or in the third-person singular, and humans are created "in His own image."

---

† All verses in this chapter are from the New Revised Standard Version (NRSV), unless otherwise specified.

Immediately following this, the human is made in this singular God's image, with the further specification "male and female He created them."

The plurality of male and female could be read as both in alignment with *Elohim*'s first-person plural "let Us … Our image" and with God and the human's singularity as God vis-à-vis the singular "man." Here however it's essential to note that the translation of "man" for the underlying Hebrew *adam* is misleading, giving the impression in Bible translations in many languages that the singular human is a biological male, rather than a description of a human who includes male and female.

God Creates Humans

The term *adam* should not be translated as the proper name of the male "Adam," nor "man" for the following reasons. First, *adam* is mostly preceded by the definite article in Hebrew in Genesis 1–4, which only consistently disappears in the narrative. Then *adam* becomes "Adam" in Genesis 4:26, possibly linked to people beginning to call on God using God's proper name YHWH,[3] the Lord.[4] So, in Genesis 1:26 and following, rather than using the gender-specific term "man," it is more accurate to use the non-gendered term "human"[5] as the best translation, as justified by Robert Alter in his translation of Genesis:

> A human. The term *adam*, afterward consistently with a definite article, which
> is used both here and in the second account of the origins of humankind, is
> a generic term for human beings, not a proper noun. It also does not auto-
> matically suggest maleness, especially not without the prefix *ben*, "son of,"
> and so the traditional rendering "man" is misleading, and an exclusively male
> *adam* would make nonsense of the last clause of verse 27 [male and female he
> created them].[6]

Furthermore, as Alter notes, the masculine pronoun "him" commonly used to reference the human in most translations is misleading, reinforcing the reduction of the first human to a biological male.[7]

Secondly, *adam* is directly associated with the Hebrew term *adamah*[8] meaning soil, ground, or earth—from which the Lord forms the human in Genesis 2:7 "of dust from the ground." This supports Phyllis Trible's compelling translation "earth creature."[9] Translating *adam* as "human" or "human being" rather than man is especially important both when we consider the meaning of humans being made in God's image, and in the fashioning of the woman as a face-to-face counterpart to the man in Genesis 2:22.

Female and Male Reflecting God

Only human beings are made in God's image and likeness. Inanimate creation is not made in God's image and likeness. Neither are the fish, birds, cattle, creeping things, or beasts of the field. Rather, each are created "according to their kind."

Humans are not mentioned as reproducing "according to their kind," in keeping with the formula used for non-humans. Rather, they are associated with God directly, almost like they are made according to God's "kind."

At the same time, in Genesis 1:27, God states that God created the human in God's image, male and female God created them, which fits the pattern of vegetation and animals designed to self-propagate. That humans are identified using the Hebrew terms for biological male (*zakar*) and biological female (*neqebah*)[10] makes procreation possible. This also suggests that God's image is not solely "male" nor "female," as God's image includes both biological male and female human beings.

In Genesis 1:28, God blessed and spoke to the biological male and female humans together, saying: "Be fruitful and multiply, and fill the earth, and subdue it; and rule over the fish of the sea and over the birds of the sky and over every living thing that moves on the earth."

Interestingly, in the Septuagint version of this text (which is the Greek Old Testament), the Hebrew terms for "be fruitful" and "multiply" are matched with Greek verbs that are never used for biological procreation in the Greek New Testament. This removes biological reproduction as the primary role for females or males, opening the way for single or celibate people to be able to obey these commands without having biological children.

The Hebrew verb *para*—"to be fruitful"—is matched with the Greek verb *auxano*, meaning "to increase, to grow, to spread, to extend."[11] This verb is used in the New Testament in Jesus' parable of the Sower, in the metaphor of the seed that falls on the good soil, that grew up and increased, symbolizing the impact of God's Word (Mark 4:8). It is also used to describe Jesus increasing in wisdom (Luke 2:40) and in John the Baptist's statement, "He must increase, but I must decrease" (John 3:30). The Word of God is described as spreading (Acts 6:7; 12:24; 19:20; Col. 1:6).[12]

The Hebrew term for multiply, *rabbah*, is matched in the Septuagint with *plethuno,* meaning "to grow, to increase greatly, to multiply" and is used to refer to the increase.[13] In the New Testament, this term never signifies procreation, but is associated with the number of disciples "increasing" (Acts 6:1, 7). The church increased (Acts 9:31), as did the Word of God (Acts 12:24), the harvest of righteousness (2 Cor. 9:10), grace and peace (1 Pet. 1:2), and mercy and peace (Jude 2).

The New Testament's appropriation of Genesis 1:28 highlights the movement of the kingdom of God through the agency of the disciples' ministry in the world, rather than through multiplying God's people through procreation!

More Than a Helper

That human beings, male and female, are created in God's image on the sixth day, after God has created the world, and that they are given these five commands, suggests that God deliberately chooses to be represented by both sexes, whom God has put over the entire non-human creation. Psalm 8, which likely precedes Genesis 1 with its language of humans made "a little lower than God," (v. 5) rather than in God's image, presents the human as "crowned with glory and honor" (NIV) with all things being placed under humanity's feet. This is well supported by contemporary scholarship. Mark S. Smith refers to a stela (or monument) of a king discovered at Tel Dan with Aramaic inscriptions of the terms *demuth* and *selem* ("image" and "likeness"), for the king's image. He writes:

> Genesis 1:26–27 may have derived its language of image and likeness notion from a similar notion of statuary by employing terminology that both bears an official's image and serves to represent an official's presence in a given place. To judge how these terms are employed, human dominion in the form of rule and service in a particular location is how the human person is seen as in the image and likeness of God. This idea of rule is also suggested by God's own words in verse 26, that precede the act of creating humanity. "Let us make the human in our image, according to our likeness, so that they might rule."[14]

The story of the Lord God forming the human in Genesis 2 further fills out this picture of how male and female were to rule together.[15] The Lord God forms the human being (*adam*) from the ground, breathes into its nostrils the breath of life and places it in the garden to serve and to guard. The Lord God states: "It is not good for [the human] to be alone; I will make him a helper suitable for him" (Gen. 2:18).

The Lord God forms all the animals, bringing them to the human. After no "helper suitable for him" is found among the animals (2:20), the narrator describes God's fashioning of woman (vv. 20–21). The language of our English translations suggests that she is made as man's subordinate to serve his needs. Here we must look carefully at both the language used and the reasons why an animal could not serve as a human's counterpart.

First, the underlying Hebrew term often translated "suitable," *nagad*, includes the primary meanings "in front of, opposite to, in sight of, before." The preposition *kaph* (meaning "as, like, or corresponding to") preceding *nagad*, followed by the third person masculine pronoun, renders the translation "a helper as before him," or "a helper like his opposite," or even "a helper like its opposite,"[16] a helper "who corresponded to him" (NET),[17] or the Septuagint's "a helper like him."[18]

Second, the meaning of the term "helper" must be interpreted in the larger context of the Old Testament. Phyllis Trible also rightly critiques the language commonly used in English translations of this text:

Traditionally translated "helper," (*ezer*) a translation that is totally misleading because the English word helper suggests an assistant, a subordinate, indeed, an inferior, while the Hebrew word "ezer" carries no such connotation.[19]

Ezer characterizes deity. God is the helper of Israel. As helper, Yahweh creates and saves. Thus "ēzer is a relational term; it designates a beneficial relationship; and it pertains to God, people, and animals. By itself the word does not specify positions within relationships; more particularly, it does not imply inferiority."[20]

In fact, the Hebrew word *ezer* is most often associated with God in the following Old Testament Scriptures, and one of the strongest identifications of God with the female:[21]

The God of my father was my help (*ezer*), and saved me from the sword of Pharaoh.

EXODUS 18:4

Blessed are you, Israel; Who is like you, a people saved by the LORD, the shield of your help (*ezer*), and He who is the sword of your majesty! So your enemies will cringe before you, and you will trample on their high places.

DEUTERONOMY 33:29

Do not fear, for I am with you; Do not be afraid, for I am your God. I will
strengthen you, I will also help (*ezer*) you, I will also uphold you with My
righteous right hand.

Isaiah 41:10

For I am the Lord your God who takes hold of your right hand, who says to
you, "Do not fear, I will help (*ezer*) you."

Isaiah 41:13

This is what the Lord says, *He* who made you
And formed you from the womb, who will help (*ezer*) you:
"Do not fear, Jacob My servant."

Isaiah 44:2

Hear, Lord, and be gracious to me;
Lord, be my helper (*ezer*).

Psalm 30:10

Our soul waits for the Lord;
He is our help (*ezer*) and our shield.

Psalm 33:20

The New Testament uses the Septuagint's term for helper, *boethos*, to designate
the Lord as helper (Heb. 13:6).

The Lord God's word that it is "not good for the human to be alone" could
not be remedied by an animal helper for the following reasons. Animals are not
made in the image and likeness of God and cannot partner with the human to
"be fruitful and multiply, fill the earth and subdue it." Since no animal is the
human's equal, it cannot be "a helper" as coequal—which is "not good." Only
one in "image and likeness" can be alongside as a helper companion.

The narrator of Genesis 2 suggests that the human is given choice regarding
its helper but cannot find one from among the animals formed by God. In fact,
the human does not choose its helper at all.

God causes the human to fall into a deep sleep, and fashions a woman from
out of the human's side as a distinct act of creation. The Lord brings her to the
human who identifies her as "bone of my bones, and flesh of my flesh; She shall
be called 'woman,' because she was taken out of man" (Gen. 2:23). The female
(*isha*) is mentioned before the now-differentiated male (*ish*).[22] Phyllis Trible
writes:

> But no ambiguity clouds the words *isha* and *ish*. One is female, the other male. Their creation is simultaneous, not sequential. One does not precede the other, even though the timeline of this introduces the woman first (2:22). Moreover, one is not the opposite of the other. In the very act of distinguishing female and male, the earth creature describes her as "bone of my bones and flesh of my flesh" (2:23). These words speak unity, solidarity, mutuality, and equality. Accordingly, in this poem the man does not depict himself as either prior to or superior to the woman.[23]

The creation of woman, as a helper who corresponds to the now differentiated man, yet is "before," "opposite," or "in the face of" the man, as God's image bearer, establishes one of the strongest identifications of God with females in Scripture.

The Lord's fashioning of the *isha* (female/woman) as equal counterpart to the *ish* (male/man) in Genesis 2:21–22, with the beautiful image "bone of my bone and flesh of my flesh" (2:23), seems almost immediately threatened. The Lord brings the *isha* to the *ha adam*, and the *ha adam* calls her (but doesn't name her) *isha*. Might this suggest that it remains possible for the *ha adam* (human) to still function as "alone," which we remember is "not good"? The text stresses here that *ish* (male/man) is to leave his father and mother and cleave to his *isha* (female/woman), "and they shall become one flesh" (2:24), "both naked and unashamed"— suggesting a deliberate process of becoming that must be intentional.

The Hebrew text mentions next that the serpent approaches and speaks falsely of God to the woman, though her husband is beside her (3:6). By submitting to the serpent's deceit, neither she nor the two of them together "rule over … every crawling thing," as God commands both to do in Genesis 1:26, 28. The immediate consequence is that their eyes "were opened, and they knew that they were naked" (3:7), resulting in an end to their one-flesh union, free of all shame. The man blames YHWH for giving him the *isha*, and he blames the woman. The resulting consequence for the woman of giving the fruit to her *ish* (3:12) is that "your desire will be for your husband, and he shall rule over you" (3:16). Male domination is not part of the created order, but a direct consequence of estrangement from God. YHWH confronts Adam in Genesis 3:17 for listening to his *isha* (wife/woman) over and above God's earlier command to "not eat," *not* for listening to her as his God-given counterpart! The *ha adam* calls the woman Eve at this point, linking this action to his earlier naming of the animals as their superior (2:19–20). It is the *ha adam*, with no mention of the *ish*, that is driven out of the garden (3:22–24) to cultivate the ground from which he was taken—suggesting a return to the starting point, from which there remains a new possibility of re-entry through being formed "from the dust," breathed into, placed in the garden, and finding himself once again before the choice of listening to YHWH, and *ish* and *isha* being before each other in God-ordained unity.

GOD'S INVISIBILITY AND GENDERED IMAGERY

God's identifications with humans does not mean that, as interpreters, we should project back onto God either an androgenous or a human female or male identity, which would go beyond the text. Scripture declares that God does not have a terrestrial form but is invisible. Yet Scripture uses terminology that is both male and female to describe God, most notably "Father." Let's look first at Scriptures identifying God as "other" (invisible and even transcendent), before looking at female and male imagery.

Moses reminds the Israelites that they could see the mountain blazing and hear God's voice, but they saw no form that was God's (Deut. 4:10–12). The New Testament affirms this, with key texts like 1 Timothy 6:15–16:

> He who is the blessed and only Sovereign, the King of kings and Lord of lords, who alone possesses immortality and dwells in unapproachable light, whom no one has seen or can see.

The first commandment expressly prohibits people from identifying God with anything in creation:

> You shall have no other gods before Me. You shall not make for yourself an idol, or any likeness of what is in heaven above or on the earth beneath or in the water under the earth.
>
> EXODUS 20:3–4

This would seem to include a prohibition of making an idol in the likeness of humans. Yet it also represents a refusal of anything else taking the place of humans as God's image bearers, established in Genesis 1 and 5.

Deuteronomy 4:15–19 expressly prohibits identifying God as a male or female, or with anything in the created world:

> So be very careful yourselves, since you did not see any form on the day the LORD spoke to you at Horeb from the midst of the fire, so that you do not

act corruptly and make a carved image for yourselves in the form of any figure, a representation of male or female, a representation of any animal that is on the earth, a representation of any winged bird that flies in the sky, a representation of anything that crawls on the ground, *or* a representation of any fish that is in the water below the earth. And *be careful* not to raise your eyes to heaven and look at the sun, the moon, and the stars, all the heavenly lights, and *allow yourself* to be drawn away and worship them and serve them, *things* which the LORD your God has allotted to all the peoples under the whole heaven.

The Apostle Paul draws from this prohibition to indict humans in Romans 1:22–23:

Claiming to be wise, they became fools, and they exchanged the glory of the incorruptible God for an image in the form of corruptible mankind, of birds, four-footed animals, and crawling creatures.

The prophet Isaiah asks: "To whom then will you liken God? Or what likeness will you compare with Him" (Isa. 40:18)?

There are Scriptures that clearly state that God is not a man, most notably Numbers 23:19:

God is not a man, that He would lie, nor a son of man, that He would change His mind; has He said, and will He not do it? Or has He spoken, and will He not make it good?

Diverse Anthropomorphisms: Human Language for God

Although God is invisible and we are prohibited from reducing God into images to worship, Scripture regularly uses both non-gendered and gender-specific human imagery (often referred to as anthropomorphisms) for God.

God is described as having a face (Lev. 20:6; Num. 6:25–26), eyes (Ps. 34:15; Deut. 11:12), ears (2 Kings 19:16; Neh. 1:6), hands (Exod. 7:5; Isa. 23:11), arms (Ps. 89:10; Deut. 4:34; 5:15), and feet (Isa. 66:1).

A man wrestles with Jacob at the Jabbok, who he identifies as God. "I have seen God face to face, yet my life has been spared" (Gen. 32:30).

God is described using non-gendered parental imagery (Hos. 11:3–4), but also overtly feminine or maternal imagery:

As one whom his mother comforts, so I will comfort you; And you will be comforted in Jerusalem.

ISAIAH 66:13

God's name is described as *El Shaddai* (or God Almighty), which literally signifies the two-breasted God.[24]

God is presented in Scripture as merciful, using a Hebrew term, *rehem*, meaning "womb." Maternal imagery for God occurs in many places.

God is like a bear robbed of her cubs (Hos. 13:8), a mother eagle hovering over her young and carrying them on her wings (Deut. 32:11–12). God is like a woman in labor (Isa. 42:14) and a mother giving birth (Deut. 32:18):

Behold, as the eyes of servants *look* to the hand of their master, as the eyes of a female servant to the hand of her mistress, so our eyes *look* to the LORD our God.

PSALM 123:2

In the New Testament Jesus himself describes God as a woman who looks for her lost coin until she finds it (Luke 15:8–10) and compares himself to a mother hen:

Jerusalem, Jerusalem, who kills the prophets and stones those who are sent to her! How often I wanted to gather your children together, the way a hen gathers her chicks under her wings, and you were unwilling.

MATTHEW 23:37, (SEE ALSO LUKE 13:34)

God as Neither Biological Mother nor Father

If God is anthropomorphized with both gendered and non-gendered imagery, then why is God identified throughout Scripture as Father, as in Isaiah 63:16?

For You are our Father, though Abraham does not know us and Israel does not recognize us. You, LORD, are our Father, Our Redeemer from ancient times is Your name.

God presents himself as a parent who raises children (Isa. 1:2) and is depicted as a father to the fatherless (Ps. 68:5–6), who adopts the abandoned (Ps. 27:10). God is a Father who forgives (Ps. 103:8, 12–13), who tenderly loves his children:

"Is Ephraim My dear son? Is he a delightful child? Indeed, as often as I have spoken against him, I certainly *still* remember him; therefore My heart yearns for him; I will certainly have mercy on him," declares the LORD.

JEREMIAH 31:20

In elaborate detail, Jesus presents God as a Father in the Sermon on the Mount—who loves his enemies (Matt. 5:44–45), knows what we need before we ask (Matt. 6:8), feeds the birds (Matt. 6:26), and clothes the fields with flowers (Matt. 6:28–29), how much more us (Matt. 6:30)! God gives good gifts to his children (Matt. 7:11). Elsewhere in the New Testament, God is described as a Father who comforts (2 Cor. 1:3), who offers to be a Father to us (2 Cor. 6:17–18).

God's fatherhood, however, never associates God directly with a biological male, but more accurately, as a motherly father who behaves in ways that are distinct from and go beyond even the best human fathers or mothers, who will always fall short.

God is presented as a heavenly Father distinct from our biological fathers, yet God is not overtly called "Mother" for the following possible reason. Since every human originates in the body of a female mother and begins in a state of physical attachment, separation is required for healthy human development. As we know from attachment theory, the health of mother-infant attachment varies widely, with "secure" attachment being the ideal originating state, and anxious, avoidant, disorganized, and other attachments being common along a wide spectrum.[25] The biological or surrogate father lacks the bodily maternal attachment and is outside the natural mother-child dyad. According to Lacanian psychoanalysis,[26] the role of the healthy mother includes desiring outside the mother-child dyad, which effectively orients the infant outward, towards whomever occupies the "place of the father." The father then is positioned to disrupt the union between the mother and the child. This helps the infant begin to develop a healthy sense of separateness, allowing for psychological and spiritual maturation.

A healthy father role includes providing security, provision, love, and nurture, so the child can naturally differentiate, separating from the mother and family to become a secure, healthy, independent adult. An unhealthy, violent, or absent father creates deep insecurity in a child's life, making it more difficult for the child to perceive God as a good and loving Father.

Scripture appears to recognize the limits of human fathers and mothers, in texts like Isaiah 49:15:

Can a woman forget her nursing child and have no compassion on the son of her womb? Even these may forget, but I will not forget you.

Here, the healthy mother is depicted as not forgetting and as having compassion on her nursing child, before being described as capable of forgetting. In contrast, God goes beyond even the ideal mother, never forgetting.

God can be said to identify as a maternal Father, offering comfort to a weaned child, similar but distinct from its mother:

> I have certainly soothed and quieted my soul; like a weaned child resting against his mother, my soul within me is like a weaned child.
>
> PSALM 131:2

In Psalm 22:9–10, God is described as a midwife, assisting in the psalmist's birth but also being cast upon as a God that is other than the biological mother:

> Yet You are He who brought me forth from the womb; You made me trust *when* upon my mother's breasts. I was cast upon You from birth; You have been my God from my mother's womb.

Jesus tells Nicodemus that his biological birth must be over-ridden by being born again or "born from above" if he is to see the kingdom of God. This reaffirms what is written earlier in John 1:12–13 about a new-birth identity and authority that comes when we receive Jesus:

> But as many as received Him, to them He gave the right to become children of God, to those who believe in His name, who were born, not of blood, nor of the will of the flesh, nor of the will of man, but of God.

While not minimizing the importance of biological mothers, God takes on the role of our spiritual Father to transition us from our innate attachment to our biological birth to our spiritual rebirth.

JESUS REVEALS THE MATERNAL FATHER AND COMMISSIONS WOMEN

In the New Testament, God is presented as invisible, as in John 4:24, "God is spirit, and those who worship Him must worship in spirit and truth." Jesus is presented as the most visible representation of God, as in John 1:18, "No one has seen God at any time; God the only *Son*, who is in the arms of the Father, He has explained *Him*."

Jesus is presented throughout the New Testament as the image of God, most notably in Colossians 1:15, "He is the image of the invisible God, the firstborn of all creation." Jesus reveals the Father, as expressed throughout the New Testament:

"I and the Father are one."

JOHN 10:30

I am the way, and the truth, and the life; no one comes to the Father except through Me. If you had known Me, you would have known My Father also; from now on you know Him, and have seen Him.

Philip said to Him, "Lord, show us the Father, and it is enough for us." Jesus said to him, "Have I been with you for so long a time, and *yet* you have not come to know Me, Philip? The one who has seen Me has seen the Father; how *can* you say, 'Show us the Father'? Do you not believe that I am in the Father, and the Father is in Me?

JOHN 14:6–10

Jesus Revealing the Maternal Father

While Jesus reveals the Father and is born male, it is interesting that the language of his conception does not present God the Father as being his progenitor, but rather the neuter Spirit. While in Hebrew the Spirit, *ruach* is feminine, in Greek it is in the neuter gender. When the angel announces Jesus' birth to Joseph, the text specifies:

An angel of the Lord appeared to him in a dream, saying, "Joseph, son of David, do not be afraid to take Mary as your wife; for the Child who has been conceived in her is of the Holy Spirit."

MATTHEW 1:20

When the angel Gabriel appears to Mary, he states:

The Holy Spirit will come upon you, and the power of the Most High will overshadow you; for that reason also the holy Child will be called the Son of God.

LUKE 1:35

The neuter-gendered Holy Spirit coming upon Mary, followed by the power (*dunamis*) of the masculine singular Most High (*hupsistos*) overshadowing her, shows the progenitor of Jesus to be the third person of the Trinity, the Holy Spirit, which is not identified as masculine. It seems that this detail makes room for seeing Jesus as a son of God in a way that is deliberately distanced from a biologically male father.

Jesus as Son of God reveals the Father; yet he comes as one whose biological sex and masculinity is not emphasized.

Jesus comes in great humility, not "recognized" by the world nor "received" by his own people (John 1:10–11), full of grace and truth (John 1:14).

Jesus did not marry, nor did he father children. Jesus calls men as his twelve disciples, yet women like Mary Magdalene, Joanna, and Susanna were among his closest allies (Luke 8:2–3).

Jesus demonstrated compassion (Matt. 9:36; 15:32; 20:34; Mark 1:41; Luke 7:13; 10:33) and great emotion, weeping at his friend Lazurus's tomb (John 11:35).

Women normally shunned by the dominant religious culture of Israel felt accepted by Jesus, who defended them before accusers (Matt. 9:20–22; Luke 7:36–50; John 8:1–11).

Jesus first revealed himself to his close female allies after his resurrection, sending them to announce the good news to his male disciples (John 20:1–2, 11–18).

Jesus clearly differentiated himself from the dominant notions of hierarchical, patriarchal power of his time. He confronted his ambitious disciples while they were jockeying for power:

> You know that the rulers of the Gentiles domineer over them, and those in high position exercise authority over them. It is not this way among you, but whoever wants to become prominent among you shall be your servant, and whoever desires to be first among you shall be your slave; just as the Son of Man did not come to be served, but to serve, and to give His life as a ransom for many.
>
> MATTHEW 20:25–28

In Luke's account of this same encounter, Jesus states:

> For who is greater, the one who reclines *at the table* or the one who serves? Is it not the one who reclines *at the table*? But I am among you as the one who serves.
>
> LUKE 22:27

Jesus embodied a way of being the Messiah (king) that differed markedly from normal patriarchal ways. He washed his disciples' feet (John 13:1–11), telling them:

> Do you know what I have done for you? You call Me "Teacher" and "Lord"; and you are correct, for *so* I am. So if I, the Lord and the Teacher, washed your feet, you also ought to wash one another's feet. For I gave you an example, so that you also would do just as I did for you.
>
> JOHN 13:12–15

Jesus' invitation to his disciples to follow his example is repeated in different ways by the Apostle Paul, who describes the Father as conforming believers into the heavenly image of his Son:

> For those whom He foreknew, He also predestined to *become* conformed to the image of His Son, so that He would be the firstborn among many brothers *and sisters*.
>
> ROMANS 8:29

> Just as we have borne the image of the earthy, we will also bear the image of the heavenly.
>
> 1 CORINTHIANS 15:49

> But we all, with unveiled faces, looking as in a mirror at the glory of the Lord, are being transformed into the same image from glory to glory, just as from the Lord, the Spirit.
>
> 2 CORINTHIANS 3:18

While born a biological male and being the visible image of the Father, Jesus shows us non-typical masculinity, overturning the patriarchy, and opening the way for us to be conformed into a renewed humanity.

Jesus Commissions Women

At the end of the Gospel accounts, right after his resurrection, Jesus appears first to a woman, Mary Magdalene, calling on her to point disciples to the Father:

Stop clinging to Me, for I have not yet ascended to the Father; but go to My brothers and say to them, "I am ascending to My Father and your Father, and My God and your God."

JOHN 20:17

Jesus tells Mary Magdalene to "stop clinging to me," to his physical, male body—because he has not yet ascended to the Father. He then gives the elevated role of being his spokesperson regarding the Father to a female other than his biological mother (interestingly, Mary Magdalene is a female who is not identified as a biological mother herself).[27] Jesus commissioned her to tell his disciples about how he will ascend to his Father and their Father, his God and theirs. This psychological role of the mother is now overtly spiritualized. Now they (and we) are called to see ourselves as both disciples of Jesus and sons and daughters of his Father and ours. This is the basis of our identity and authority, according to the Spirit. And the "promise of the Father," the non-gendered (neuter) Holy Spirit, is announced as being sent so we will be "clothed with power from on high" (Luke 24:49).

Since Matthew ends with Jesus commissioning his disciples to "make disciples ... baptizing them in the name of the Father and the Son and the Holy Spirit" (Matt. 28:19), who would in turn carry forward the commission to make still more disciples, might Mary Magdalene's message also need to be transmitted to future disciples?

The role of Mary Magdalene remains open like a placeholder for women to fill. The purpose of this role is to reorient future disciples back to their baptismal identities—not primarily according to their biological sex, or to a gender marked by strife between the sexes, trauma, gender confusion, or the good and bad of our generational heritage according to the flesh. Now is the time to find our truest non-biological, non-gendered identity as daughters and sons of God, where "there is neither Jew nor Greek, there is neither slave nor free, there is neither male nor female; for you are all one in Christ Jesus" (Gal. 3:28).

8

THE HAND THAT ROCKED THE MESSIAH'S CRADLE

Scot McKnight

(PhD, University of Nottingham) is a world-renowned speaker, writer, professor, and equipper of the church. He is a recognized authority on the historical Jesus, early Christianity, and the New Testament. His books have been translated into Chinese, Korean, Russian, and Portuguese. He is the author of *The Jesus Creed*, *The Blue Parakeet*, *The King Jesus Gospel*, *Revelation for the Rest of Us*, numerous commentaries, and is now writing a sixteen-volume series of reflections called *The Everyday Bible Study*.

Scot blogs on Substack and hosts the *Kingdom Roots* podcast.

The hand, so the adage goes, that rocks the cradle rocks the world. Actually, the line, which comes from a poem by William Ross Wallace, raises the bar more than a little:

> For the hand that rocks the cradle
> Is the hand that rules the world.[1]

That 1865 poem may be forgotten but his line is not. Jesus certainly rocked the world, and the Christian faith claims he will someday rule the world with absolute benevolence, peace, and justice. Today, there are some 2.6 billion people connected to Jesus. The one who rocked Jesus' cradle was Mary, and her rocking contributed mightily to her son rocking the world. In this exploration on Jesus and women, and how his vision empowers women today, I reduce the study to Mary because she was the most influential woman on Jesus. Not only that, she has been minimized, ignored, and even silenced by most evangelical preachers, pastors, and parents. As we consider Jesus' empowerment of women today, we must surely understand the importance of Jesus' mother and teach ourselves and our children about the mother of all mothers.

SOME THINGS WE GUESS AT

We don't know Mary's age at the time of her engagement. It was not unusual in those days for a young woman to be given in marriage at the age of twelve.[2] So, though we don't know Mary's exact age, she was most likely young, and any age under twenty would be a reasonable guess.

In spite of what is said on the platforms of many churches, we don't know if or how Mary was educated. The higher the social level of a young woman the greater likelihood for some education. What we do know is that knowledge was less connected to formal education and more connected to primary socialization. That is, the family. Children learned what it meant to be a Jew and how to behave as a Jew—not in classrooms, but in the home, in the facial expressions of their significant others, and in the stories they heard on the playground or in gatherings, including the synagogue.

We don't know if Joseph married Mary as his first or second wife. Early Christian traditions have at times suggested he was older and had children— Jesus' brothers and sisters—from a previous marriage. Some suggest otherwise. The early Christian tradition that maintained Mary remained a virgin her entire life is the least likely explanation of the relations between Joseph and Mary.

SOME THINGS WE KNOW

One thing I know, yea two, are that most Bible readers don't know much about Mary and most evangelical preachers don't preach about Mary. And yet, other than Jesus and Peter, we are told more about Mary in the Gospels than any other character. This has not changed the Protestant impulse to ignore or silence the mother of Jesus.

Here is a quick sketch of the life of Mary as found in the Gospels.

Luke's first chapter tells the complementary stories of the arrivals of John the Baptist and Jesus, of Zechariah and Elizabeth, and Mary and her fiancé, then husband. Mary visits Elizabeth in the hill country of Judea and then Mary sings the Magnificat. In Luke 2, Jesus is born in the midst of a heightened political situation, with angels and shepherds adoring the child; Jesus is named; and then he is presented as the firstborn in the temple. The family returns to Nazareth. Then at age twelve they take Jesus to Jerusalem where he becomes the *wunderkind* in a circle of temple authorities. Joseph and Mary make their trek home to Galilee only to discover at nightfall that Jesus was not in the caravan, a common way Jews of Galilee traveled to Jerusalem for festivals. The parents return to find Jesus in debate with the leaders in the temple courts where he effectively tells Mary and Joseph his mission was to be about his Father's business. They return to Galilee. In these stories Mary is the uber-faithful, observant Jewish woman.

John's second chapter tells us about Mary and Jesus at a wedding where the wine runs short. Jesus miraculously turns the water in six stone jars into wine (equivalent to some 907 bottles of wine, if you care to know), and everyone was stunned. In Mark's third chapter we learn that Jesus is making waves, and stories are getting back to the family; Mary and the siblings of Jesus (notice the absence of Joseph in John 2 and Mark 3) make the two-day trek down to Capernaum. They think Jesus is losing his mind, and if he's not careful the leaders are going to put him down. They discover Jesus is in (presumably) Peter's home. Instead of welcoming them, Jesus informs them that his family is composed of those who are doing the will of God as taught by Jesus. In these two episodes, Mary is the uber-protective Jewish mother who has some reasonably based expectations of what her future-king son ought to be doing. After all, she sang the Magnificat and we're about to discuss the power of that song in forming Jesus.

We hear not a word about Mary again until the cross. Jesus is on it. She's watching. She hears from Jesus that she has been assigned to John's care (John 19:25–27). She's at the upper room prayer meeting in Jerusalem in Acts 1:14, and she was thus present at Pentecost. Outside of the Gospels, we would deduce that she is present in Revelation 12 when we see a depiction of a woman about to give birth to the son who will rule the world, that is Jesus. But that woman of Revelation 12 morphs before our reading eyes: She's Israel, she's Mary, she's the church.

So, as I indicated above, Mary appears quite often in Scripture, and she deserves better among evangelicals. She was the prototypical Jewish person—encountering God's plan in Jesus—who learned to respond as each new moment of revelation was made clear. She shows us the path of struggling faith, confident faith, and proclaiming faith. The history of Christian art has done us all a disservice. Mary is most often depicted in a blue robe—"Duke blue" as a friend once told me—with a white headscarf, both perfectly pleated and perfectly in place. She's got a pensive, unexpressive face. Gentle, if not piercing, eyes. A little blush on her cheeks. Put together, she's perfectly pious. Yet the Gospels do not present that image of Mary. Maybe Luke 1 and 2 have a bit of that image, but after that she's pushy, confident, opinionated, determined—nothing like the stereotypes we conjure of her today, where she is limited to the Christmas tableau or occasionally the weeping mother at the cross.

MARIAM'S SONG, OR *THE MAGNIFICAT*

Mary's song, the Magnificat, reveals her theology. It was this theology that rocked the cradle of Jesus and presumably influenced much of his early upbringing—so much so that the theology and practice of Jesus (his lived theology) can be hung on the various themes of Mary's song. Mary's song can be understood as the primary socialization vision of Jesus and is therefore worthy of exploration as we discover what her song taught her son.

I will be using *The Second Testament*,[3] my recent translation, to take us through Mary's song. This translation's aim is to take readers back to the first century, to the Greek language, and to break apart some of our familiarity so we hear the New Testament afresh—as if for the first time. I transliterate names. Hence, it's Mariam, not Mary; Yisraël, not Israel; Abra'am, not Abraham. (Incidentally, the Greek translation for my name is *skotos*, meaning "darkness," so I prefer not to use it for myself!)

> Mariam said,
> "My self magnifies the Lord,
> My spirit was overjoyed in God, my Deliverer, because he looked upon his impoverished slave.
> For Look! From now all generations will bless me, because the Powerful One did greatnesses for me, his name is devoted.
> His compassion is for generations and generations who are awed at him.

He made a grip with his right arm, he scattered status-mongers in their hearts' intelligence.

He took down the powerful ones from thrones and raised the status of the impoverished.

He filled in the hungering ones with goods and commissioned the rich ones away hollow.

He attached himself to his young servant, Yisraël [Israel], to remember compassion, just as he spoke to our fathers, to Abra'am and to his seed to the Era."

Mariam remained with her [Elizabeth] about three months and returned to her house.

LUKE 1:46–56

If you read each line and then pause to consider the whole life of Jesus, you will find instance after instance of Jesus implementing the Magnificat-vision of mother Mary—albeit, I cannot say mother Mary and not begin to intone the song of Eric Clapton, who sang the song *Holy Mother* with the great Pavarotti.

Let's now look at each element of The Magnificat and what it reveals about the nature and significance of Mary.

God of Mary, God of Jesus

Mary looks to God, her God, the God of Israel, the God of her fathers, as the "Lord" and the "Deliverer" (or Savior), and as the "Powerful One." The word "Lord" is so common to the Gospels—appearing some 235 times—that it goes unnoticed. But this term evokes *YHWH*, the name of Israel's God (Exod. 3:14), a word so holy that the term *Adonai* was substituted for it. So, to use the term "Lord" puts Mary into the covenant God has made with Israel. Her God is the Savior, and the Powerful One who—as the song continues—makes all things right.

More than this, the God of Mary looks with grace and compassion on the marginalized and poor; this God is holy ("devoted" in the sense of self-glory) in that God is a one-of-a-kind God whose fierce presence burns away all sin and injustices; this God is known for his "greatnesses." What can go unnoticed and unlived for Protestant evangelicals, with their history of polemics with Roman Catholics, is that Mary announces with utter clarity that "from now on all generations will bless me." Except, as I have hinted already, Protestant evangelicals do not engage in this practice. I mean this to our shame. Our polemics have spoiled us on Mary, and in so being spoiled we have failed to teach the truth about her significance and influence.

Now to look at how these words are manifest in Jesus' life. Jesus calls God "Lord" (Matt. 9:38; 11:25) and is himself called "Lord" (Matt. 8:2, 6, 8, 21, 25). Of course, as a Jew, Jesus would automatically have called God "Lord." Jesus is also called "Savior" (Luke 2:11; John 4:42) because one of the most common activities of Jesus was to "save" or heal or, as the *Second Testament* translates, "deliver" (Matt. 8:25; 9:22). Jesus learned from Mary that God was Savior, and that God had called her son to do the work of deliverance. Mary's God was an omni-savior, in that deliverance, redemption, and salvation were holistic. Joseph hears from the angel that the son is to be called "Jesus" because he will "deliver his people from their sins" (Matt. 1:21). If you read Matthew's eighth and ninth chapters in one sitting, you can see how holistic his deliverances were: He delivers people from skin diseases, he cures a military leader's "young servant" who was "tossed down in the house, paralyzed, tortured terribly" (8:6), he delivers Peter's mother-in-law from fever, he delivers those who are demonized, he delivers the disciples from a storm on the water, he delivers two men stuck in a cemetery, he delivers a man paralyzed from sins, he delivers some from their riches and tax exploitations, he delivers from death and from blindness and from pastoral neglect. Indeed, the hand that rocked his cradle sang songs of deliverance to Jesus. He was surely shaped by the song.

God is also named as the Powerful One. Have we not seen the displays of God's mighty powers in all these deliverances? And there is more. With God all things are "possible," but the word used is the same word for "power," here in the plural: With God all things are powers! (Matt. 19:26). Jesus taps into the Powerful One to do mighty acts of power (Mark 9:23). In Luke's last scene, we hear the witnesses say of Jesus that he was "a prophet, powerful in work and word before God and all the people" (Luke 24:19).

Mary's God was Lord, Savior, and the Powerful One. Jesus' God was Lord, Savior, and the Powerful One. As God's agent of deliverance, Jesus, too, was Lord, Savior, and filled with the powers of the Powerful One.

The Poor

Mary has two reasons for emoting her magnification of the Lord and being overjoyed in God, her Deliverer: 1) Because she knows she will give birth to a baby boy destined to become deliverer and ruler of God's people, and 2) because God "looked upon his impoverished slave" (Luke 1:48). That word "impoverished" tells a story—tapping into a social marker for both Galilee and Judea—and summons those who recognize the story and social marker to do something about it. The issue is poverty—at times desperate as a result of famines and at other times the simple reality that the rich had an abundance while the ordinary Galilean made do. Mary was poor and the offering Joseph and Mary made to buy back their son in the Temple was a reflection of this (see Luke 2:24; Lev. 12:8). When they did present Jesus to the Lord, they were quickly surrounded by two elderly poor persons: Simeon and Anna (Luke 2:22–38). They were part of a sector of Jerusalem's society sometimes called *Anawim*, that is the "pious poor," who trusted in God for justice, and who longed for the days of deliverance. Even in his early years, Jesus attracted the lowly and those seeking God's justice, and Mary was willing for these people to bless her son.

One more observation. When the brother of Jesus, James, describes "Worship that is clean and unstained with the God and Father is this: to care for orphans and widows in their trouble" (James 1:27), the word "widow" pertains almost certainly to his and Jesus' mother, Mary. The word "orphan" in the Jewish world described any child who had lost a parent. In our world the term tends to refer to a child who has lost both parents, but in Jesus' world it would have referred to himself and his siblings (Mark 6:3).[4] What is moving about this passage in James is that it suggests he learned from his childhood what true worship was: He learned it from those who cared for his poor family.

This provides the backdrop to Jesus beginning his first public sermon in his hometown synagogue by quoting his mission-for-life passage, referencing Isaiah 61:

> Spirit of Lord is upon me,
>> because of which he christened me to gospel to the beggars,
>> he commissioned me to announce release for captives,
>> and sight-recovery for sightless ones,
>> to commission the broken with release,
>> to announce a year of Lord's reception.
>
> LUKE 4:18–19

Jesus' mission-for-life passage is to "gospel" (or preach the gospel, one word in Greek) to the beggars. The customary translation of *ptōchos* is "poor." These are not just regular poor but the destitute, begging poor. The unemployed, the unskilled, the oppressed. These are people trapped by the economic disparities of Galilee, and Jesus saw them and cared for them *because his mother taught him to do so.* She taught him this by how she lived, what she sang, and by pointing to those who embodied the way of grace and compassion. The others identified in Jesus' cited text from Isaiah 61 are "captives" and "sightless ones" and "the broken." They flesh out versions of the meaning of beggars, and they are associated with the impoverished and the *Anawim.*

So, when Jesus offers his understanding of the Law of Moses in the Sermon on the Mount, he opens with blessings on specific people groups—groups Jesus knows are the apple of his Father's eye … and his mother's, too! First up, "God blesses the beggars in spirit" (Matt. 5:3). Luke has just "God blesses the beggars" (Luke 6:20). When John the Baptist wants to know if Jesus can get him out of captivity (Luke 7:19), no doubt he has Jesus' mission-for-life passage in mind. But Jesus wants John to know that his mission is a reframing of that opening sermon in Nazareth. We read in Luke 7:22 how he responds to John's question:

> *The sightless see again,*
> The lame walk around
> The scaly are cleaned and
> *The deaf hear,*
> *The dead arise,*
> The beggars are gospeled. (Italicized words are citations from Isaiah).

Notice the last line: The "beggars" are the ones who are to hear the great news of God the Deliverer through the Messiah Deliverer, Jesus, and his deliverance is utterly holistic in body, soul, mind, and spirit. He urged his followers to invite the *beggars* to their feasts (Luke 14:13, 21), and called out the rich who don't see the *beggars* at their gates (Luke 16:19–31).

When the rich leader approaches Jesus asking how he can enter into the future kingdom of God, Jesus gives him some of the Ten Commandments (Luke 18:20). The man claims to be in control of such commands. Jesus' stunning, memorable response follows: "One order still remains for you. Everything whatever you have, sell and distribute *to the beggars!*" (Luke 18:22). Only then could he join the gaggle of followers with Jesus. Later, Jesus praises Zacchaeus because he donates half of what he's got to the *beggars* (Luke 19:8–9). At another point, Jesus blesses "this widow, the begging one" (Luke 21:3).

It is no surprise then that the followers of Jesus who were baptized into the Spirit at Pentecost formed a community that cared for the poor (Acts 2:42–47). No surprise, too, to wonder if Mary was not leading that ministry to the poor among them (Acts 1:14). The hand that rocked the cradle, sang a song about care for the poor. Jesus knew that song well.

Compassionate

In Mary's Song we learn that God is a God of "compassion" (Luke 1:50, 54; see also 1:58, 72, 78), and the Greek term is often translated "mercy." The term points us to actions done to those in need that alleviated those needs. The Greek term is *eleos*, which I translate as compassion. God shows mercy and compassion to those who, in need, are not even aware of their need. His mercy acts to resolve their needs.

There are a few terms Gospel writers use to describe the emotions of Jesus, a couple of which point us to his care for those in need. The first is compassion. He heals out of compassion (Matt. 9:13; 12:7) and he summons those who want to be like the Samaritan to be compassionate (Luke 10:37). Those in need appeal to Jesus for his compassionate mercy toward them. The Canaanite woman cries out to Jesus, "Show some compassion on me, Lord, son of David. My daughter is demonized terribly" (Matt. 15:22; see also 9:27; 17:15; 20:30, 31). Often then, in the Gospels, the act of Jesus to deliver someone is an act of mercy; he is clearly known for his compassionate nature.

The other emotion that points to Jesus' care of those in need is *splanchnizomai*, which I translate as "empathy." It describes a visceral response of the lower organs to someone's pain, distress, and suffering. Jesus is one who exhibits, almost certainly with facial expressions, if not tears, empathy for the suffering. A noticeable instance is his empathy for those who have suffered pastoral neglect (Matt. 9:36). But the term is also used for Jesus when he observes fellow humans in need (Matt. 14:14; 20:34). In both compassion and empathy, we encounter a Jesus who sees someone suffering, who exhibits a visceral response, who does something to alleviate the suffering ... and the delivered person displays a similar response to Jesus among those who observe the act of deliverance.

Mary knows of a God who is compassionate for the people of God in their suffering. This theme appears twice in the Magnificat and it shows up in spades in the ministry of Jesus. One has to think his mother had at least something to do with Jesus learning the art of compassion and empathy, as we all learn approvable emotions, like compassion and empathy, from our parents and siblings.

Dispersing the Powers and the Rich

Mary knows that when God sends the Messiah, that Messiah will wreck the existing powers. Notice these three verses again:

> He made a grip with his right arm, he scattered status-mongers in their hearts' intelligence.
> He took down the powerful ones from thrones and raised the status of the impoverished.
> He filled in the hungering ones with goods and commissioned the rich ones away hollow.
>
> LUKE 1:51–53

If Mary believed this is what God would do when the Messiah arrived—and she believed her baby boy would be that Messiah—she would have taught Jesus the art of prophetic critique of unjust powers, whether she sang the Magnificat over him or not.

Jesus was clearly schooled in this prophetic critique. I mention a couple of examples. First, Jesus followed hard on the heels of his relative, John the Baptist, who cut into the fabric of economic exploitation when he was asked what repentance looked like: "The ones soldiering were asking him, saying, 'And what should we do?' He said to them, 'Don't shake anyone down or commit fraud, and consider your fees enough'" (Luke 3:14). Jesus followed John in this kingdom-is-near vision, by having a similar attitude toward those who needed to hear about economic injustices. Second, Jesus seemed to have a mission to the rich in a double sense: He both called them to cease their exploitation of the poor and he called them to become generous with their funds. He not only blesses the beggars, but he also warns the wealthy (Luke 6:20, 24). He castigates the Pharisees because they were "silver-lovers," that is, greedy (Luke 16:14). Nothing reveals this more crisply than the story of Zacchaeus in Luke 19, for whom repentance means economic justice-making: "Half of my possessions, Lord, I am giving to the beggars, and if I defrauded someone, I am giving back four times" (19:8). This, Jesus says, is "deliverance" (19:9).

In Mary's Magnificat this section of the song ties together the status-mongers in their arrogance, the powerful who sit on thrones, and the rich who have blocked food to the hungry. Mary, a Galilean woman who would know poverty in her search to provide for her many children, had the *chutzpah* to stand with her feet planted and speak out and up against the oppressing powers of her day. That power was Herod the Great. She was but a young woman. But she caught the vision of the kingdom of God in her son. She was emboldened by the Spirit of God to speak up. She had the courage to resist the powers and to lead a dissident movement against economic exploitation. Her method was to sing a song to her children, beginning with Jesus, and to teach them that the way of God is justice. Her sons—Jesus and James—we know caught that vision.

God's Covenant Faithfulness

At the bottom of Mary's song, both literally and theologically, was confidence in the God of Israel to remain faithful to the covenant arrangement with his people: a covenant that entailed the blessing of the nations, a nation too numerous to count, a king too just to be exploitative, and a people too righteous to be sinful. One can read Genesis 12 just to get a whiff of that covenant.

Jesus, too, knows this covenant-making God. He knows this God as his Father, his *Abba* (Mark 14:36), which suggests a familial, intimate relationship. He knows this God is holy, and one who deserves to be approached with reverence and worship. He knows this God listens to prayer, and he knows this God's mission is to deliver humans from their sins, to rid the world of systemic injustice, and to conquer the evil one. He knows this God is the God of the kingdom. This faithful God of his mother is the One who has promised to turn the world into the kingdom of God. Such a kingdom requires the following features for anyone who has been spiritually formed by the song of Mary.

First, the kingdom needs a *king*.[5] In the vision of Jesus, the king is not the emperor of Rome, is not Pontius Pilate in Judea, is not Antipas in Galilee, and is not Caiaphas and his family in Jerusalem. The kingdom's God is the God of Israel who has sent his Son, Jesus, to be the King of God's kingdom.

Second, the kingdom needs a king *who rules*. The God who rules is the God who delivered; that is, the ruling God is the Deliverer—the one who liberated the children of Israel from the economic exploitations of Pharaoh in Egypt. The God who rules is the Lord Jesus who holistically delivers humans from sin, Satan, diseases, and systemic sins, and does so by becoming one of us, by living our life and dying our death, by being raised for us, and by ascending to rule for us as the Deliverer.

Third, the kingdom needs a king who rules *a redeemed people*. The story of the Bible is the story of God creating a people for himself—Israel. God creates this people through a person—Abraham. He does this in a covenant and for a purpose—to bring glory to the name of the God of Israel. The Bible's story moves from the people of God being Israel to the incorporation, *a la* Genesis 12, of Gentiles into the people of God. Not by erasing Israel's privilege but by qualifying Gentiles who believe in Jesus as God's Messiah to be on par with Israel in God's plan for this world. That is, Israel expanded by the church. Mary's song anticipates a people who will live out the vision of the Magnificat.

Fourth, the kingdom needs a king who rules a redeemed people by *living out the law or ethic of the kingdom*. From the beginning, God not only redeemed and ruled his people, but the covenant gave the redeemed people of God a rule for life. There are four major moments in the revealing of this rule for life in the story of God's people: 1) the giving of the law of Moses, found in Exodus 19–24, supplemented as it were by Leviticus and Numbers and Deuteronomy; 2) the vision of the prophets, which heightened the laws of Moses by calling out the systemic failures of the kings and the temple authorities; 3) Jesus' presenting his ethical vision for the kingdom of God as summarized in the Sermon on the Mount (Matt. 5–7; Luke 6), and the calls after that sermon to follow him to the cross and beyond; and 4) the apostles' visions of living the way of Jesus in the power of the Spirit, most especially in the Apostle Paul's expression of the fruit of the Spirit (Gal. 5:22–26).

Finally, Mary's song imagines a kingdom with a king (her Son) who has redeemed a people who live out the kingdom life *in a place*. The covenant God makes is a covenant with a people, not so they can escape this life or this world but so they can indwell this world and embody the way of God. So, Mary's song takes root in the land promised to Israel—a land that finds its central node in the temple, where the glory of God is destined to dwell. But the radical newness of the kingdom vision of her Son means glorious Spirit-indwelling humans who are sent on mission into the whole world to take up residence—to occupy a place in this world to embody the kingdom life.

Those kingdom people know not only the song of Mary and her Son, but they also know the experience of the blessing of God, the compassion of God, the justice of God, and the holistic deliverance that is embodied in the way of life for this people of God.

Now, to ask: What has this to do with women? Everything! The kingdom plan of God and the kingdom mission of God that was incarnated in the Son of God was mediated to Jesus through his mother. She sang a song of deliverance to her relative Elizabeth with a sparkle in her eyes that communicated with the joys of full expectation, "Finally, the kingdom of God has come. I get to be part of it. My son is its king. May it be!" The irony of so many Bible readers who dismiss women from teaching and pastoral roles in the church is that, in their claim to be biblical, they have failed to be biblical with the very teacher of Jesus, his mother. What we have seen in the Magnificat is a proclamation of God's covenant faithfulness and kingdom vision, imparted and embodied in the life of Jesus and a practice we are invited to participate in as part of God's people. Perhaps this is a lesson not just in the wonders of Jesus' life and ministry, but in learning from Mary—and women like her—who are passionately pursuing a kingdom life that ushers in more of God's presence and power, transforming the world around them.

9

WHAT DO WE DO WITH PAUL?

Aaron White

is the author of *Recovering: From Brokenness and Addiction to Blessedness and Community.* He teaches at Westminster Theological Centre and, with his family, has served in Vancouver's Downtown Eastside for the past twenty years.

This chapter draws heavily on the remarkable theological work of Dr. Lucy Peppiatt, both from her written work and through ongoing conversations.

In our faith community in Vancouver, we are committed to wrestling with the full voice of Scripture. It's not always easy. One Advent, the liturgical calendar presented some of Mary's words to lead us into worship—specifically, her cosmos-changing response to the Annunciation (Luke 1:38), and her fiery prophetic rap in the Magnificat (Luke 1:46–55).

So far, so good. Those bits are always fun and challenging and put one in the mood to celebrate Christmas and overthrow oppressive systems.

But our preaching schedule, either through bad planning or divine arrangement, had led us simultaneously into 1 Corinthians 14:34–35: "Women should remain silent in the churches. They are not allowed to speak, but must be in submission, as the law says. If they want to inquire about something, they should ask their own husbands at home; for it is disgraceful for a woman to speak in the church."

So. This was awkward.

How can Paul's words exist alongside the story and teaching of Mary? Would the mother of our Lord be permitted to speak in one of Paul's churches? Would she have to wait and ask Joseph questions back at home? Would Paul insist on checking to see if Mary's head was veiled when she prophesied the Magnificat? And what about all the women Jesus regularly interacted with and amongst whom he found amazing faith? Was it okay for them to boldly talk with Jesus, but not okay to make a peep in front of brother Tim in the third pew? And then there is Peter quoting the prophet Joel at Pentecost, announcing in Acts 2:17–18: "In the last days, God says, I will pour out my Spirit on all people. Your sons and daughters will prophesy, your young men will see visions, your old men will dream dreams. Even on my servants, both men and women, I will pour out my Spirit in those days, and they will prophesy."

What are we supposed to do with Paul?

HOW PAUL'S WORDS HAVE BEEN USED

There are a few passages in the Pauline letters that are really hard to read aloud in mixed company, yet they have been used to shape church teaching for two thousand years. Paul, his thinking, and the effects of those letters, for good or ill, have to be reckoned with one way or another.

We know how Paul can be used as a theological hammer and as a gatekeeper for supposed "true doctrine." Many have insisted that their understanding of Paul is the only lens through which Jesus may be understood. On the other end of the spectrum, some people claim that the angry little man from Tarsus took Christ's beautiful message of freedom and love and transformed it into a repressive religious system of his own devising. It is this system, they suggest, rather than Jesus' message, that has become the standard Christian expression throughout the world. If this is true, then Paul should only ever be used with the greatest caution, and much of his writing should be dismissed as culturally biased, and anachronistic—irrelevant at best and actively misogynist and harmful at worst.

What makes Paul's apparent teaching on women even more galling and bizarre is that Paul seems to apply the radical leveling message of Jesus to relations between Jewish and Gentile believers, between rich and poor, and even between masters and slaves, but then appears to double down on the culturally prevalent ideas of the inherent inferiority and subjugation of women. I remember a friend at university expressing her frustration that Paul gives all this freedom to others, but then seems to take it all away from women. Can this be right? Are these the only options available to us with regard to Paul?

Let's look first at Paul seemingly forbidding women from speaking in the church.

Few churches act out the literal reading of these verses, which is that women should remain *absolutely silent* in church. That doesn't just mean preaching or teaching; that means praying, singing, doing children's time, reading announcements, saying hello, passing the peace, hiccupping, etc. Even those who believe that women shouldn't preach or teach have mostly given up on this most simplistic reading, along with the instruction for women to cover their heads (or wear their long hair up) in 1 Corinthians 11:2–16.[1] Therefore, our inconsistent adherence to women being completely silent or being forced to wear head coverings shows that we have already practically rejected an exact reading of the text.

The denomination I grew up in, for instance, encouraged women to preach and teach, and had women leading at the very highest levels. But they also required women to wear hats and had rules for keeping long hair safely bound up, while men were discouraged from having long hair and forbidden to wear their hats in worship unless we were outside. There was obviously great confusion in our church when it came to knowing which passages to follow or not, and how strictly.

These are no light or theoretical matters. Contained within the passage on head coverings, for instance, can be found a potentially serious danger for women who do not comply. Paul says in 1 Corinthians 11:6: "For if a woman does not cover her head, have her also cut her hair off; however, if it is disgraceful for a woman to have her hair cut off or her head shaved, have her cover her head" (NASB). According to theologians Bruce Winter and Philip Payne, head-shaving was an actual punishment meted out upon adulterous women within various cultures of the time, to the extent that the offending women should be seen as (or actually be forced to *be*) prostitutes.[2] Notably, the same threat is *not* given to men in this scriptural passage, even though they likewise are told what to do about their heads/hair in worship (1 Cor. 11:4, 7). Theologian Lucy Peppiatt says bluntly, "If we take this to be the voice of Paul then we must face up to the coercive nature of his statement ... Paul is recommending here that women who pray and prophesy unveiled/loose-haired should be treated by the community in the same way that they used to treat whores and adulterers."[3]

This type of punishment still happens in my neighborhood—Vancouver's Downtown Eastside. Women who find themselves on the wrong side of a drug debt are in danger of having their hair shaved off or torn out, and then being forced to sell their bodies. There is simply no possibility that we could ever look at this as a reasonable, fair, appropriate, or godly thing to happen to our beloved sisters and neighbors. It is not a thing that a good person would threaten, even if they were using hyperbole. Encountering the Scriptures alongside our neighbors makes this reading impossible. Some have run to our own faith community to find liberation from these exact threats, and they trust us when we tell them that both God and we see them as precious, beloved, and worthy of protection and honor. We treasure their voices. Does Paul *really* claw all of this back? Is this the Word of the Lord?

APPARENT CONTRADICTIONS IN PAUL'S LETTERS

The temptation, again, is just to do away with these passages altogether, to avoid speaking and teaching on them, or to actively teach against them. But I am convinced we should address the text, including the really tough bits, and to try to do it better. People are going to come across these ideas either through their own reading of Scripture or through the efforts of those committed to the idea that women are inferior. Many ministries, not to mention Western cultures and societies, have also been shaped by these interpretations. If we still dare to hope that the message of Scripture is ultimately liberating, joyful, and hopeful, we need qualified people doing the hard work of helping us read Paul in that light. Thankfully, my friend Dr. Lucy Peppiatt, principal of Westminster Theological Centre where I teach, is one of those people, and she has developed an alternative reading of Paul that begins to address the apparent contradictions and harm within this section of 1 Corinthians.

In her book *Women and Worship at Corinth,* Peppiatt addresses the wild variety of interpretations confidently held by a vast number of Pauline scholars on these contested passages.[4] There is simply no scholarly consensus on these issues, but rather much confusion and contradiction. It isn't that we shouldn't seek answers, or that they could never be found; but if anyone asserts that the easiest thing to do is read and accept the "plain meaning of the text," you should at the very least look at them funny. Our "plain sense" of what Paul means in his letters, Peppiatt argues, largely stems from our prior conception of who Paul was: "Was Paul a misogynist? Was he just committed to a gentle patriarchy? Was he confused? Or was he a radical?"[5]

Instinctively, we are searching for a better meaning than the blatantly obvious one we see in the passages, because it is impossible to believe Paul is saying that women must remain totally silent in the church. Paul's own letters belie the idea that women in his own churches were silent. In 1 Corinthians 11:4–5, Paul assumes that women will pray and prophesy. In other letters, Paul commends various women as prophets, deacons, even apostles (e.g., Rom. 16:1–12; Phil. 4:2–3). And in Acts 2:17–18 it is announced that sons and daughters, and male and female servants, will prophesy. All believers who are filled with the Holy Spirit can prophesy, and the context for this prophecy is the building up of the church. In fact, if women are not allowed to speak at all in the church assembly, then it must mean that the rest of 1 Corinthians 12–14, which instructs believers on how to build up the church with their Spirit-given gifts, must apply only to the male members of the body of Christ! Some have suggested that women were allowed to prophesy and pray, but not to teach, preach, or weigh the prophecies of others. But Paul does not limit the gift of discernment (nor any other gift) to men alone. And prophecy was designed at least in part to teach everyone (1 Cor. 14:31), so women who were prophesying *were* teaching. In fact, prophets are described in 1 Corinthians 12:28 as taking precedence over teachers. So why could women prophesy but not teach? It seems the verses in front of us cannot mean that all women should never talk in church. What do we do with them, then?

The church in Corinth was apparently toxic, and Paul's letters to them are filled with stark rebuke, argumentation, and even pulling rank to get his point across. New Testament scholar Ben Witherington makes a list of the problems Paul addresses there: partisanship; lawsuits amongst believers; unequal treatment of the poor, especially at the Lord's table; pride and arrogance around spiritual gifts; sexual misconduct; and eschatological disagreements.[6] Their meetings, according to Paul, were doing more harm than good (1 Cor. 11:17). Peppiatt characterizes the Corinthian practices addressed in the letter as "oppressive, bullying and childish."[7] Perhaps this kind of toxic church culture sounds familiar to some in the present day and age? It probably sounds more familiar when we realize that Paul appears to specifically target the men who were leaders in the church in Corinth with his critiques.[8]

The claim that the male leaders of the church in Corinth were causing problems might be troubling to some, but we are quite used to making speculative claims about the behavior of the women of the church in Corinth. Commentaries are rife with suggestions that the women in Corinth had taken liberties with the freedom offered in the gospel and were getting all wild and bare-headed and talkative in the church gatherings. While there is no actual evidence of this, we are simply asked to imagine that this is what happened, and then to assume this was a big problem because it was either offensive to the surrounding culture, or to the created order, or to both. We do this to try to make sense of Paul's apparent restrictions on women. I have taught this speculation in the past, even in an attempt to demonstrate that these restrictions no longer apply. Yet as I look back on my notes from those talks, I see the number of times I had to say things like "What if …?" and "It is possible that …" and "Our best educated guess suggests …." In order to make this interpretation plausible, I had to draw on all kinds of speculation about the behavior of the women in the church, the expectations of the surrounding culture, and Paul's intentions. Those interpretations require us to assume more certainty than we actually have.

This point cannot be overstated. We don't have the letters the church in Corinth sent to Paul (the letter we have from him is the second one he wrote, and we don't even have the first); we aren't privy to the conversations and debates they had together over the course of Paul's eighteen months there; we don't know the referents that could make some of what Paul says make sense to our context. One example: If someone asks you why women are expected to wear head coverings or wear their long hair up in your church and your response is, "Well, obviously, because of the angels …" how would that go? Are we confident we know what Paul is implying when he says, "It is for this reason that a woman ought to have authority over her own head, because of the angels" (1 Cor. 11:10)? Scholarly opinions abound, from increasing the shame women should feel at letting their hair down because even the angels are witnessing this; to the notion that a woman's hair or head covering is a witness to the angels of her authority and power in Christ (the angels need a special reminder of this?); to an indication of a woman's role in the order of creation; to an effort not to offend human messengers (a different interpretation of "angel").[9] There really isn't a consensus, nor is there a common practice in the church today that applies this teaching. Maybe the Corinthian Christians knew exactly what Paul was referring to here, but we surely don't.

The problem goes far beyond an uncertain cultural context. If Paul gave this teaching to the church in Corinth because the women's behavior was offensive and damaging within that culture, then we could say we no longer live in that culture, so these restrictions no longer apply. That seems to be what we *are*, in fact, saying, as few churches require women to cover their heads when prophesying or praying, for instance. But Paul strongly insists in 1 Corinthians 11:16 that his teaching is true for all his churches; and in 1 Corinthians 14:33–34 the prohibition on women speaking appears to be applicable "in all the congregation of the saints." This negates attempts to make these restrictions time or culture-bound. And the argument in 1 Corinthians 11:2–10 invokes the created order rather than the immediate context, suggesting that the requirement for head coverings rests in some way upon the hierarchical descent from God to Christ to men to women,[10] and from the idea that women were created for men and not the other way around: "For a man ought not to have his head veiled, since he is the image and reflection of God; but woman is the reflection of man. Indeed, man was not made from woman, but woman from man. Neither was man created for the sake of woman, but woman for the sake of man" (1 Cor. 11:7–9, NRSV). Paul is apparently contradicting the creation account from Genesis 1:27 by saying that men are made in the image and glory/reflection of God, but women are not.

Peppiatt highlights the absurdity of this last point, and its supposed resolution, in the following way:

> Whichever way you read 11:7, and the implications and application of this verse, the message of the text as it has most often been understood is that the woman lacks something that the man does not, and that this is rooted in the creation order. It might be a physical deficiency in an Aristotelian sense, a symbolic positioning below the male, a lack of authority in a spiritual sense in the sight of the angels, a creational deficiency in her own image and glory, or maybe all of the above in some way. Furthermore, this lack is a source of shame.
>
> And the remedy to this: a head covering, a hairstyle, a scarf? To approach God in prayer, she covers her head, and thus becomes acceptable. Woman's cosmic cultic infraction against God via her relation to man, merely by virtue of being a woman, is annulled through her wearing of a veil."[11]

This is some bizarre theology, and I think we all know it.

But even if this argument *was* just cultural and contextual, and we could be totally sure of those cultural and contextual factors, is that something with which we should be comfortable? There remain cultures around the world where women are required to be silent, veiled, and even separated from men in worship, and it is only recently that Western culture has begun to move toward greater gender equality, often against the wishes or practices of many churches. Are we prepared to say that this teaching no longer applies only because the surrounding culture has progressed? Does that sound like a liberating message of truth, or more of a reaction to keep up with the times?

Perhaps our confusion is understandable because Paul himself seems to assert certain contradictions in the letter. Only three verses after we hear that women were made from and for men, and not vice versa, we find this: "Nevertheless, in the Lord woman is not independent of man, nor is man independent of woman. For as woman came from man, so also man is born of woman. But everything comes from God" (1 Cor. 11:11–12). In truth, the whole section of 1 Corinthians 11:2–16 seems to contain serious discrepancies around things like headship and glory. For instance: Do women need a head covering when they pray and prophesy, as is claimed in 1 Corinthians 11:5–6? Or have they been given a headful of glorious hair *instead* of a head covering, as Paul says in verse 15? There is no end to scholarly debate and translational obfuscation on these issues, and again, we mostly just ignore the embarrassing implications.

But these implications of inferiority, whether cultural or creational, also stand in vivid contrast to Paul's repeated arguments about the equality of men and women *in the Lord*. In 1 Corinthians 7:4, for instance, Paul makes the radical claim that a wife has authority over her husband's body. Everyone would have agreed with the statement in verse 3 that a husband has authority over his wife's body, but to argue that this authority is mutual is utterly shocking. It is difficult to reconcile the liberating power of this statement with the restrictions expressed concerning female clothing and speech later in the letter.

RHETORICAL ARGUMENT

If these are really Paul's beliefs, they just do not make sense. At the very least, they are extremely unclear and confusing. Happily, Peppiatt has proposed an elegant and plausible solution to this dilemma: What if Paul was employing rhetorical argument in his letter? What if, in this reading, some of the contentious verses are not the actual thoughts of Paul, but rather Paul citing the arguments of the Corinthians in order to reveal their absurdity? In other words, Paul quotes the incorrect views of the toxic church leaders in Corinth to demonstrate how they are not in line with the teaching he has given them, and so that he can refute them definitively.

The argument is subtle and cannot be fully reproduced here, but I will give an example of how it works. In 1 Corinthians 14:26–33, Paul discusses order in worship and outlines how everyone should be expected to be able to bring a word of instruction, a hymn, a revelation, a tongue, or an interpretation to share. *Everyone.* He goes on to discuss how those who are sharing prophecies should take turns, with only two or three per meeting (with interpretations), but there are no restrictions on who can prophesy. Quite the opposite. We already know from 1 Corinthians 11 that Paul *expects* women to pray and to prophesy. Then suddenly, in 14:34, we get a complete reversal: "... women should remain silent in the churches. They are not allowed to speak, but must be in submission, as the Law says. If they want to inquire about something, they should ask their own husbands at home, for it is disgraceful for a woman to speak in the church." Putting aside the questions of which women are being referred to here (all women or just wives who have husbands to ask later?); and the bizarre idea that Paul would be leaning on the Law for his support (which Law?); this section contradicts what Paul has just said. Just how women are to prophesy while remaining silent is a mystery.

Peppiatt therefore argues that the most sense can be made of the letter if we accept that Paul is quoting the leaders from Corinth in 1 Corinthians 14:34–35, and then responding to them in a devastating manner in verses 36–40. Verse 36 (ESV) asks, "Or was it from you that the word of God came? Or are you the only ones it has reached?" Theologians Flanagan and Snyder contend that, in the Greek, the phrase *only ones* is masculine.[12] This suggests that verse 36 is explicitly directed in a gendered way, but surprisingly not to the women of Corinth who were referred to in verses 34–35. If Paul was correcting the women for talking out of turn, one would expect this rebuke to address them. Instead, the rebuke in verse 36 appears to be addressed specifically to the men, those who had presumed themselves to be super-spiritual prophets and were seemingly domineering over the church. Paul, then, is asking these men if they think they are the only possessors of the Word of God. Do they really think they are the *only ones* holding the key to understanding the gospel? Peppiatt points out that this is fundamental to understanding the rest of the passage, if Paul is indeed quoting these men in verses 34–35 and then rebuking their practice of keeping the women quiet in verse 36. How dare they prevent anyone from sharing the gift that they bring to worship? There is nothing that disqualifies someone who is submitted to the Lordship of Jesus from using their gifts in the body of Christ: not gender, not background, not ethnicity, not social status. Everyone can bring a word.

OBJECTIONS

I understand the immediate objections to this argument. One is that there is no clear evidence these verses are quotations from the Corinthians. It is, of course, true that there are no quotation marks or obvious breaks in any of these verses to indicate a change in voice from Paul to his opponents. But Douglas A. Campbell asserts that "... it is widely if not universally conceded that Paul behaves in exactly this fashion—quoting the positions of others, often unannounced—in the rest of his letters ... it seems that Paul does quote texts from others when composing his letters, and that he does not always signal those overtly with written cues."[13] It is actually uncontested that Paul quotes the people of Corinth in the following verses: 1:12, 3:4, 6:12–13; 7:1; 8:1, 10:23; and he might also be doing this in 4:6b; 8:5a; 12:3; 15:12, 35. We also know that the rhetorical strategy of quoting and refuting the words of your opponents was an accepted form of argument at the time.[14] Critics point out that Paul typically uses shorter quotations in this letter, but that does not rule out Paul doing the same with longer quotations. Peppiatt, for instance, convincingly shows an example of Paul quoting his Corinthian opponents at length on the issues of tongues and prophecy in 1 Corinthians 14, and likewise on head coverings in 1 Corinthians 11:2–16.

Another objection asks: Isn't this just a little too convenient? Isn't it just that we don't like something that Paul says, so we put it into the mouth of his opponents and have Paul refute it? Using this technique, we can make Paul say whatever we want him to say. Well, there of course have to be very good reasons to say that these are quotes from Corinth rather than statements from Paul— say, for instance, a passage that is full of contradiction and confusion, whose argument doesn't scan and doesn't fit within the rest of the letter or the message of the New Testament.

Furthermore, need it be pointed out that the traditional reading has been *awfully convenient* to men in positions of power who would prefer women to remain silent? And recall, we know that there was a group of leaders within the Corinthian church who were toxic: They are immature, arrogant, partisan, believing themselves to be super-spiritual. It is they who were causing the problems that Paul wrote the letter to correct. The traditional interpretations already require us to use our imagination and to speculate about the situation in Corinth. So, what is easier to imagine? That some women had become unruly, and Paul had to lay down severe restrictions that ran contrary to the message of freedom and equality in the rest of his letters, and which jar sharply against things he writes within the same paragraph? Or that the abusive and bullying male leaders who are being rebuked and corrected throughout the letter had expressed these restrictive ideas to Paul, and he was using all his rhetorical skill to combat them? The question before us is: Does this rhetorical approach genuinely make more sense of the contested, confusing passages? I believe it does.

But I also believe that this reading makes far more sense within Scripture's (and Paul's) deeper message of liberation, hope, and joy. It is this that convinces me we should be open to the rhetorical argument.

THE FULLNESS OF THE GOSPEL

When we are confused by a passage of Scripture, we need to read it amongst the fullness of the whole gospel. The passages that seem to prohibit women from speaking in the church and make them cover their hair lest their head be shaved are found in 1 Corinthians 11–14 which is concerned with the presence of the Spirit of God amongst the believers and how that should manifest itself in love and edification as they meet together, share with one another, and honor each other. This theme is especially pronounced through the practice of table fellowship. In 1 Corinthians 11:17–34, Paul rebukes the church for the way they exclude the poor and give preference to the wealthy and privileged in their midst. He insists upon a Lord's Supper that honors those who are normally shamed, and later on a picture of the church as a body that specifically and intentionally cares for and honors members who have been neglected. Paul also specifically highlights those who were considered foolish and the lowly in his letter to the haughty leaders of the Corinthians: "But God chose what is foolish in the world to shame the wise; God chose what is weak in the world to shame the strong; God chose what is low and despised in the world, even things that are not, to bring to nothing things that are, so that no human being might boast in the presence of God." (1 Cor. 1:27–29 ESV). And he bookends the two contested passages on women with his great ode to Christlike love in 1 Corinthians 13, which describes the more excellent, humble, and sacrificial way of Christian life.

These themes are all present in the rest of Paul's letters as well. The major controversies he courted centered around his stark refusal to allow discrimination or separation at the table. He even rebuked Peter to his face in Antioch when he withdrew from eating with Gentiles (Gal. 2:11–19), and later exclaimed that "there is neither Jew nor Greek, there is neither slave nor free, there is neither male nor female, for you are all one in Christ Jesus" (Gal. 3:28 ESV). In Romans 12:6, Paul commanded the followers of the Way to "associate with the lowly," and in 1 Corinthians 4:13, he essentially called himself and his fellow apostles the "scum of the earth, the garbage of the world." Here was a man who knew what it was to identify with the shamed and dishonored, who stood in stark contrast to the divisions of the world around him, and who untiringly taught others to do the same. Can we believe that this same Paul, who insisted on boundary-breaking love and fellowship, is likely to have also insisted women be silenced and covered or shamed in all churches? Does it not make more sense to read Paul's letter to the Corinthians in a way that honors rather than shames women? This is why Peppiatt argues that Paul, in response to the male troublemakers from Corinth, made the strongest possible case for freeing women from restrictions, shame, and silence.

But let's go even further. One is put in mind not just of Paul's emphasis on an inclusive, equal table and fellowship, but also of the table ministry of Jesus. Who was invited to Jesus' table? How were they treated? We have story after story in the Gospels of women, many of them vulnerable within their own societies, feeling safe and welcome to approach Jesus, to speak with him, to join him at the table, to be in his fellowship, to participate in his mission. The woman in Mark 5 who was bleeding for twelve years isn't rebuked, but rather called daughter and healed through her faith. The Canaanite woman in Matthew 15 is praised by Jesus for her boldness in speech and action.

I remember sharing the story of the Samaritan woman from John 4 with a group of volunteers in our neighborhood. A Muslim woman from Syria, hearing the story for the first time, was amazed that this Samaritan woman and this Jewish man were conversing alone at Jacob's Well. She understood the danger of this encounter. But then she said: "There must have been something about Jesus that made this woman feel safe to talk with him." The Samaritan woman became the first evangelist in John's Gospel. Even in Jesus' genealogy in Matthew 1, we see the inclusion and centering of scandalous women like Tamar, Rahab, Ruth, Bathsheba—and Mary, the mother of Jesus, the prophet who announced the downfall of the mighty and the exaltation of the humble, the one who carried this promise in her womb. If Paul was likewise a faithful carrier of the gospel of Jesus, the freeing and honoring of women would be a significant part of his message.

This is just one example of how to begin reading difficult passages from Paul's letters in a way that liberates rather than oppresses. It requires, in my estimation, a great deal more exegetical humility and hope than the traditional readings, and in the end makes a lot more sense of both the text and of life as we live it. It is not a *definitive* reading, but we should accept that neither are all of the equally speculative, and often contradictory, traditional interpretations. The rhetorical approach treats the text with the greatest respect while also acknowledging the incredible difficulties of interpretation and the long-standing harmful applications of these contested passages. It also allows my community to read this letter from Paul to Corinth alongside our beloved female friends and neighbors in a way that offers life, joy, honor, and freedom, and resonates with the rest of Paul's message and the message of the gospel.

LUCY PEPPIATT'S WORK

- *The Imago Dei: Humanity Made in the Image of God* (Wipf and Stock, 2022).
- *Rediscovering Scripture's Vision for Women: Fresh Perspectives on Disputed Texts* (IVP Academic, 2019).
- *Unveiling Paul's Women: Making Sense of 1 Corinthians 11:2–16* (Wipf and Stock, 2018).
- *Women and Worship at Corinth: Paul's Rhetorical Arguments in 1 Corinthians* (Wipf and Stock, 2015).
- *The Disciple: On Becoming Truly Human* (Wipf and Stock, 2012).

10

CRUCIAL CONVERSATIONS BETWEEN EGALITARIANS AND COMPLEMENTARIANS

Dr. Mimi Haddad

currently serves as president of CBE International. A graduate of Gordon-Conwell Theological Seminary (*Summa Cum Laude*), Mimi holds a PhD in historical theology from the University of Durham, England. An award-winning author, Palmer Theological Seminary recognized Haddad with an Honorary Doctor of Divinity in 2013. Haddad teaches for seminaries and institutes worldwide. A founding member of Evangelicals and Women at the Evangelical Theological Society, Haddad served as a gender and theological consultant for World Relief, World Vision International, and SASA! Faith Beyond Borders. For her full bio see: https://www.cbeinternational.org/primary_page/dr-mimi-haddad/.

Because of our differing interpretations of Scripture, egalitarians and complementarians present opposing worldviews, complicating dialogue and understanding in significant ways. These divergent worldviews affect how we see our church history, theology, and human flourishing.[1] But before we examine the sources of our divergent perspectives and the outcomes of egalitarianism and complementarianism, we must define our terms.

Egalitarianism: Holding to biblical authority, egalitarians believe Scripture teaches that women and men are both equally created in God's image—an ontology (the nature of being) that directs their assumptions about the purpose of men and women: to share dominion over the animals and plants, not each other. For egalitarians, *both* Adam and Eve disobeyed God. Their sin ruptured and distorted their shared dominion. Significantly, male rule—the consequence of sin (Gen. 3:16)—obscures and demeans woman's nature as created in God's image and this upends human flourishing. Shifting from human sin to God's rescue, Scripture foreshadows the birth of a child—a Savior, born of a woman, who will crush evil (Gen. 3:15). This hope accompanies woman and man as they navigate a fallen patriarchal world. For egalitarians, man and woman's shared rule fosters human flourishing.

Complementarianism: Holding to biblical authority, complementarians interpret Scripture to teach that women and men are both created in God's image—an ontology—the nature of being) that directs their belief that a distinct yet *different* purpose exists for each of them. Men are given authority over women in the church, home, and (for some) in the world, and women are to submit to male authority. This is God's original design, observed in a sinless world—one that remains unchanged after the fall. Complementarians believe that male authority and female submission is evident throughout Scripture and will continue in eternity.[2] Said to be part of God's design, complementarians believe male authority is essential for human flourishing. There is a range of ways complementarianism is taught and practiced. Some complementarian communities extend leadership to women but reserve the highest position of authority to men. In some complementarian marriages, husbands are tiebreakers only when they encounter a serious impasse or issue. This somewhat limited expression of male authority is referred to as "soft complementarianism."[3] Regardless of how male authority is practiced, *most* complementarians agree that male headship does not presume the inferiority of women.

DISTORTING HISTORY

From an egalitarian viewpoint, complementarians too often present a truncated view of women's leadership through history, one that obscures the scope and impact of their gifts, calling, and achievements. For more than fifty years, egalitarians have pioneered research recovering women's history. Women's achievements are astonishing, given the prevalence of patriarchy. For egalitarians, historical research is a "telling by showing" of God's design and purpose for women. God's purpose for women and men is not submission to men, but to the person of Christ.

As missiologist Dana Robert notes, women outnumbered men two to one in the evangelical movements of the 1800s and 1900s, thus shifting the density of Christian faith to broadly scattered regions throughout Asia, Africa, and South America.[4] Women founded mission organizations, funded its work, and served in all areas of leadership. Yet, the historical research published by egalitarians collides with that of complementarians over a *full* account of women's achievements in many occupations—but especially as evangelists, preachers, and church planters.

Consider Lottie Moon (1840–1912), a Southern Baptist missionary from Virginia whose leadership in China pioneered the first key initiative of the Foreign Mission Board at the *first* Southern Baptist Convention in 1849.[5] The Southern Baptist Foreign Mission Board, today's International Mission Board (IMB), celebrates Lottie Moon as the "namesake of Southern Baptists' international missions offering ... [since] she was like today's missionaries. She labored tirelessly so her people group could know Jesus."[6] For Lottie, there was "no greater joy than that of saving souls."[7] Without ordination, Moon could not officially lead the churches filled with believers she evangelized; so, she focused her energies on training pastors who, several decades later, baptized more than 2,000 Christians in Pintu, China. A stellar example to aspiring women evangelists, Moon launched a successful campaign to recruit more women missionaries. As her final act of solidarity with her beloved community in Pintu, ravished by famine, Lottie shared her food and refused to eat while others were starving. As a result, she died of starvation on Christmas Eve and was henceforth celebrated worldwide for her sacrificial leadership. So much so, she was referred to as "the best man among our missionaries."[8] Every year since her death, a Lottie Moon missionary offering is held on Christmas Eve in Southern Baptist churches.[9] Clearly, there is more of Lottie's story that needs telling among Southern Baptists—and especially the IMB, as it continues to raise funds in her name.

One might expect the SBC's International Mission Board to acknowledge, in the fullest terms, their own history which includes God's gifting and calling of women like Lottie Moon. Lottie's history also includes her fearless challenge to Southern Baptists to treat women missionaries as equals to men. Historians, like Ruth Tucker, reveal that Lottie once said, "What women want who come to China is free opportunity to do the largest possible work … What women have a right to demand is perfect equality."[10] Her expectation for equality inevitably motivated Lottie's insistence that women missionaries receive equal voting privileges beside their male coworkers. According to Moon, "Simple justice demands that women should have equal rights with men in mission meetings and in the conduct of their work."[11] Inevitably, Moon confronted her field director on the scope and location of her work with a stated willingness to part ways and "go it alone." But even with her persistently challenging the patriarchal structures, Moon's work in Pintu was viewed "as the 'greatest evangelistic center' among the Southern Baptists 'in all China.'"[12]

The history IMB paints today is one colored in its own complementarian image. Though raising funds based on Moon's legacy since 1913, would the IMB today tolerate women like Lottie Moon who expect equal voice beside their male coworkers and who challenge male field directors? Thankfully, Moon's legacy has inspired countless women missionaries in the SBC. But as complementarians gained control of the SBC, women leaders (and their male allies) were forced out of the IBM when they refused to sign the *Baptist Faith and Message 2000* statement that restricted leadership to men.[13] Because of this, CBE honored these individuals for their decades of service at their 2001 and 2003 international conferences.[14] Still, year after year, the leadership of Lottie Moon is distorted to fund a male-led missionary agency at odds with the values and legacy of a woman who preached, married, buried, planted churches, and trained the next generation of pastors.

Further, the historical example of Lottie Moon challenges the distorted history of complementarians[15] who argue that egalitarianism is the product of modern secular feminist ideology, when in fact, her example echoes the many women who have played significant roles throughout church history.[16] As George Orwell wrote: "Who controls the past, controls the future: who controls the present, controls the past."[17]

DISTORTING THEOLOGY

Over the last fifty years, four theological issues have been prominent in egalitarian-complementarian dialogue, including the meaning and relevance of:

1. The maleness of Jesus and its purpose in Christ's salvific work.
2. Male language in Scripture—particularly Christ's use of "Father" for God in the Lord's prayer (Matt. 6:9–13).
3. Man as "head" of woman (1 Cor. 11:3; Eph. 5:23); and God as "head" of Christ (1 Cor. 11:3).
4. Male leaders cited in Scripture.

For each theological issue, we will examine the complementarian assertions against the full witness of Scripture and history.

The Maleness of Jesus

Concerning the gender of Jesus as Messiah: To support male leadership, complementarians too often conflate maleness with God's being.[18] Examples include:

- **Mark Driscoll** (2010): "When it comes to leading in the church, women are unfit because they are more gullible and easier to deceive than men ... ."[19]
- **John Piper** (2012): In his lecture titled, "'The Frank and Manly Mr. Ryle'—the Value of a Masculine Ministry," Piper states, "God has revealed himself to us in the Bible *pervasively* as King, not Queen, and as Father, not Mother. The second person of the Trinity is revealed as the eternal Son. The Father and the Son created man and woman in his image, and gave them together the name of the man, *Adam* (Gen. 5:2). God appoints all the priests in Israel to be men. The Son of God comes into the world as a man, not a woman. He chooses twelve men to be his apostles. The apostles tell the churches that all the overseers—the pastor/elders who teach and have authority (1 Tim. 2:12)—should be men; and that in the home, the head who bears special responsibility to lead, protect, and provide should be the husband (Eph. 5:22–33)."[20]
- **Owen Strachan** (2014): "Satan hates testosterone. You can't blame him—after all, he's seen it used to crush his head."[21]

- **David Mathis** (2020): "God became man, and not woman. Jesus was a son, not a daughter; a brother, not a sister … the manhood of Christ is a stubborn, objective fact of history that unsettles modern sentiments, and holds important lessons."[22] For Mathis (the editor of desiringGod. org), *only men can represent humanity* because Adam, the man, was formed first. Adam received the moral mandate to eat of every tree but the tree of good and evil (Gen. 2:16–17). Being created first, the man Adam, and not Eve, named the animals—demonstrating his authority as head of the human race. Eve, being formed second, had a submissive role as "helper" to the man Adam.[23] And just as the man Adam was head of humanity, so, too, the man Christ is head of a new race (1 Cor. 15:22; Rom. 5:12–21; Eph 2:15).

While Mathis asserts that by naming the animals (Gen. 2:19–20) Adam was given authority, this complementarian reading omits the first creation account (Gen. 1:26–31) in which *both* Adam and Eve are created in God's image and *both* are given rule over "the fish in the sea and the birds in the sky, over the livestock and all the wild animals, and over all the creatures that move along the ground" (v. 26). "God blessed *them* and said, 'Be fruitful and increase in number; fill the earth and *subdue* it. *Rule over* the fish in the sea and the birds in the sky and over every living creature that moves on the ground'" (v. 28, italics mine). In the first creation account, God gives both image-bearers rule over the animals, not each other. Before Eve was created, Adam (the human) received the moral mandate regarding which trees to eat from. After Eve was created from Adam (the human), both man and woman were commissioned together to rule over creation (Gen. 1:28). Further, both were held accountable for their disobedience (Gen. 3:16–19). Created in God's image, both woman and man are moral agents, with moral capacity, moral choice, and therefore moral accountability (Gen. 3:11–19). Thus, both bear the consequences of sin.

Through Christ's death and resurrection, sinners become a new creation. Alive in Christ (Eph. 2:1–10), both women and men share authority through the Spirit which Christ promised to send (John 14:26). The Spirit's gifts are not limited by maleness or femaleness.[24]

While Mathis cites 1 Corinthians 15:22, Romans 5:12–21, and Ephesians 2:15 as examples of male headship or authority, Paul used the term *anthropos* (human), not *aner* (male), for Christ's self-disclosure as Savior of humanity. Though Jesus was male, he was first and foremost human (*anthropos*) because, as Savior, Christ represented *all humanity* on Calvary. To center Christ's maleness over his humanity opposes the teachings of Scripture and leaves women without a representative on the cross—a stunning theological failure the early church avoided.

Gregory of Nazianzus (329–390) writes, "For what he has not assumed he has not healed."[25] To absolutize the maleness of Jesus called into question access to Christ's atonement—available for *everyone*. To deem essential any aspect of Jesus' embodiment (his sex, ethnicity, etc.) posed a serious threat to what the early church had achieved in articulating Christ's victory on behalf of sinners both male and female.

Male Language in Scripture

Complementarians also elevate male authority by emphasizing that Christ taught his followers to pray to God as "Father." However, egalitarians counter in five ways. First, God's self-naming in Scripture is "I AM WHO I AM" (Exod. 3:14), a name without gender. Second, Scripture teaches that God is Spirit (John 4:24) and not a man (Num. 23:19).[26] Third, the Bible warns against graven images of any kind, including men or women (Deut. 4:15b–17). Fourth, Scripture uses metaphorical language for God, mindful that metaphors have points of meaning, and points of *no* meaning. Fifth, Scripture employs feminine language for God to illustrate God's fierce nurture and maternal protection. God is likened to a mother bird (Deut. 32:11), a she-bear and she-lion (Hos. 13:8), a pregnant woman (Deut. 32:18), and a mother hen (Matt. 23:37). God who gives us birth also comforts and trains us like a loving mother. We understand, of course, that *God is not* an *actual* bird, bear, lion, hen, or human mother; but because mothers are overall fiercely protective and nurturing of their children, this quality originated with and characterizes the motherly love of God for us, God's children.[27]

Not only does Scripture use mothering language for God, Christians throughout history have also used mother images and metaphors for God.

- **Clement of Alexandria** (150–215) wrote: "The Word [Christ] is everything to His little ones, both father and mother. The Word is all to the child—both father and mother, and tutor and nurse."[28]
- **Anselm** (1033–1109) wrote: "And you, Jesus, are you not also a mother? Are you not the mother who, like a hen, gathers her chickens under her wings?"[29]
- **Julian of Norwich** (1342–1423) wrote: "As truly as God is our Father, so is truly God our Mother. Our Father wills, our Mother works, our

good Lord the Holy Spirit confirms ... so Jesus is our true Mother in nature by our first creation [source of life], and he is our true Mother in grace by taking our created nature." [30]

- **Teresa of Avila** (1515–1582) wrote: "For from those divine breasts where it seems God is always sustaining the soul, there flow streams of milk bringing comfort to all the people."[31]

Søren Kierkegaard (1813–1855) showed how language "bursts and cracks under the strain of expressing God's greatness."[32] God is self-revealed in terms we can understand through experience, sometimes using gender. We should not, however, treat metaphors, which are implicit comparisons, as absolutes. Perhaps that is why Scripture offers various metaphors in describing an infinite God, mindful that metaphors retain the tension of what "is and is not." God is our rock; but God is not granite. God is our Father; but God is not a biological father since God is neither male nor female but Spirit (John 4:24). Given Israel was surrounded by people who worshiped gods and goddesses, the concept of God as Father was rare in the Old Testament. To insist that God is male is to make God in our image, which Scripture condemns as idolatry (Exod. 20:4). The Jews most often referred to "God of our fathers," and avoided calling God father or mother lest the image be taken literally. Yet Jesus called God *abba* (or "daddy")—an expression of intimacy, trust, and also birthright, as egalitarians note.

Male Headship in the Trinity and the Church

Complementarians like Wayne Grudem and Bruce Ware perceive a hierarchy in the Trinity, insisting that God the Father is "head" or authority over God the Son whom the Son obeys.[33] Given this, Ware directs Christians to pray to God the Father rather than to Jesus.[34] Thus emerges the eternal functional subordination that God the Son is presumed an ontological equal with God the Father yet is functionally subordinate.

Conversely, Phillip Carey, of Eastern University, raised serious concerns for Trinitarian subordinationism in his 2006 *Priscilla Papers* article, stating that a masculine Christianity is "determined to see in God, what they wish to see in humanity, a subordination in role or function that does not compromise (they insist) an essential equality of being."[35] Complementarians aim to justify the subordination of women to men by claiming the eternal functional subordination of God the Son to God the Father, while denying any devaluation in women or in the persons of the Trinity. Yet, the *homousia* (or essence) of God the Father and God the Son has been expressed throughout history in language that declares that the "Son is equal with the Father in status, power and glory."[36] It was the Arian argument that "human sons are subordinate to their fathers that led to their contention that the Son is subordinate to the Father. The church rejected the conclusion as heretical and opposed the premise as mistaken."[37]

Whether it is persons of the Trinity, males or females, slaves or free, Jews or Greek—how can you be equal in your being but *forever* unequal in authority or purpose? To do so renders the word "equal" meaningless! If US history teaches anything, it shows how essentialist rhetoric of "separate but equal" divided schools, restaurants, restrooms, hotels, buses, and even churches along racial lines, creating a country that was anything but equal and just! Claiming men and women can be "equal in being but unequal in purpose" is illogical, duplicitous, unjust, and at odds with Scripture's teachings. To deny women or people of color authority not because of their gifts, calling, or character but solely based on a fixed and unchangeable condition is not only biblically flawed, it also distorts human purpose and creates communities that are *inherently unjust and too often put people at risk*—a point we'll return to.

Male vs. Female Leaders Cited in Scripture

Finally, what is the significance of the twelve male disciples? Piper notes, "There is a masculine feel to Christianity" given Jesus our Savior was male who "chooses twelve men to be his apostles."[38] Yes, the twelve disciples were male, but equally important they were Jewish. If you insist leaders today should resemble the Twelve, leaders should be *both male and Jewish*. The point of the Twelve was not their gender but to demonstrate God's faithfulness to Israel's twelve tribes. Piper rightly notes the Twelve were also apostles, those who witnessed the risen Christ. But egalitarians remind us that on Easter morning, the beginning of a new creation, Jesus first appeared to women.[39] Further, Christ told Mary Magdalene to declare his resurrection to the disciples, thus making her the first apostle.[40] Women were commissioned as apostles ahead of the men.

Unlike the rabbis of his day, Jesus welcomed women like Mary of Bethany to learn at his feet (Luke 10:38–42)—preparing them as disciples, evangelists, teachers, apostles, and church planters. Jesus unhesitatingly engages women as fully human: as Abraham's daughters[41] and heirs of his new creation. Jesus challenged the patriarchal devaluation that demeaned and restricted women's being and purpose. To argue that Christianity has "a masculine feel" is to *fail exactly where* the Twelve failed: They were slow to realize that Christ redeemed and liberated the identity, value, and purpose of those at the margins. Scholars view the writings of the New Testament as the most emancipatory texts on women coming from antiquity.[42]

The female disciples often succeeded where the male disciples floundered. The twelve male disciples grasped for power, asking to sit at Christ's right and left hand (Mark 10:37); they forbade children to approach Jesus (Mark 10:13); they were outraged when Christ spoke to and welcomed women openly as heirs and daughters of Abraham (John 4:27, Mark 5:34, Luke 13:15); they stole money (John 12:6); and one betrayed Jesus (Matt. 26:14–16). When Christ was arrested and crucified, the Twelve dispersed, one denied Christ openly (Luke 22:54–62), and others hid behind locked doors. Not the women. They anointed Jesus just as Samuel and Zadok anointed Israel's leaders (Matt. 26:6–13, 1 Sam. 16:1, 1 Kings 1:34). They remained with Christ through his crucifixion. They wrapped his corpse and returned the next morning. Mary Magdalene was the first to meet the risen Lord who sent her to tell the disciples (John 20:17). She became an apostle to the apostles, but the disciples did not believe her. Even as Jesus appeared to them, Thomas asked to touch his wounds as proof (Mark 16:14, John 20:24–27).

Women were also prominent at Pentecost, the birth of the church: United and equal without gender, ethnic, or age barriers, all were anointed by the Spirit for service (Acts 2). Paul reminds us to "fan into flames" the Spirit's gifts (2 Tim. 1:6) which empower men *and* women as evangelists like Lottie Moon, as prophets like Deborah and Huldah (Judg. 4:4–16, 2 Kings 22:13–20, 2 Chron. 34:22–28), and as pastors (or coworkers, deacons, and apostles) like Priscilla, Euodia and Syntyche, Phoebe, Junia, Persis (Rom 16:1–12), and Apphia (Philem. 1:1–3)—women who functioned as pastors since Scripture calls no one "pastor."[43] Through the Spirit's equipping, Priscilla was a teacher (Acts 18:18–28), and Mary Magdalene (John 20:11–18) and Junia (Rom. 16:7) were apostles. These women demonstrated that God (the Son) is the source of their newness of life, just as God (the Spirit) is the source of their spiritual power for service.

FOSTERING HUMAN FLOURISHING

What is the impact on human flourishing that results from the differing teachings and practices of egalitarians and complementarians? Clearly, egalitarians and complementarians disagree on what constitutes a fair representation of history and theology. When history and theology are distorted to privilege a class of people, it not only fosters bias and power imbalances, but it also furthers a trajectory of marginalization and abuse.

In 1994, egalitarians considered the impact of complementarian theology at the CBE conference titled, "Women, Abuse, and the Bible."[44] CBE's first president, Cathie Kroeger, described her shock at the number of women who attended the conference and disclosed their experiences of abuse.[45] Paper presentations were published in 1996 by Baker Publishing under the same title as the conference. The response from complementarians was a *stunning silence*— even as egalitarians continued to address the abuses of male headship biblically, at events, in research, and in publications beside egalitarian partners worldwide. Research showed how male headship resulted not only in marital dissatisfaction but also in abuse and violence.[46] The egalitarian interpretation of "headship" as mutual submission (Eph. 5:21) and Christian service as shared authority (Gen. 1: 26–29) had support from both biblical and now sociological data.

Eventually, some complementarians tried to tackle the topic of abuse and male headship by proposing a "third way." In 2003, former complementarian Steven Tracy wrote an article for *Christianity Today* titled "Headship with a Heart: How Biblical Patriarchy Actually Prevents Abuse." In it, he advocated for this "third way" that framed male headship as reflecting Christ's sacrifice and service.[47] In 2016, Biola professor Michelle Lee Barnewall published another "alternative position" themed, *Neither Complementarian nor Egalitarian.*[48] Like Tracy, Lee Barnewall views male headship as self-sacrifice that initiates unity, love, and oneness between husband and wife and all Christians. But while Tracy's "third way" was rooted in a concern for abused women, Lee Barnewall never mentioned abuse. Lee Barnewall also criticized post-1970s egalitarian's focus on "rights" and "equality" as out of step with first-wave biblical feminists of the late 1800s and early 1900s whose aim was serving others through abolition, suffrage, and laws against rape.[49] On closer scrutiny, however, the focus on women's rights and equality by post-1970s egalitarians did in fact serve others, especially the abused and those at the margins.

Consider that in the 1970s, women's full-time annual income was 59 percent of men's with median income for women only 33 percent of the median income for men, with women of color being paid even less.[50] Most women also shouldered a "second shift" at home. During this time, women experienced less pay, but more violence. Prior to the 1994 Violence Against Women Act (VAWA), domestic violence data was almost non-existent; but through the VAWA and activism of second-wave feminists and post-1970s egalitarians, violence against women declined 48.2 percent between 1994 and 2000.[51]

The tension between "third way" complementarians and post-1970s egalitarians persists. Just as "third way" pro-slavery Christians attempted to address the abuses of slavery while retaining the system as God-approved, "third way" complementarians oppose the abuses of patriarchy but wish to retain male headship. In contrast, egalitarians opposed slavery and Christian patriarchy as biblically and ethically flawed. As Richard Hays observed, the New Testament calls the powerful and privileged to:

> *Surrender* it for the sake of the weak ... it is *husbands* (not wives) who are called to emulate Christ's example of giving themselves up in obedience for the sake of the other (Eph. 5:25) ... [interpreting this] as though it somehow warranted a husband's domination or physical abuse of his wife can only be regarded as a bizarre—indeed, blasphemous—misreading ... the followers of Jesus—men and women alike—must read the New Testament as a call to renounce violence and coercion.[52]

Post-1970s egalitarians focused on political and legal rights as a means of serving women who were abused physically and economically. In this way, post-1970s egalitarians are in-step with the first-wave biblical feminists who advanced abolition, suffrage, and women's rights to protect the vulnerable of their day.

Even more, with the emergence of #MeToo and #ChurchToo, egalitarians produced lectures and resources to evaluate, expose, and prevent abuse theologically and socially.[53] Groups like Barna reveal the significant obstacles that still make it harder for women to flourish economically: "In our research, women point out inequality in promotions and in pay ... women are still under-represented in executive suites and paid less than men for the same jobs. Additionally, women continue to disproportionately feel the tension of work/family balance."[54] Significantly, Barna reports that "evangelicals are the most skeptical of the existence of barriers for women in the workplace." Evidence also shows that women are underrepresented in theological and leadership fields among evangelicals.[55]

Personal experiences of women in the Evangelical Theological Society (ETS) also reveal humiliating assumptions that women are not themselves scholars but are simply married to one; unvoiced sentiments that women do not belong; a "general feeling of being unequal, unnoticed and even invisible"; women's "very presence [being] too different and difficult to include"; and difficulty talking to married professors, who seemed to create barriers to conversations, collegiality, and collaboration.[56]

The above data exposes barriers that make it more difficult for women to gain professional equity in Christian spheres even as secular business research shows that a diverse workforce increases performance and workplace ethics![57] Without the shared leadership of women and men, not only is human flourishing at risk but these environments can also become a breeding ground for abuse— as John Pryor of Illinois State University showed in his "Likelihood to Sexually Harass" scale. Based on answers to the question, "What causes some men to harass and not others?" Pryor identified four characteristics of harassers:[58]

1. a tendency toward power, dominance, and authoritarianism;
2. a lack of empathy;
3. environments that foster impunity; and
4. an enforcement of traditional gender roles.

For decades, scientists have recognized that authority and dominance are consistently part of an abuser's profile. While complementarians like Ware believe that male-headship protects women from abuse,[59] organizations like Prepare/Enrich, with the most prominent premarital worldwide research of over four million data-points, consistently shows that partner dominance is a *key* indicator for physical and sexual abuse.[60] Power and privilege are also known to foster impulsive behaviors, altering an abuser's perception.[61] Dominant men, with authority and power, wrongly believe that their subordinates desire sex with them.[62] This explains why those with privilege often behave impulsively, lunging at women ... and more. Sadly, repeated use of porn—as common among Christian men as non-Christian men—feeds a narcissistic impulse to control and dominate others for self-pleasure.[63]

Putting this all together, when men who score high on dominance, low on empathy, and high on support of traditional gender roles, make their way into environments without accountability, where they can act with impunity, they often do. Pryor's data is crucial since both egalitarians and complementarians have celebrity pastors in our communities who have abused women.

WOMEN'S SHARED RULE REVEALS GOD'S VERY GOOD CREATION

While egalitarian and complementarian dialogue continues to address differences in theology, Scripture, and history, increasingly these conversations reveal flawed assumptions, teachings, and practices. As theological, biblical, and historical accuracy becomes increasingly prevalent, more women and men have the confidence and assurance that women's gifts and calling constitutes God's path for ministry in the church, home, and world—one that is not limited by gender, but shaped and empowered by God's Spirit. As women use their gifts in any sphere, they bring the Spirit's gifting and power for God's purposes to foster human flourishing—as modeled by women leaders and leadership teams not only in Scripture (Rom. 16) but throughout church history (like Paula and Jerome, Teresa of Avila and John of the Cross, Sojourner Truth and Fredrick Douglass). Releasing women's service in church, home and the world aligns profoundly with the creation account that women, like men, are created in God's image and called to shared rule ... and this, God said, is very good (Gen. 1:31).

IN CONCLUSION

How can we work together as Christians?

While egalitarian and complementarian dialogue will continue to address history and theology, it's crucial that we invest new effort in upending abuse and creating environments that allow women to flourish. We can help families and churches combat the four horse-riders of abuse that John Pryor identified. Here are six simple ways.

Challenge dominance boldly as Jesus did. In all four gospels, Jesus tells his followers that the Gentiles lord their authority over others, but not so you (see Luke 22–27). Churches can agree that leadership is service and service is based on character, exhibiting the fruit of the Spirit (Gal. 5:22–23).

Model and rehearse the capacity of male-female leadership teams seen in Scripture (Rom. 16) and history (like the examples I listed, above). Male and female teams have inherent accountability; they're more productive and ethical; they foster empathy; and they challenge dominance and impunity.

Discern and protect against abuse by requiring screening, training, certification, *and systems* of accountability for leaders. Catholics have done this, we can too.

Discuss porn from the pulpit, in adult education, and in youth programs. Be honest about personal temptations and failures.

Work to improve legislation to defend and protect victims by removing the statute of limitations in sexual abuse cases of minors.[64]

Pray as leaders, despite our differing views of leadership. Pray to end abuse.

THE COST OF PATRIARCHY

The adverse experiences some women encounter in Christian environments extend beyond mere individual interactions—they are ingrained within a system that reinforces inequality and male dominance. Many refer to this system as a "patriarchy"—a "hypothetical social system in which the father or a male elder has absolute authority over the family group; by extension, one or more men (as in a council) exert absolute authority over the community as a whole."[1]

As Anita Giardina Lee conveys in her opening letter to this section, these systems can easily lead to dysfunction that weighs heavily on those who serve in these contexts. Rev. Dr. Elizabeth Rios goes on to highlight the roles of empire and patriarchy and their impact on the church, pointing to a way forward that encompasses a collaborative leadership model that benefits all. Beth Allison Barr shares her motivations for writing *The Making of Biblical Womanhood* and the ongoing injustices for women within denominations such as the Southern Baptist Convention. Janet Munn further exposes the prevalent inequality in organizations that intend to be equitable but don't take care to embed equality in their values and practices. She highlights how this negatively impacts everyone in the organization and points to practices for change.

As we listen to and learn from these examples—both personal experiences and lessons from history—we must consider how systems of inequality can be dismantled in our spaces, allowing us to embrace a way forward and become more centered on how God calls us to operate as the body of Christ.

11

WHAT I NEED YOU TO KNOW

Anita Giardina Lee

is passionate to amplify and celebrate the voices of women in the church: past, present, and future. When she's not tending to her young family or working with the team at Boundless Enterprise, she is excitedly researching the legacy of discipleship women have in the history of Christianity and dreaming up ways we can be the church Jesus intended us to be.

It was fun. It felt like love. It felt like family. I was honored to serve alongside good, kind, and brilliant people. It felt like we were doing something important—life-altering and world-changing—and that I had a special role to play. It seemed worth giving up important things for: time, sleep, rest, financial security, dating prospects, and even a future family. *This is my family, right?* It felt anything but toxic. At least not at first.

So, when the opportunity arose, I had no qualms resigning from my comfy corporate job and taking on a role I'd never expected: pastor. Despite the change of direction, I felt enchanted by the vision of kingdom building I saw before me. A part-time position as an associate pastor grew into full-time ministry when, less than six months later, I was encouraged to become lead pastor for one of our church campuses. The main church staff and the satellite community where I served were two very different ecosystems, and I welcomed the challenge of finding ways for them to thrive together. I didn't expect it to be easy, but I assumed it would be healthy.

But as time went on, I noticed that colleagues who left were usually sick or angry. I felt deeply concerned about them and almost never saw them again. As the reasons for their departures made their way through the team, those who left were somehow labeled as the problem. Few relationships lasted beyond their last day. When I met former staff or adjacent ministry leaders, I expected instant camaraderie, yet more often felt treated like I had the plague. They appeared to want to get away from me as soon as possible.

I was aware that people had been hurt, but I had explanations for all of that. In fact, I had scripts to counter anything that caused me to question my full investment. These were scripts I'd acquired early on and adopted as my own. It was part of the culture to defend the main church and its important people. When leadership was questioned, I had ready-made excuses for their behavior: *It's just their personality, it's just their nature—don't take it the wrong way.* In reality, we were constantly pushing aside the obvious. In fact, there were leaders whose "personality" was part of their charm tactic—a way to build trust, disarm others, and create a culture with no accountability to challenge their lack of boundaries.

Meanwhile, I continually deferred my questions to the powers that be. They were, after all, much smarter, more *Jesus-y*, and more experienced than I was. Nevertheless, my conversations with fellow female colleagues led me to believe I wasn't the only one struggling. I wondered if we weren't cut out for ministry. But seeing the caliber of these gifted leaders questioning themselves and their vocation compelled me to advocate for a healthier environment for us all. It stung when our male colleagues seemed to be having such a great time and our superiors attributed our concerns to perfectionism or misplaced expectations.

I also lamented that the church system itself seemed to be the biggest obstacle to our ministries. Because as well as the toxic behavior of leaders, there was no real plan to help us pursue the vision we said we had. There were only meetings that led to piles and piles of more busy work that didn't amount to anything of consequence, except burned-out pastors.

I desperately wanted to be a part of what we *said* we were doing. But, as time passed, I didn't see this translate into action. I didn't see it in the workload, in the budgets, in the perpetual last-minute rallies to make things happen, in the way people were cared for, or in the responses to my questions. I didn't see it, but I still believed it faithfully.

I wish I could say I stopped because of the gaslighting, the violation of boundaries, the victim-blaming, or the failed promises that let so many people down. I wish I could say I stopped when I was told I "care too much" when raising concerns about how others were treated. I wish I could say I stopped because I trusted myself, but I didn't know I was in danger, even when my body was telling me so. She tried to tell me when my teeth started breaking in my sleep. She tried to tell me when it took me days to physically recover from certain meetings. She tried to tell me when she froze after a superior snapped at a fair question. My body, she knew. I just couldn't hear her, even though she was screaming.

What I did trust was that Jesus cared about people and it seemed clear to me that Jesus wouldn't continue in this way; he would change the course of the church. I assumed the people around me hadn't realized it yet—I just had to keep going so I could help them. And I did, diligently, until my body gave up.

I just need a few weeks' break, I told myself. But I never really made it back, not fully. A few months into my return from complete burnout, I met with a trusted leader and friend. She gave me the words I needed to hear: "If you need to go, we bless you to go. We don't need you to stay for us." I had been praying that I would know when it was time and I felt released. When I finally put in my resignation, I was heartbroken and spent weeks in deep grief. I was leaving a community that I loved but also a world in which I could not thrive. I tried with everything in me, and it wasn't enough. That was difficult to accept.

With distance, I saw more clearly the toxic culture in which I'd been. In time, I learned of abuse and deception that ran rampant under the surface. Brave truth-tellers finally brought light to the darkness. If I'm honest, amid the horror, I breathed a sigh of relief—I finally knew it wasn't that I just couldn't cut it.

I need you to know that I am better now. I have a family. I have dreams, boundaries, and priorities. I am working in a vibrant ministry. I also need you to know that I am still unequivocally convinced that Jesus is enough. Jesus wouldn't be rushed and bogged down with projects and busy work. He wouldn't be sucked into a system of exploitation in the name of God. He wouldn't allow toxic behavior to be overlooked in the name of "gifting" or "keeping the peace." Jesus is enough, and we are enough for him already.

Despite my experience, I'm excited and hopeful for the future of Jesus' church. I believe that, because of Jesus, none of this will go to waste. I also believe it is possible to prevent other women from having similar experiences. I know there are women ready and willing to give their all to build the kingdom of God here and now; heaven forbid that we, the church, be their biggest obstacle. We need men, alongside women, who pull down the barriers, who call out the injustices, and who make space for each person to thrive. To pursue that hopeful future, we must advance together.

12

COLLABORATIVE LEADERSHIP: MORE KIN*DOM, LESS EMPIRE

Rev. Dr. Elizabeth Rios

is an Afro-Boricua, native of Manhattan, NY, now living in South Florida. She is the pioneering founder of Passion2Plant, one of the only national church planting networks in the US founded and led by a woman, that trains global majority leaders to start holistically-minded, justice-oriented churches. As a writer, her articles have appeared in *Sojourners, Influence, Called, Christianity Today*, and in the materials of Pentecostals and Charismatics for Peace and Justice. She has been featured or quoted in *The Atlantic, The Washington Post, Religion News Service*, and *Outreach Magazine*. She is an author and has also contributed to many books, including most recently, *Rhythms of Rest: 40 Devotions for Women on the Move*, published by Our Daily Bread Publishing. She has been married for thirty-four years to Hiram, and has two boys, Samuel (26) and DJ, who transitioned to heaven in 2022.

The status of women in the United States continues to lag behind that of men on a consistent basis; notwithstanding certain advancements in recent decades, women continue to earn lower wages than men, endure greater poverty rates in comparison to men, encounter distinct adverse health conditions, and remain underrepresented in political office nationwide.[1] Although complete gender equality has not yet been attained by any nation, certain countries are making greater progress than others in narrowing the divide between the sexes. The United States is not among them, currently ranked 43rd out of 146 countries by the World Economic Forum, according to the Global Gender Gap Report 2023, which is in its seventeenth year of comparing gender disparities across four dimensions: economic opportunities; educational attainment; health and survival; and political empowerment. Unfortunately, the position of the US on this list is worsening as the ranking was 27th in 2022.[2]

Meanwhile, the church continues to engage in dialogues and deliberations regarding the position of women in pastoral leadership, eldership, preaching, and ministry. Amidst a backdrop of numerous sexual abuse cases, and incited by Pastor Rick Warren's ordination of three women at Saddleback Church, the Southern Baptist Convention (SBC) voted overwhelmingly in June 2023 to prohibit churches from hiring women pastors and to expel the few churches that had them.[3] However, the SBC is by no means the only organization that continues to debate the position of women. The Lutheran Church—Missouri Synod, The Church of God in Christ, The Presbyterian Church in America, The Reformed Church in the United States, The American Baptist Association, and The Evangelical Free Church of America all refuse to ordain women.[4]

Further, even those churches and Christian organizations that claim an egalitarian position on women in leadership can perpetuate environments where women are treated as less than men. In church traditions that do not distinguish responsibilities or clergy positions by biological sex, the congregational culture can be male-centric and leave women feeling excluded and powerless to live out their calling. Women are typically seen as a threat to men. Their bodies are strictly policed, unlike men's, which can foster abusive cultures and lead to marginalizing women. This is why we must be careful not to presume that a congregation is "egalitarian" and without male-centric attitudes that disadvantage women. Some think that seeing women in a leadership position (usually in children's, youth, or hospitality ministry) means the senior pastor is fully embracing of women. Yet when asked outright, many of these same pastors believe that women can be "directors" or "ministers" but not pastors and elders (who have a voice in the direction of the church). The truth is that a leadership culture of top-down, command-and-control decision-making, zero-sum power games,[5] honoring of "set-man" thinking,[6] and intolerance to vulnerability and transparency often epitomize a patriarchal culture. These patriarchal cultures have stemmed from the influence of empire over the centuries.

As a Generation X, Afro-Boricua born in Brooklyn and raised in Manhattan, NY, who is now living in the hotbed (literally and politically) of Southern Florida, I am no stranger to many of the -isms women face in the world—and sadly, in the church. It is within these contexts that I discuss an alternative to the empire-based perspectives so prevalent in our churches, in favor of a kin*dom-based approach that centers around collaborative leadership.[†]

THE PREVAILING INFLUENCE OF EMPIRE

Most of what we have learned about Jesus, and even the image we have of him, was developed in the context of empire. That's how much influence empire has had on Christianity. Many of the stories we read in the Bible were of people living under empires—including the Assyrians, Babylonians, Persians, Greeks, and finally Romans. Although many American Christians have viewed themselves as biblical people, most have never been taught how to read the Bible from a decolonized lens. This makes it difficult for them to see the stories of the Bible from a decolonized perspective, even though empire is a major subject in the Bible and appears from the story of Pharoah in Egypt to Israel's monarchy to the exile of Israel to Roman Empire and to what many are waiting for as "the end times" in the battle described in Revelation. And, while the Bible talks a lot about empire, it has never been anything particularly good.

In his book *God's Reign and the End of Empires*, Antonio González breaks down what empire looks like and what feeds it. Essentially, there are four features attributed to empire: 1) a fixation on military power; 2) a love of capitalism,

---

† Kin*dom may not be a familiar term to us, but it has been used for decades by people who have wanted to get away from the imperialistic, patriarchal language of kingdom. Unlike a kingdom, a kin*dom is inclusive, non-hierarchical, relational, compassionate, justice-oriented, and anti-imperial. See Dr. Ada María Isasi-Díaz, *Mujerista Theology* (Orbis Books, 2005).

which is the engine that drives the economy; 3) a political infrastructure estab-lished for power and control, usually with a key individual believed to be the best/strongest/most powerful; and 4) an ideology that shapes a narrative that the best life is the one you can live when you fall in line with what they say is truth: "manifest destiny," their right to rule over others and oftentimes, their right to kill anything that stands in their way, even if it means genocide.[7] Empire living puts trust in the sword (power and control) while kin*dom living trusts in the power of the cross and the one who gave his life for others. An empire aims to expand its dominion extensively, encompassing not only geographical, political, and economic aspects, but also intellectual, emotional, psychological, spiritual, cultural, and religious dimensions.

Christianity emerged during the early stages of a vast empire that was among the biggest in history. The Roman Empire, which was less than fifty years old at the time of Jesus, would continue to exist for about 1,500 more years. While initially the notion of collaboration between Christianity and empire seemed inconceivable, during the ongoing reign of the Roman Empire, Christianity emerged as the dominant religion of the imperial state, laying the foundation for the establishment of entities such as the Holy Roman Empire in Western Europe, which lasted until the early 19th century.[8]

Throughout history, empires continued to exert influence, particularly through colonialism. This manifested in our indigenous communities through the appropriation of our lands, the disregard for our culture and values—often stigmatizing what was not comprehended—and the subjugation of our people. Rather than standing in opposition to this work of the empire, Christianity was central to its justification.

Professor of Theology Joerg Rieger highlights this:

In the history of Christianity, many have died because people worshiped a god of servitude who sanctioned slavery; a god of violence who endorsed torture, mass killings, and war; or a god of privilege who underwrote the "superiority" of white people, straight people, men, or privileged elites at the expense of everyone else. These are only a few of the most detrimental images of God. Others include a god who embodies unilateral power that allows no human agency, blatant insensitivity in the face of suffering, or smothering love that leaves no room to breathe—the power, the insensitivity, and the love of empire.[9]

Further instances of Christianity and empire can be observed in contemporary times through phenomena such as the Doctrine of Discovery,[10] justifying colonial conquests; Manifest Destiny,[11] promoting a so-called "God-given" right for American dominion; and the more recent emergence of Christian Nationalism, the conflating of American and Christian identities and the belief that the US was founded as a Christian nation and has God's special favor.[12]

The impact of the influence of empire and its compounded damage through Christian doctrine has been seen throughout history. As Rieger notes, "The truth is that worshiping and serving the wrong god has done tremendous damage to people and the earth, and has even led to killing and death."[13] Who is the "wrong god" we have been serving? Caesar. The conflict between Caesar and Jesus has significantly transformed Christianity, leading to a profound alteration in the way we practice our faith and carry out religious activities in the name of God. "The tension at the heart of Christian faith is the tension between ways of life that are life-giving for all—not just a few—and ways of life that are not. This is the tension between Jesus and Caesar."[14] From the looks of much of what is happening in North America, we are neck deep in empire ways and on our way to drowning. We can see empire ways in our churches when they prioritize institutional growth, wealth accumulation, and political influence over spiritual depth and discipleship or service to the marginalized. These modern practices often mirror corporate models, focusing on hierarchical structure, celebrity-pastor leadership, and a consumerist approach to faith. These empire ways have already led to a culture where success is measured more by numbers and financial prosperity than by transformational impact on individuals or the social transformation of our communities. These practices align more with earthly empires than with the radical, counter-cultural teachings of Jesus. Unless we promptly recognize the identity of the One we worship and the manner in which we ought to worship and follow his ways, we will eventually lack any resemblance to Christ. We are almost already there. Essentially, empire is Satan's principal weapon against God; and the church has fallen for it time and time again.

This is why examining how our theology has been influenced by empire is crucial. Empire's influence on our theology has impacted our understanding of the nature of God, the essence of humanity, and the interconnectedness between ourselves and God and the natural world. Furthermore, responding theologically to the current issues of empire is imperative considering the historical context of colonialism and the ongoing process of globalization. Empire, which is an undeniable reality in our daily lives, must be actively opposed in order to achieve the type of justice that Jesus aimed to establish, particularly in solidarity with those who are marginalized by the power dynamics of empire. These days, we witness firsthand or through the media how many people who claim to be followers of Jesus actually have more in common with the ideals and practices of empire. Here are a few examples:

1. *Preference for violence over promotion of peace.* The Roman Empire was known for its military might and use of force to maintain control. Jesus, on the other hand, taught and practiced nonviolence and peace. His famous teachings like "turn the other check" (Matt. 5:38–39) and "blessed are the peacemakers" (Matt. 5:9) emphasized this.

2. *Authoritarian rule over servant leadership.* Empires typically operated under a system of hierarchical, authoritarian rule. Jesus introduced a different model of leadership—one based on humility and servant-hood. Washing the disciples' feet during the Last Supper is an example of this (John 13:1–17).

3. *Exclusivity over inclusivity.* The Roman Empire was known for its class distinctions and often oppressive treatment of colonized peoples and the enslaved. Jesus, however, reached out to the marginalized of society—including tax collectors, the sick, and women—promoting a message of love for all and everybody belonging.

4. *Revenge over forgiveness.* Empire was almost always focused on vengeance and punishment. Jesus emphasized mercy and forgiveness, especially toward those considered enemies!

5. *Accumulation of wealth over sharing with the community.* The Roman Empire was characterized by wealth accumulation and economic disparity. Jesus advocated for resources to be shared, the poor supported (Mark 10:21) and the hungry fed (Matt. 15:32–39; Mark 8:16–21), and often taught about the dangers of wealth (Luke 12:34).

6. *Celebrity over humility.* The leaders of empires often sought glory, honor, and public recognition. Jesus, however, lived a life of humility and simplicity. He was born in a manger and associated with the lowly, in stark contrast to the pomp and circumstance of imperial rulers.

7. *Disempowerment of women over the promotion and celebration of women.* Empire ways have had a profound impact on women throughout history, often in ways that perpetuated gender inequality and limited

women's rights and opportunities. Women have often been victims of exploitation and violence under imperial regimes. The Bible offers numerous instances that highlight Jesus' revolutionary treatment and empowerment of women, especially when contrasted with the societal norms and attitudes of the Roman Empire and the patriarchal structure of ancient Jewish society. Two prominent examples come from the Gospels: The Woman at the Well (John 4:4–26) and Mary Magdalene and the Resurrection (John 20:1–18).

8. *Lastly, an "it's-about-me" over "it's-about-you" heart.* Empires conquer through force. The ultimate act of Jesus' life, his crucifixion, was in direct opposition to the values of the empire. He conquered through sacrificial love, offering his life for the sake of others. Kin*dom is radical love!

Understanding and knowing the difference between this earthly empire and the kin*dom of God and the theologies of each is not only of importance in the life of a Jesus-follower; it will also help everyone involved in ministry in any capacity to discern if they are attempting to do kin*dom things in empire ways.

The ministry of Jesus exemplified an alternative path to the ways of empire, revealing that no empire can ultimately achieve absolute dominion, as they are all flawed systems. None possesses the capacity for wholly just dominion that genuinely considers the well-being of all members of society. Jesus opposed the subjugation imposed by the Roman Empire and should be a source of inspiration for church leaders, as well as their people, to seek alternative lifestyles and align themselves with those who are marginalized and oppressed. This resistance against the empire remains relevant in present times. If our theology fails to acknowledge the impact of empire on Christian history and its ongoing influence on the beliefs and actions of present-day Christians, then it is likely to perpetuate and justify the ways of empire and endorse contemporary imperialism under the guise of divine authority.

The reason we find ourselves in this situation within North American ministry is partly due to the inability of many individuals to verify whether the teachings delivered from our pulpits align with the true gospel. Instead, we are influenced by celebrity pastors, personal biases stemming from our cultural or spiritual background, and our political alignment. The consequences of this have particularly played out in the role of religious influence in recent political cycles.

Like Joshua, we must make the decision that will determine everything for us: "determine this day whom you will serve" (see Josh. 24:15). Will we serve the god of empire or Jesus?

KIN*DOM COLLABORATION

Despite empire's prevalence throughout much of church history, whenever there is a state of dominance, the innate prophetic instincts and principles of Jesus-followers emerge to counteract the expansion.

In recent times, the cultivation of a kin*dom-oriented outlook has grown in significance for the North American church as a consequence of the waning influence of Christendom (another symptom of the influence of empire). The kin*dom of God can be defined as the ongoing and active rule of God throughout history, as he fulfills his intentions in the world through the actions of Jesus. It is the realization of God's ultimate vision for humanity and the fulfillment of Jesus' purpose in sacrificing himself.

I believe a key element to pursuing kin*dom will be the collaboration of men and women in church leadership. Patriarchy is yet another product of empire theology which sees the subordination of women to men. But if we want to return to God's intentions for kin*dom living, patriarchy will have to be subjugated. Research in anthropology tells us patriarchy is not the "natural order of things" as some may suggest. Researchers have uncovered that hunter-gatherer communities may have been relatively egalitarian, at least compared to some of the regimes that followed. And female leaders and matriarchal societies have always existed.[15]

Within the church, we have seen women as key figures since its inception,[16] and in contemporary times we can assert with certainty that women have been the fundamental support system of the church. According to George Barna's data, there has been a slight drop in this trend,[17] but it is still insufficient to claim that women are no longer the main support of the church. Women are more inclined than men to make up the majority of churchgoers, volunteers, and Sunday school teachers. I was raised in a predominantly Puerto Rican Assembly of God church called Iglesia Cristiana Primitiva, located on the Lower East Side. Interestingly, the church was primarily led by women. I never witnessed the disregard of women's talents and abilities in my spiritual formation at this church. Women played a significant role in all aspects of this faith community. Although there were no female pastors when I arrived at the church in 1975 at the age of ten, by September 1999, my sister-in-law had been appointed as the first full-time executive pastor; and now there are six women serving as ministers and four women holding the position of pastor. As with the increase in female leadership my church has seen, more women are looking to lead in churches today. Journalist A. J. Willingham believes this points to a hopeful future for the church. She says, "Women—and men—in the church have seen abuse and suffering. They've seen the role of the patriarchy in the church. They want to address constructively some of these challenges that have been facing both the church and our society."[18] Perhaps it is time for us to consider a new age of women's responsibility in the church and find ways for men and women to work together to overcome the challenges we face.

To fully experience the profound impact of the gospel, it is crucial that we develop the ability to actively participate and work together in the church. This will surely be the way we can fully experience the inclusivity prophesied about the last days, where "sons *and* daughters" will prophesy (Acts 2:17, emphasis mine), and "every nation, tribe, people, and language" (Rev. 7:9) will stand before the throne of God.

So, what does collaboration really look like?

The term "collaborate" is derived from the Latin word *laborare*, which means "to labor, toil, or struggle," and the prefix "co-," which denotes "with" or "together."[19] Collaborating involves the act of working together to achieve a shared goal. Collaboration involves a deliberate and purposeful effort to work together harmoniously.

I often find there is a significant amount of confusion surrounding the concept of collaboration. Individuals employ terms such as "connect," "coordinate," or "cooperate" in a manner that is interchangeable with the word "collaborate." This often curtails the potential of true authentic collaboration. When we establish a *connection* with someone, we come together in a meeting and exchange concepts. We may possess a profound understanding of another individual, however, that does not constitute a collaborative partnership. When organizations *coordinate*, it signifies their intention to work together on an activity or event with each group assigned tasks for efficiency to produce a better outcome than doing it alone. However, this differs from collaboration, as the achievements of the two groups remain distinct. *Cooperation* is generally associated with passivity rather than activity. We acquiesce to the desires of others.

Collaboration, or co-creation, entails using the dynamics of relationship to bring together individuals to create something from nothing in a way that invites ideas in a shared power structure. The goal of co-creation collaboration is to produce something new, useful, and meaningful in a collective experience. Interdependence is required in order to achieve collective benefit. Instead of simply adding resources, we seek synergy, demonstrating that when we collaborate and work together, the combined effect is multiplied. The entirety is consistently greater than the aggregate of its individual components.

WHAT COLLABORATIVE LEADERSHIP LOOKS LIKE

If collaboration is about pursuing kin*dom, the objective of collaboration in ministry is to see spiritual and social transformation in all aspects of the world around us. Spiritual transformation is the result of individuals developing a deep and unwavering love for God, encompassing their entire being—their hearts, souls, brains, and strength, as stated in Luke 10:27. Societal transformation occurs when individuals demonstrate love and compassion toward their fellow citizens, leading them to actively work toward repairing and improving the damaged aspects and structures within their community.[20]

Collaborative leadership between men and women is a concept that causes some leaders to head right out the room. But even amongst those who widely accept it, it is not commonly practiced. Bringing up collaboration often includes lengthy discussions with little direction that go nowhere. Some individuals view collaboration as a passing trend and enthusiastically embrace it without adequate expertise or training on how to practice it. It is not surprising that individuals tend to leave when the concept of this type of teamwork is brought up.

Effective collaboration most often occurs when a situation reaches a level of importance, urgency, or complexity that seems beyond the capabilities of a single individual, and existing forms or resources are deemed insufficient. Isn't that ministry in today's society? Collaborators and co-creators have often pioneered innovative ideas, and that is surely what is needed at this time.

Collaboration in the Bible

In Judges 4, Deborah and Barak exemplify the potency of collaboration. Barak is an example for contemporary male leaders to emulate. His actions demonstrate the importance of a male recognizing and valuing the leadership of a female. Due to Deborah's indisputable divine connection and adept leadership qualities, Barak, as the commander of Israel's forces, seems aware that Deborah's assistance would guarantee triumph and refuses to engage in the fight without her, despite being informed he would not receive recognition for victory (Judg. 4:8–9). Deborah's prompt and modest reaction serves as proof that she recognized her importance in securing the triumph of the Israelite army. Contrary to some commentators insisting that Barak was a timid individual, I maintain that he was a person of strong religious conviction who recognized the significance of God's guidance and leadership in warfare. His inclusion in the list of heroes of the faith in Hebrews 11 (v. 32) seems to make this more likely. Furthermore, he showed respect for women in positions of power and is unafraid to acknowledge and share credit for his achievements with them.

I appreciate how the Matthew Henry commentary describes Barak and Deborah's collaborative efforts: "The work and honor of this significant activity are divided between Deborah and Barak. Deborah, as the leader, provides the instructions, while Barak, as the executor, carries out the tasks. God distributes his blessings in many ways. The team overpowers their adversary with divine intervention."[21] This example is in stark contrast to male leaders who insist on their right to give orders because they claim it is the God-ordained way.

Some individuals experience apprehension toward the concept of engaging in collaborative work due to feelings of vulnerability and insecurity. We may question whether we will receive recognition for our contribution. Who desires to be just another insignificant part of a larger whole? We must liberate ourselves from the mindset of being a superstar and adopt a humble attitude. In our current era, characterized by self-centeredness and the prominence of "influencers" and celebrity pastors, the pervasive impact of social media and television has undeniably infiltrated our religious congregations. It's about me and the name I make for myself vs. Jesus and the glory we give to his name. Decades ago, a speaker at a conference I was attending said these words, which have been imprinted in my mind ever since: "May the mention of my name bring glory to his name." Now that is the mindset we should have in doing anything in the Kin*dom!

Collaboration involves leveraging many talents and pooling them together to work toward a shared objective for our churches, neighborhoods, cities, and states. As believers in the kin*dom, it is crucial for us to acknowledge that we are united as a team and our success is dependent on the contribution of every individual within the community. It is necessary for individuals, regardless of gender, to set aside personal issues or burdens, present their most exemplary selves, and concentrate on the shared objective of ushering in God's kin*dom transformation.

New Models of Collaboration

While there have been models around the country that have granted women the authority to be ordained as pastors and elders, as well as to actively participate in shaping the church's future, true collaborative models are few.

Yet one model of collaboration is a church plant, The Church We Hope For, in Pasadena, California, which began a mere two months before the global pandemic in 2020 and is co-led by Inés Velásquez-McBryde and Bobby Harrison (a female and male leadership team who are not a married couple). When I asked Inés what initiated this setup for pastoring her new church, she said,

> The reason we chose this co-lead pastor collaborative approach is because of the Trinitarian model in Genesis of three persons in leadership, leading out of unity, shared equity, and respectful mutuality. Even the Trinity does not work in isolation.
>
> White men in church planting invented solo-celebrity-pastor leadership models where all the power lands on one solo-leader. I believe that all hierarchical structures are misogynistic in nature, which affects power distribution and sets up organizations for abuse of power and all the demons birthed from abuse of power: racism, sexism, ableism, and homophobia, to name a few.
>
> This model of leadership is subversive to the historical church planting approaches where patriarchy has dominated the pulpit. We desired and envisioned a more equal pulpit, with shared equitable leadership, that moved to the slow rhythms of La Espiritu Santa, because the Spirit slows the roll of potential narcissistic, manipulative pastor-leaders. There are checks and balances, accountability, transparency, and equitable systems set in place so that the church does not revolve around the power of one voice.[22]

Inés credits this model for getting their church through the pandemic while she saw eleven of her colleagues close their churches. She also heralded this model for providing care for her own soul because she gets to sit and receive; she doesn't have to run at the crazy pace of solo-pastors who usually do everything, including preaching every Sunday. Presently, the church is sustainable as they hit the four-year mark and expect to be able to hire two more pastors for worship and youth/kids ministry soon.

She has also seen many join their church, having experienced church-hurt trauma in the past. Inés believes their collaborative model has been one of the reasons these members (who were giving church one last try) have been able to trust a faith community again.

WHY LEADERSHIP MATTERS

Despite prevailing cultural, societal, and ecclesial practices that perpetuate the marginalization of women, your church has the power to defy this trend. You may just need to start by acknowledging that something needs to change.

According to Timothy C. Geoffrion, a professor and minister,

> Churches and organizations may be growing and expanding, yet missing out on God's will for them because of an unwillingness to change. Power brokers are satisfied with the status quo and don't want to change much of anything. Perhaps the credo of their leadership team or board is, "If it ain't broke, don't fix it." However, if God has something else in mind for these organizations and the leaders are not listening or changing, then something is "broke." A process of corporate discernment may be needed to determine whether God is calling the organization to something new, but if the leaders are not truly open to God's leading, unwavering devotion to the status quo is another kind of "stuckness."[23]

How can we avoid being "stuck" upholding the status quo? First, it is crucial to acknowledge that patriarchy is not an unavoidable condition, despite the assertions of certain leaders who present it as the way things must be. The individuals in positions of authority who perpetuate the patriarchy are the ones responsible for its continued existence. This is the reason why effective leadership is crucial in any organization, and it is imperative for everyone to be attentive and not assume that the church they attend completely values women. For me, the phrase "completely values women" means no lids for women, anywhere, at any time; a complete absence of limitations or restrictions on women. Women have the freedom to pursue and fulfill the divine purpose assigned to them by God, regardless of what that may entail for them.

Working against the prevailing culture is the responsibility of leaders—both male and female—even if you have women in leadership positions in your church. The sad reality is that empire and patriarchy impact the way some women view other women in the pastoral role. Inés mentioned a story of a beautiful young woman who had been with her church for over a year and recently confessed that she couldn't call Inés "pastora" because of her conservative upbringing in a Latino church. Inés went on to say, "I don't care about titles, and was not offended. However, it made me sad for her, because she doesn't realize the internalized machismo she still carries and needs healing from. This type of internalized sexism/racism/any-ism is normal for people recovering from church hurt who still show signs of what I call 'church-PTSD.'" It is crucial that we create environments where our female siblings no longer have to unquestioningly accept what they have been taught as absolute truth. Instead, we should together [in conjunto] seek to understand God's perspective on women, bringing liberation to these views as we uncover the truth about our equality.

In order for these challenges to be overcome, we require the presence and support of our male siblings to observe and advocate for us. Each male leader determines their approach to collaborating with women. Dr. Saehee Duran suggests male leaders can successfully champion women by becoming advocates/allies or champions. She goes on to describe each:

> Male Advocates or Allies: Men who publicly support, promote, or stand in the gap for women to help reverse the barriers or challenges in their leadership journey. They often collaborate and cooperate with women to accomplish common goals, objectives or causes. However, not all advocates or allies are champions depending on their level of understanding, involvement, or consistency of championing practices.
>
> Male Champions: Men who intentionally engage in ongoing cross-gender training, empowering, advocating/affirming, and mentoring opportunities to advance women called to ministry while onboarding aspiring male champions. While not all advocates or allies are champions, all champions are advocates or allies.[24]

I believe, by adopting a kin*dom framework, there will be more of these kinds of men collaborating with women. It will enhance our witness in serving God and we will shine brighter representing the fullness of the body of Christ.

COMMENCING COLLABORATIVE LEADERSHIP

If you feel moved by the Spirit to work against the prevailing influence of empire, here are some preliminary steps you can take.

1. CHOOSE the Right People

Collaboration is a collective endeavor; therefore, it is imperative to assemble the appropriate individuals for the team. At this stage, one of my guiding principles is that life is too short to collaborate with others with whom I lack chemistry and compatibility. Interpersonal discord is an unavoidable aspect of being a leader, but I have the ability to use discernment when it comes to selecting individuals with whom I wish to collaborate. I discern the suitability of individuals to include in my life, whether friend or ministry partner.

I prioritize individuals with strong moral values or a high level of spiritual development over those who possess only professional competence. Within the pastoral epistles, there are a total of forty-four distinct *character attributes* deemed essential for those assuming leadership roles within the church, but only two *skills* are specified (teaching in the context of 1 Tim. 3:2 and 2 Tim. 2:24; and managing money, mentioned in 1 Tim. 3:4–5 and Titus 1:7). While there may be some overlap in certain character attributes, it is evident that character is more important than competency.

Furthermore, I desire a diverse range of inputs. Collaborative teams consist of individuals with a wide range of talents, backgrounds, and character traits. It is imperative that you seek the valuable insights and unique viewpoints that the people around you can offer, such as teachers, business professionals, and others. You just might find after working with these people for a while that they could be excellent co-leaders with you at a higher level.

Ultimately, I desire to connect with those with whom I share a strong rapport and compatibility. Chemistry refers to the possibility for people to enjoy working together. Ministry is hard enough and life is too short to do otherwise. Although issues may occur even in highly skilled teams, we can mitigate them by selecting individuals with whom we have chemistry.

2. CHECK Your Ego

In empire culture, individualism thrives partly because it fosters a sense of personal responsibility and a prioritization of one's personal goals. In empires, individualism fuels motivation to pursue ideas tied to economic prosperity and influence. This has been the perfect breeding ground for celebrity-pastor and influencer culture in society. However, individualism often hinders collaboration because collaboration necessitates a significant relinquishment of personal control and ego. The key to this is surrendering our individual ambitions and preferences to collectively pursue the optimal path as guided by the Lord. We should decide to collaborate due to the enormity of the issues we face in this world, which surpasses the capabilities of a single individual. Think of this as waving a white flag which symbolizes a blank piece of paper, representing our individual ideas, objectives, and timetables. Similar to Timothy's relationship with the apostle Paul, our primary focus is not on our own desires, but on the interests and priorities of Jesus Christ (Phil. 2:21). Prayer is certainly necessary to do this.

3. CAST the Vision

Collaborative leaders exhibit a strong sense of vision and purpose. Once we have chosen the right people, and all parties have checked their egos, we must share the vision of what we want to complete collaboratively. Not being clear and having ambiguous objectives pose the greatest obstacle to achieving effective collaborative performance. Effective communication is key to collaboration. Determine what the focus will be.

The term "focus" refers to having a clear understanding of shared goals and recognizing the mutual benefits of working together. Once there is clarity, there can also be fun!

Collaboration can be a fulfilling endeavor when it is appropriately employed with the right people, and executed effectively. It is the utmost demonstration of faith, wherein we place our trust in God to bring into being something that now does not currently exist. Collaboration unites individuals to dream and do great things for God.

4. CONNECT with Others

To aid each other on this kin*dom journey, we can connect with like-minded others to learn from and resource them. Daniel Yang (formerly of Wheaton's Church Multiplication Institute), Len Tang and Corey Lee of Fuller Church Planting, Lori Ruffin of Movement Leaders Collective, Carl Johnson and Yucan Chiu of Ethnos Network, and I have collaborated to bring church planters together to pray, hear from each other, and work together. While representing diverse organizations, we gather for collaboration and kin*dom partnership. Influential Global Ministries, founded by Dr. Efrem Smith and his wife Donecia, gathers Black leaders from across the country to pray and prepare for movement that uplifts Jesus and addresses Black Americans' problems.

In building these connections, you could also consider how you might collaborate with others in relation to funding. Oftentimes, when a woman is in a top position or equal with a man in leadership, we come up against empire theology because, at its core, it leads patriarchal men to mistrust women in leadership. In the church planting world, some networks even demand a signed contract that the "lead" planter/pastor will never appoint a woman as a pastor, else they will forfeit any money the network has given to the church.

Inés experienced this challenge. She explained, "I disorient and disrupt systems that would otherwise give advantage to white-male-cis-het church planters, and in the last three years I have lost much potential funding in the amount of $670,000, simply because an organization/process/denomination/church-planting system/foundation could not handle my pushbacks as a female pastora. It's problematic to patriarchy to support a woman of color like me! But I'd rather be poor and free, honestly. By God's grace we have made ends meet."[25]

"Poor and free" is the attitude many women church planters have taken. Had they not, their churches would never have been planted or their ministries wouldn't exist. As a leader of the only Afro-Latina, female-founded church planting network in a predominately white male space, this is also the attitude I have taken. As Inés said, it is by God's grace we are still here. This also illustrates our determination to oppose empire to the extent that it endangers our very survival as church plants and ministries. Empire ways have survived in Western Christian ministry because people need jobs and church planters need money; so, they take what's offered knowing they will support many of the ideals they internally oppose.

Movements that promote collaborative leadership in pursuit of kin*dom transformation need funding because most gatekeeper organizations and funders don't prioritize what they do or who they serve. Resourcing also goes beyond money. Connect with these leaders, find out what their resource needs are, and consider how you might help. This might not look like giving directly; it might involve opening up opportunities for these leaders to expand their influence and networks to bring in the resources they need.

DREAMING OF TOMORROW'S CHURCH

Following the Spirit and rejecting empire ways can lead the church to fresh ground. I believe kin*dom churches will include women at all levels of leadership and encourage them to participate in the church's future, not just for growth but to establish a safe environment for women to work alongside men in cooperation with the Spirit to make disciples. Because God didn't limit women, tomorrow's church should allow them to serve at all levels. In John 14:12–28, Jesus stated, "Truly, whoever believes in me will do the works I have been doing, and *even greater things than these*" (italics mine).

As a former church planter and pastor, phygital faith community experimenter,[26] and church-planting-network educator for prospective church pastors, I encourage other leaders to follow God's model, listen to his voice, and move forward with the community of witnesses who have already confirmed their gifts and calling. Despite the prevailing debates around women in leadership, I will keep following the advice of Dr. Martin Luther King Jr.: "We must accept finite disappointment, but never lose infinite hope."

Greater days are ahead—if we can get our act together, quit debating minor issues, and focus on the major ones: serving God and doing our part for individual and social transformation. Collaborative leadership is the kin*dom way. Tomorrow's church, both male and female, should work together as equals for the kin*dom's greatest work.

13

THE MAKING OF *THE MAKING OF BIBLICAL WOMANHOOD*

Beth Allison Barr

is the James Vardaman Professor of History at Baylor University. She earned her PhD in Medieval History from the University of North Carolina at Chapel Hill and is the bestselling author of *The Making of Biblical Womanhood: How the Subjugation of Women Became Gospel Truth.* She is also a pastor's wife and mom of two great kids.

This chapter is adapted from a conversation between Beth Allison Barr and Danielle Strickland that took place on the *Right Side Up Podcast with Danielle Strickland*, titled, "Burn Down the Patriarchy with Beth Allison Barr."[1]

I'm not sure if people really believe me, but I never intended to write *The Making of Biblical Womanhood*.[2] It was not something I ever saw in my future when I thought about my life. I'm a medieval historian. The 15th century was my world, and I was fine with that. But I also grew up in the evangelical world;

I grew up Southern Baptist. The Southern Baptists are a large denomination in the southern part of the US—Virginia, the Carolinas, Kentucky, etc. They have about 16.7 million members and it's a very prominent, if not the main, denomination of the South. It was born in the era of slavery and was forged in defense of it, which is why it's no surprise they are so strict on gender roles. Patriarchy and racism are closely interwoven.

So, I grew up Southern Baptist and I got married to a Southern Baptist pastor. Ten days after we got married, we moved to North Carolina so that he could start at Southeastern Baptist Theological Seminary. We were so young. It never even occurred to us to look and see who the president of the seminary was. It just wasn't on our radar. While my husband started at Southeastern under Paige Patterson, I started a medieval history and women's studies program at the University of North Carolina at Chapel Hill. It was quite a difference in perspective.

I was at Chapel Hill between 1997 and 2004, and it was during that time that the Southern Baptist world was writing *Baptist Faith and Message 2000*.[3]

In the 1970s, something happened called "the conservative resurgence," where Baptists decided that their seminaries had become too liberal. In response, the conservative movement launched a takeover of all seminaries. Then, in the 1990s, they began moving toward rewriting their statement of faith with *Baptist Faith and Message 2000* solidifying it all. A key part of this document says that women cannot be pastors and that women are required to submit graciously to the authority of their husbands, enshrining male headship in the home and in the church.

When this happened, my husband was in the seminary where the orchestrators of this movement were based. The Pattersons—Paige Patterson and Dorothy Patterson—fought on the convention floor for this statement to be included in the updated version of the *Baptist Faith and Message*. Paige was the president of my husband's seminary.

You don't always think critically about the church you've known as home; it's just how you grew up. There are often all these good people, and this good church, and this beautiful faith—all of those things can be true. But we often live with a simplistic worldview that says, "it's either good or it's bad." And yet there are complexities within our church experiences and our faith. So, I felt that I was experiencing beauty in my church experience, my husband was finding his calling, and I was free to pursue my education; and, in our marriage, we felt free to work it out together. Well, this is the irony of being Southern Baptist. There are tons of women who have power outside of the church, contributing their gifts and skills in their own fields of expertise, but are unable to exercise those in the church setting.

Once you step back from the experience and analyze it from a distance, you realize it was such a strange culture to be in and that it just doesn't make sense. That's exactly what happened to me. So, when you ask me, "Where was this book born?"—it was born when I began to see my Southern Baptist world through the eyes of my studies at Chapel Hill. And I also began to see the inconsistencies.

One of the very first things my husband and I confronted was local. We found out that a woman who was our friend, also getting a degree at Southeastern, couldn't get her masters of divinity *because she was a woman*. She was in the chaplaincy program there, but they would not allow her to access available scholarships. She had to pay more tuition because she was a woman. And this really struck us as unjust. We thought, even if she's not going to be a pastor, she's just doing ministry, shouldn't she get the same scholarship? And so, we began to be confronted by these inconsistencies.

As I say early on in the book, I began to be struck by how the way the Southern Baptist world treats women just looks like how the rest of the world treats women. My journey started there. I didn't know where it was going to take me. And I don't think I would have written this book if it hadn't been for the fact that we were essentially thrown out of the church we were in when we put forward the idea of a woman teaching Sunday school. My husband was fired three weeks after we tried to get that forward.

We didn't actually sign anything that forbade us from speaking about what happened, but we were told that our severance pay was conditional on our behavior. That was something we really struggled with. We were clearly expected not to tell people what happened. In fact, everything we did—our interactions with everyone (including the youth group we led)—was monitored until we left. The elders came and "babysat" us the whole time. It was horrible. It was crazy. Some of them were really good friends of ours! The hurt that caused is still with us. It's hard to think about it now, but we were in trauma, which I didn't really understand at the time. It's clear to me now that you don't make good decisions when you're in trauma. I'm really pleased by the decisions we did make, because at least we didn't sign anything—even though it was costly.

Once the separation was in effect, and our severance pay ended, there were no longer any strings. I had been writing on my blog since 2015, but you can see a shift in the spring of 2017, when I first posted about Paige Patterson. I began writing, not really sure where I was going, but I knew I couldn't be silent anymore. I had to speak out about what I knew, for the sake of other women.

Danielle: Oftentimes, when we try to shift power in response to a deep injustice, some people will say, "Oh, it's just because you're a woman." But I love how this was a journey that you took together. It wasn't just a "women's issue," because as you deconstructed the system, you realized how dangerous and harmful it was for everyone.

That's exactly right. My husband was a major part of this. He was a social work major as an undergrad and went into his religious vocation with that background. Justice has always been deeply embedded in what he does. He's been connected with Mission Waco for a very long time; he was on their board for six years and president for a term. This has also been part of the DNA of our marriage. Part of our mutual calling is around justice; we loved showing students that their small world was within God's global church where God was working in a much bigger way. We wanted them to know that they were invited into that. Because of this, it became impossible for us to ignore injustice in our own system of patriarchy that we began to see was harmful to women. As a social historian, I study power structures. It became impossible for me as I was studying power structures outside of the church to not be applying what I was learning in my own life.

One example is when I was involved in conversations that epitomized a concept I teach in class called "the patriarchal bargain." It's where women choose to support systems of oppression for one of two reasons:

1. The woman's identity is so wrapped up in the system of oppression that they honestly believe this is the way it should be. This is what often happens to women in complementarian movements.
2. The woman chooses to support the systems of oppression because it benefits them or their family. You might think they shouldn't do that; but sadly, women make choices like this all the time. They'll stay with an abusive husband because they know that they need to protect their children. They might be afraid that if they try to get out of the marriage, their husband will get control over their children, or their finances, and so they make hard choices to protect themselves and their family. That's part of the patriarchal bargain.

I was studying this and having conversations about this in my work, and I couldn't help but draw parallels to my church experience. As a woman who grew up in this system, it was very hard when I began to realize that what I had been taught about being a woman and what a woman should be might be reinforcing "the patriarchal bargain." Furthermore, it might not actually be what God has called women to. Although it didn't cause a crisis of faith for me, it took me a long time to accept it. I was so enculturated, so much a part of that system—it was pretty much all I knew.

Danielle: What was the tipping point? How did you move from the internal dissonance between what you read in the Scriptures and your own culture, to speaking out?

That is a great question, and it mostly manifests when people begin to ask, "When should I leave?" Particularly, "When should I leave my church?" I can't tell you when you should leave your church. What I can tell you is what I realized.

I realized that even though there were good things in this system, those things did not come from the oppressive parts of the system. Those good things would still be there without the oppression. The oppression hurts women. It hurts men. The danger is real. And it harms the gospel.

We can see the impact of that harm through the mass exodus represented in the ex-vangelical movement in the US today as well as listening to the harm that's been done to many individuals by the church through these oppressive teachings.

I'm still going to a Baptist church. There are a lot of different Baptist churches. Technically, our church is still Southern Baptist, but that's because it's never been removed from the Southern Baptist list. I suspect they'll probably cross it off before too long. We're such a small church, nobody pays attention to it.

But I also believe in redemption. I believe Christianity is about redemption, that anyone can be saved, and that Jesus came for all of us. I believe that this system could be redeemed. I don't know if it *will* be, because people are so entrenched within it and are refusing to listen; but I think what is inevitably going to happen is people are going to have to leave the system. I don't want people to leave their faith. My goal is for them to realize the things that are good and true and beautiful about the story of how God came to save us—and that those things are separate from the oppressive structures we have enforced within our churches.

I hope that people will realize that they can continue to stay a part of this faith, even an evangelical faith (a faith that emphasizes sharing the good news). I hope they know they can be a part of that without being part of the oppression. That's my ideal. I'm still afraid though. Afraid that the Southern Baptist Church is set on upholding oppressive structures.

I wrote a blog post last year about this small little Texas town that had died because of the decline in the mining industry, but then had been reborn into something else.[4] It was a metaphor for the hope we can have that, if we're willing to change, something new can be reborn. Within the Baptist world, there are a lot of different kinds of Baptists. I believe that you can still be a Baptist and support God's calling on all people. There is hope that something new may rise up, despite the challenges facing a movement for change.

People ask, "Why do you stay Baptist?" Well, you know, I like Baptist ecclesiology. I love theology, and I love looking at different practices throughout denominations and the world. So that's why I stay. But it doesn't mean that I think the only true Christians are in the Baptist church. I don't think that at all. We have this legalistic foundation within American evangelicalism that it's all or nothing, and that's a very dangerous sentiment. It's also a relatively new sentiment. Even in the medieval church there was always a safety valve. For example, monasticism, in some sense, served as a safety valve to allow people to have new ideas. And the church essentially said, "Okay, go over there and do it. But you're still part of the church." We've lost that. We've lost that elasticity. In fact, when we think about the origins of the Reformation, part of it was because the medieval church was no longer elastic.

Danielle: You have a chapter devoted to Paul, and much of the oppressive systems of the church use Paul's words in the New Testament as foundational texts to support their practice. Tell me about your discovery of Paul and why you included it in your book?

With Paul, instead of reading him the way he intended to be read, we have read him through the lens of our culture. We keep reading him through a patriarchal lens because our culture continues with that patriarchal bent. One of the ways I think we have completely missed the point with our modern eyes is how Paul talks about the church using maternal imagery. If you think about how Paul talks about God, and even about himself, he refers to himself as a mother (1 Thess. 2:7). This maternal imagery that he uses, which Beverly Roberts

[Gaventa] points out Paul uses more than paternal imagery, should really stop us in our tracks.[5]

My students look at the Bible through a modern, patriarchal lens. When you stop and show them the maternal imagery, and how medieval Christians saw this maternal imagery, they're like, "Whoa, how did I miss this?" What I was trying to draw out in the book is that our culture blinds us to what is actually in the Bible. The Bible hasn't changed. People have seen the maternal imagery in the Bible from the very beginning, but we don't pay attention to it because we focus on the masculine aspects. I'm just trying to get people to look differently. And, to me, that's the beginning of wisdom, of genuine learning. It doesn't mean that every time you stop and look differently you have to accept that different vantage point. But it helps you see the broader perspective, and helps you better understand your own.

The main question to ask yourself is: Why do I believe this? Why do I decide to do *this*? That's really what I'm trying to do with the chapter on Paul in the book. I had one New Testament student ask me, "Well, you know, there's all this scholarship here, how can you say that this is the one way to read Paul?" And I said, "I didn't say this is the one way to read Paul, I asked questions. I asked, what if we look at Paul differently? What if we look at Paul from the lens of the perspective of women in the first century, as well? He was speaking to them first."

If we look from the Old Testament to the New Testament, one of the continuities that we see is how God always fights for women. It's an incredible thread that you can see throughout the Bible, even, for example, putting Rahab in the lineage of Jesus. This is amazing! The fact that there are so many women listed in the Bible who are not listed by their affiliations with men is also something that is really remarkable. Shocking. Yet instead of pulling on those strings and asking, "What do we see going on here?" we choose to focus on the oppressive parts of the Bible that come from the cultures in which people lived. Instead of focusing on what God is doing and what God has always been doing with women, we focus on what humans have always done.

Danielle: This whistle-blowing work is difficult and taxing. I've watched you take a lot of abuse online and I can only imagine the things I can't see. How are you taking care of yourself and do you have advice for others?

I have to be honest. I'm not going to say this has been easy. I mean, it was scary for me to sign the writing contract, because I didn't know how big the book would be. There's no way I could have known. But I did know it had the potential to get people's attention because it put this all in a different light. And, if I did this, I knew it could be hard on our family.

So, I brought it up to my husband that this could happen and we needed to be aware of how putting our story out there could cause people to be angry with us. I don't think we could ever have anticipated the Council for Biblical Manhood and Womanhood going after our church and us personally.

I think part of taking care of yourself when you embark on truth-telling is being honest in your marriage and being honest with the fact that it's hard work. The other issue was actually just writing the book. I have a full-time position, which meant I wrote the book at night. There were a lot of nights that I didn't get to do things with my family and I didn't get to spend time with my husband. I would sit outside from where we live—we live in a dorm because we're faculty and residents—in the seminar room and write until two in the morning sometimes. Then I'd get up at four in the morning. It was hard.

There was one time I remember my husband saying, "I just want this to be over." And I said, "I know, but you also want me to finish this book." The cost is real. It's not always fun. I think that it helps in marriages for everyone to not pretend that everything's happy all the time. That's been helpful to us. It's also helpful that our world doesn't live in the world of the book. Our lives are bigger than this one issue. We have many things to attend to besides this one thing. We have real lives. We're at a tiny church that's been struggling during COVID. I'm an administrator as well as a historian. I have students. The fact that our life is full of all these different things keeps us from living in the world of the book.

But there was a mental toll. For me, every time I got a really big attack on me, which seemed for a while to be happening every week—whether it was social media or articles being written attacking me—I would lose my concentration and ability to focus. It took a toll on my work and I had to finally realize that this was hard on me, too. Sometimes I needed to just stop and do something else.

I've stepped away from social media now—that's been helpful. And there are a lot of people I talked to behind the scenes, which has been helpful, too. But, you know, it was harder than I thought it would be. I'm at a moment now where I've got a little bit of a breather. Part of me wonders, *Is this going to last? Are things going to pick up again?* I don't know. But I get as much work done as I can right now.

Danielle: This book is rooted in a southern US context but has resonated around the world. Why do you think that is and what does it mean?

The Southern Baptist Church took its theology to the world. So, this message must get to all the places we took our oppressive theology to, as well. There is much to do. This is one of the systemic and oppressive issues within the structures of our church that have been explored by many others. But taking complementarian theology and adding it to places that already have a very strong patriarchal bent—that are already harmful to women—ends up a toxic recipe for more harm. Then you make it "gospel truth" and it's a tragic distortion of the gospel. There are all sorts of stories. Lots of people around the world (particularly in Asia) have contacted me about this book.

Danielle: How has social media been helpful and harmful in this season and with this message?

I think social media has done a wonderful thing in allowing people's voices to be heard. Of course, this makes it harder to fly under the radar and easier to become a target. But at the same time, it elevates and connects voices in a way that is historically unprecedented. Part of this shift is that people and systems can't hide—they can't hide what's going on in their churches, they can't hide the harm. The "good-old-boys" club that used to control things can't control the narrative anymore. That is what is making this shift possible. And it is also forcing those who have controlled the narrative to examine what they have been doing.

14

MIND THE GAP

Janet Munn

is a leader, author, speaker, and mentor, focused on empowering the next generation of leaders, especially women and girls. She has served as director of the International Social Justice Commission for The Salvation Army, has written and co-written several books, including a doctoral dissertation on "Theory and Practice of Gender Equality in The Salvation Army." Janet has worked for justice and formation locally and globally for more than thirty years.

As I stepped onto the platform, a voice came over the loudspeaker: "Mind the gap" it warned, in a formal, disembodied male voice, almost drowned out by the London tube as it roared out of the tunnel. This mundane announcement, so familiar to locals, can be quite a thrill for first-time visitors, although it's an unnerving warning as it cautions passengers from stepping into the perilous space between train and platform. Not minding the gap can cause serious injury.

Mind the gap, indeed.

BEGINNING BY MINDING THE GAP

As a teenager, working at a summer camp for underprivileged children in greater Boston, I first encountered a world of dynamic and powerful women with gifts and access to leadership, making decisions for their organization. This left a lasting impression on me; one that was reinforced many times in the ensuing years, and that strongly influenced the direction of my life to this day. The camp was run by The Salvation Army.

I have been delighted to learn more about the remarkable history of The Salvation Army in the nineteenth century and how it disrupted the status quo in terms of gender roles and access to power. The Salvation Army established itself early on as a movement where women could preach and lead in spiritual ministry, as a powerful advocate for the rights of women and girls in the wider political arena, and as having a willingness to confront the hypocrisy of the surrounding Victorian culture. For example, in 1885, The Salvation Army held a major, very public, role on behalf of vulnerable young girls in the successful campaign to raise the age of consent in Great Britain from thirteen to sixteen years old.

By 1895, the following statement was published by the young movement:

> One of the leading principles upon which the Army is based is the right of women to have the right to an equal share with men in the work of publishing salvation to the world ... She may hold any position of authority or power in the Army from that of a Local Officer to that of the General. Let it therefore be understood that women are eligible for the highest commands—indeed, no woman is to be kept back from any position of power or influence merely on account of her sex ... Women must be treated as equal with men in all the intellectual and social relationships in life.[1]

The values of The Salvation Army stood in marked contrast to those of the surrounding culture. In Victorian England, women weren't generally empowered to lead; rather, they were marginalized and restricted to the separate sphere of domestic life. But, according to historian Pamela Walker, The Salvation Army "disrupted and refashioned gender relations in many facets of its work ... as Salvationist women challenged and resisted the conventions of femininity and enhanced women's spiritual authority."[2] In claiming the right to preach, women "disrupted a powerful source of masculine privilege and authority."[3] Walker concludes, "Virtually no other secular or religious organization in this period offered working-class women such extensive authority."[4] Consequently, The Salvation Army has an unusual and significant history of advancing women's rights in relation to the surrounding culture, be it popular or religious, in many parts of the world.

Even today, a position statement on sexism, developed in 2019 by the international Salvation Army, affirms:

> The Salvation Army believes that both male and female are made in the image of God and are equal in value and therefore is opposed to sexism. We reject any view that subordinates women to men, or men to women.
>
> The Salvation Army believes that our world is enhanced by equitably valuing, equipping and mobilising all human beings. While valuing gender equity, The Salvation Army acknowledges with regret that Salvationists have sometimes conformed to societal and organisational norms that perpetuate sexism.[5]

Historically, The Salvation Army has made it a priority to "mind the gap" in gender equality.

DRIFTING INTO THE GAP

Despite its history, there is considerable current statistical evidence of systemic sexist practices which contribute to a grievous gender gap within The Salvation Army.

Consider—in recent years, a survey was sent to all the national leaders of The Salvation Army, a charitable/religious organization present in over 130 nations worldwide.[6] The survey asked the leaders about their views on the importance of gender equality as well as their own efforts to bring about improvements in gender equality in their sphere of influence. The purpose of the survey was to determine two things: first, the beliefs or theoretical views of the leaders in relation to gender equality; and second, the actual practices of those leaders in improving gender equality in their spheres of influence.

The overall results of the survey indicate widespread agreement among the leaders participating in the survey, across all nations, with responses from both women and men, as to the importance of gender equality. The respondents perceive themselves as committed to gender equality in belief and in their own current practice. In other words, from the worldwide survey, Salvation Army leaders think gender equality is important and believe themselves to be active and intentional in using their power to improve it.

However, this self-perception is not supported by international statistics of the organization, which indicate that 53 percent of the human resources (Salvation Army officers specifically) are women, while less than 10 percent of *senior leadership* roles are assigned to women.[7] This power gap has been consistent internationally over many years. The needle has not moved significantly at the time of this writing.

The Salvation Army is an example of a movement that began as a remarkable and radically counter-cultural world leader through the empowerment and equal opportunities for women, yet which has, in some respects, lost that sense of courageous example in such matters, and instead, has too often conformed to local, societal, and cultural norms.

The change we see in The Salvation Army, from working against the cultural norms in its early days to experiencing gender inequality similar to the wider society, can be described as drifting out of the "Lydia phase." The "Lydia phase" describes a period in the early years of a developing movement in which women begin in positions of leadership, as was true of a woman named Lydia, the key person in the establishment of the church in the city of Philippi (Acts 16).[8] But with time, the very women who were founding leaders in the church are "relegated to secondary roles in order for the movement to gain cultural legitimacy and to diminish the feminizing effect of women's leadership."[9]

The irony of widespread, significant female leadership in The Salvation Army being a "Lydia phase" which came to an end for the sake of cultural legitimacy is obvious in view of the unseemliness of the early Army's actions relative to its cultural contexts. Their actions stood in defiance of worldly cultural conventions, often deemed "secular" and "unconventional" by the established church. Further, the initial "feminizing effect of women's leadership" was such that in many towns nearly all the pubs went out of business because "the whole population had gone to the 'Hallelujah Lasses!'"[10] Yet, a drift from the "Lydia phase" did indeed take place in The Salvation Army within the first few decades of its existence. By the 1930s, the percentage of females in leadership was relatively minimal.

While The Salvation Army experienced explosive growth largely due to the active involvement of tens of thousands of (mostly young) women in its mission—including the release of these women into the work of The Salvation Army spearheaded by Catherine Mumford Booth—the challenge of consistently acting in accordance with the proclaimed principle of gender equality was apparent early on in Salvation Army development and remains today.

THE COST OF NOT MINDING THE GAP

Why should organizations like The Salvation Army address these inequalities, both for the benefit of their own members and workers, but also as part of their work and witness to wider society? To answer this question, we must see the real harm that is caused when we fail to mind the gap.

The gap in opportunity and resources for females begins early. Studies of classrooms ranging from kindergarten through graduate school reveal that teachers are more likely to call on male students, even when female students raise their hands; wait longer for male than for female students to respond to questions; and give male students more eye contact.[11]

> From our televisions to our textbooks, the stories we're told about power and influence almost always center on men—and, most often, white men. Women in movies and TV are significantly less likely to be depicted as professionals, and female characters who have jobs are six times more likely to be secretaries than men are ... Fewer than 3% of the words in history textbooks are specifically about women ... By the time children are six years old, they already tend to guess that a story about "a really, really smart person" is about a man, not a woman. If you associate smartness with men, and you're *not* a man, then you might think certain career paths are less available to you.[12]

Sexist attitudes may result in everything from a pay gap to sexual harassment. Globally, women earn less compared to similar male workers, according to median hourly earnings.[13] The feminization of poverty is a direct consequence of women's unequal access to education and economic opportunities.[14]

Sexist behavior can include a man talking condescendingly to a woman with the automatic assumption that he knows more about the subject than she does—a credibility gap; or a deliberate pattern of manipulation that makes a woman doubt her own perceptions or sanity.[15] This behavior is frequently associated with male emotional abuse of females.

For millennia, women in general have not been in control of their own bodies, including their sexuality and reproductive capacity. They have not had access to education, the right to vote or own property, or opportunities to be financially self-supporting. Even today, by and large, men control the economic and political environments in which women live and work.

Inattention to minding the gender power gap has real and costly consequences. Consider the following:

- Women often experience systemic social injustice because of their gender. Sexism can result in extreme human cruelty and even death.[16]
- In some cultures, infant girls do not receive the same medical care and attention that boys receive.[17]
- Globally, women aged fifteen through forty-four are more likely to be maimed or die from male violence than from cancer, malaria, traffic accidents, and war combined.[18]
- Women have been doused in kerosene and set ablaze or burned with acid for "disobedience." So-called "honor killings" take the lives of thousands of young women every year.[19]
- The majority (71 percent) of people trapped in modern slavery every year are female, many being exploited for sexual purposes.[20]

Not only does the power gap put women at more physical risk, women experience a huge financial imbalance as well. The United Nations estimates women perform 66 percent of the world's work and produce 50 percent of the food yet earn only 10 percent of the income and own 1 percent of the property.[21]

A gender pay gap is a discriminatory reality that has been documented worldwide. It ranges from a low of 15 percent in the European Union to a high of 51 percent in Latin America.[22]

According to the Gates Foundation, globally women do three times more unpaid care work than men.[23] The gap is largest in Northern Africa and Western Asia, but it exists in every region. This work is currently valued at $10 trillion per year, but even that huge number doesn't capture the full extent of women's lost economic potential.

According to recent United Nations statistics, women and girls remain the most vulnerable members of society—disadvantaged in employment, health, and education provision, and victims of extreme violence and oppression. Women are also often discriminated against by religious practices and traditions.[24]

Not only do women lose out when inequality exists, but there is evidence that its impact is felt by society at large. New York Times bestselling authors of *Half the Sky: Turning Oppression into Opportunity for Women Worldwide*, Kristof and WuDunn, reference a series of studies indicating that "when women hold assets or gain incomes, family money is more likely to be spent on nutrition, medicine and housing, and consequently children are healthier."[25] The US State Department, as well as the president of the World Bank, have asserted that giving females access to power economically, politically, and educationally "yield(s) large social and economic returns" and is key to fighting global poverty.[26]

There is considerable evidence that empowering women yields substantial benefits, not only for women but for societies. According to World Bank statistics, women have been found to be less likely to abuse power. For example, increases in female participation in government leadership correlate with decreases in corruption. Research in Indian villages demonstrates that female-led village councils deliver public services more effectively, matching the needs of the community with available resources.

Prioritizing gender equality in organizations and in every sphere of society aligns with the key indices of global gender disparity according to the World Economic Forum: economic empowerment, access to education, and political influence. The indices are monitors to track the correlation between "a country's gender gap and its national competitiveness. Because women account for one-half of a country's potential talent base, a nation's competitiveness in the long term depends significantly on whether and how it educates and utilizes its women."[27] When women are equally empowered, everybody wins.

Further, social scientists define effective leadership as evidence of the ability to build and maintain high-performing teams, and to inspire followers to set aside their selfish agendas in order to work for the common interest of the group.[28] These are the very qualities demonstrated by women in the studies referenced earlier by Kristof and WuDunn, and many others.

Evidence shows that development indicators improve significantly when women make an equal or greater contribution than men. In fact, when women and men have equal opportunities and rights, economic growth accelerates, and poverty rates drop more rapidly for everyone. Of equal importance is the social and spiritual contribution women often encourage within their families and communities, resulting in the building of more stable, peaceful, and productive societies.[29]

CLOSING THE GAP

So, what can be done today, to close the gap of gender bias, discrimination, stereotyping, and sexualization between women and men? Implicit bias, that is so prevalent in our society, can be circumvented through creative means and simple changes.[30] These shifts pertain to organizations and individuals.

Organizational Next Steps

Across all aspects of American life, it is most often men who set policy, allocate resources, lead companies, shape markets, and determine whose stories get told. Although progress has been made globally toward gender equality in terms of education and primary health care, Melinda Gates has recognized the broad, systemic, culturally embedded nature of sexism, and rightly concludes:

> All the human capital (primary health care and education) in the world, though, won't lead to equality and prosperity if healthy, well-educated girls are subject to social norms that disempower them.[31]

All the access to education and health care in the world won't make a difference if women still hit a glass ceiling and fall into the gender gap. Men in positions of leadership and power can help break the glass ceiling and close the gender gap by regularly practicing the following:

- Teach sound, biblical egalitarianism—and make choices to live it out.[32]
- Tell the stories of the influence of women and girls in non-stereotyping roles.[33]
- Notice and point out who is interrupting whom, and who gives credit to whom.
- Assign opportunities on merit—not informally, based on who people know or with whom they are associated.

Organizations can also shift their entire culture through redesigning human resource procedures based on research evidence. This can be done by:

- Informing leaders and managers of their past track record of promotion by gender which can change the way they hire and promote in the future. This should include measurable data of actual empowerment and promotion of women by the manager(s) and throughout the organization.
- Setting quantifiable goals for improvement in gender equality in an organization, large or small, and sharing these goals often, with necessary and appropriate accountabilities established so that this issue remains in the consciousness and in the discourse of the movement.
- Establishing an ongoing organizational audit pertaining to improving gender equality. This would demonstrate that individual leaders' practices of gender equality are interconnected with institutional practices.
- "Blinding" persons to the demographic characteristics of job/appointment applications (name, gender, race, etc.). For example, blind auditions helped increase the fraction of women in our major symphony orchestras from about 5 percent in the 1970s to almost 40 percent today.[34]
- Overcoming the "groupthink" prevalent in panel interviews by requiring evaluators to make independent assessments.

One systemic obstacle to gender equality includes a lack of intentionality in preparing women for greater leadership responsibilities. Part of the solution to this problem could be a decision, taken at the highest levels of an organization (where most of the power is held by men), to intentionally train and prepare women, especially younger women, to equip them for greater responsibility—and to implement this decision in a systematic way throughout the organization. This would include men intentionally mentoring, coaching, and advocating for women to prepare and equip them for greater leadership.

Individual Next Steps

While much can be done at an organizational and leadership level to close the gap of gender inequality, there is also great power in the everyday, individual responses of men. Jackson Katz, a thought-leader in the growing global movement of men working to promote gender equality and prevent gender violence, has written a book entitled, *The Macho Paradox: Why Some Men Hurt Women and How All Men Can Help.*[35] His intended audience is *not* violent men who need help to change their ways, but *all* men, who, he says, "have a role to play in preventing male violence against women." His basic assertion is that rape, battering, sexual abuse, and harassment are so widespread that they must be viewed as a social problem rooted in our culture, not as the problem of troubled individuals. He urges men to directly confront the misogynistic attitudes and behavior of their peers.[36]

Katz asserts men have a powerful role to play in this work and calls on men to put aside the notion of a gender war and stand side-by-side with women—to speak up for women and for men to influence the culture around them by making abusive behavior unacceptable to society, not just illegal. He says, "there's been an awful lot of silence in male culture about this ongoing tragedy ... we need to break that silence, and we need more men to do that."

Jesus' example teaches us that the empowered are not to grasp at or cling to power and privilege but, instead, to exercise power by creative self-giving, for the sake of others. As theologian Walter Brueggemann said, "There is nothing [in Jesus' example] of coercive or tyrannical power," but rather a costly demonstration of the caring for the world.[37] For the sake of others, Jesus laid down his life (Mark 10:45), emptied himself of privilege (Phil. 2:7), washed others' feet (John 13:1–17), and empowered them for greater works than he did (John 14:12).

I have sometimes been asked about my perseverance in the struggle for the empowerment of women in the face of systemic gender inequities. I have been asked how I continue to be hopeful and have faith. Some ask me why I have not quit. Madeleine Albright said it well: "It took me quite a long time to develop a voice, and now that I have it, I am not going to be silent."[38]

Men, what does this mean for you today—in issues personal and practical, as well as societal and systemic? Dr. Martin Luther King Jr., in the context of the struggle for civil rights, said, "In the end, we will remember not the words of our enemies but the silence of our friends."[39]

Men, can you be counted on to be friends of females by speaking up, confronting toxicity in male culture, using your power to establish systems to improve gender equality, and at times, by stepping back? How can you use your power to close the gap? By bringing more women to the decision-making table;

by providing leadership opportunities for women; by intentionally mentoring women, formally and informally; by including women in educational and developmental opportunities, equally with men; by ensuring that in discussions, women's voices are heard, their words not interrupted; by heeding and honoring the counsel and input of women, recognizing that women often bring a different, valuable, and needed point of view, for the greater good.

ANTI-ABUSE AND ADVOCACY

The prevalence of abuse within religious spaces is now well-documented. Movements such as #churchtoo, as well as investigations into larger institutions, have exposed abuse and given survivors some acknowledgment of their experiences, following years of cover-up, silencing, and victim-blaming. Yet despite our awareness, it's easy for us to think that abuse is a problem that happens "over there" in someone else's church, school, or organization. It surely couldn't happen to us. However, this can lead to complacency—assuming that we know our people and their well-intentioned hearts, and missing the existence of abuse in our spaces or the potential that it could happen. We're often poised to dismiss an allegation, disregarding or explaining away the situations we encounter.

The authors of this section share their raw experiences, expert knowledge, and hopes for a way forward. Lori Anne Thompson knows firsthand the profound damage abuse can inflict—but moreover, how the mishandling of abuse can further compound a survivor's trauma. Angela Lam shares her wealth of knowledge from her work with Hagar's Voice, detailing the many ways abuse can manifest and sharing practical, expert advice on how we can shape our organizations to both combat abuse and advocate for survivors. And Rev. Dr. Julie Faith Parker unpacks some of the biblical examples of abuse—confronting the true brutality of passages we may prefer to skim over or avoid. She helps us find a way to draw from the Bible in our pursuit of safer spaces and practices in our own context.

We may find the words on the pages that follow difficult to read. But if we long to banish abuse and oppression from our churches and communities, we must read, we must reflect, and we must act.

15

WHAT I NEED YOU TO KNOW

Lori Anne Thompson

lived a life marked by adverse childhood experiences of physical, sexual, psychological, and emotional abuse; parental separation; alcoholism; incarceration; domestic violence; and devastating deprivation. Upon turning to the evangelical faith community for help and support, she was revictimized spiritually, financially, and sexually by clergy in adulthood. Lori Anne now seeks to serve the survivor community through selective speaking, extensive writing, and in her professional role. She graduated from Queen's University, Canada, earning a bachelor of science degree in kinesiology (with honors) and a master's of child advocacy and policy (magna cum laude) from Montclair State University. She is a distinguished member of Alpha Epsilon Lambda Society. She works as a registered kinesiologist in private practice and as an intake specialist for a survivor-centric law firm. She is devoted to her family, continuing education, and empowering her fellow survivors.

Today is Holy Saturday.

I have risen in the darkness as one who was woken from within. Compelled, but not coerced, to the keyboard to communicate the incommunicable, to define the undefinable, to speak the unspeakable. This is how we overcome—the blood of the lamb and the word of our testimony. The blood is all over the floor. Whose blood? Mine? His? Ours? I can't tell anymore. My words, his, or ours? I know not for sure. The hemorrhage of harm has me here hanging head; drenched in red. It gurgles in the veins of victimization.

Friday passed without the historical heaviness. The weight of it no longer crushed me; the stagger had steadied; the crowd had long since left the hell of my hill; the stripes, they have mostly healed. There is no need, however, to run my fingers far to feel the scars.

I remember the stench of the sneers. I hear the accusation and I taste the humiliation. Recall of these comes easy to me: to suffer in the garden of your private Gethsemane; to be kissed unto death; to be lied about by lips that spoke of love; to stand defenseless in judgment; to watch cruelty be set free; to pay the price silently; to be mocked in your helpless estate; to be scorned by those who know you not; to be led in silence to the site of your own suffering; to carry a cross meant not only to crush, but to crucify; to stagger under the weight of it all and to succumb to the slaughter.

To write to you on Holy Saturday is to descend into despair, to return to the scene of my own crime, to name hell and to hear its names for me. None of it is pretty, none of it is pious, all of it is not only crushing—it is crucifying. Such is the truth of Saturday.

My brothers, I have much against you.

You have left your sisters in harm of, but not the holiness of, Saturday.
Many of you have stoned us.
Some of you stone us still.
Most of you have denied you knew us.
Some of you deny us still.
Others have torn our garments and told us to go home.
You have covered yourselves in cloaks and left our bodies bare.
You have contributed to the seductive system that has become Christendom.

I came to you hungry—you consumed me.
I came to you naked—you took photos of me.
I came to you captive—you reinforced my restraints.
I hungered and thirsted for righteousness—I hunger still.
You sought the ninety-nine and you left me for dead.

You took what little I had left.

You cast me out to wander bewildered in the wilderness.

You lowered me under your feet while you raised your hands in worship.

You denigrated me with your lips fervent in prayer.

You did all in his name.

Because of you, I cannot speak or hear the name of the Christ without cringing.

I who sought him with all my heart, I who love him still.

The name above all names was used to brutalize me and many.

I urge you, my brothers, speak not of him until you love like him.

Seek not others only to crush them—

Under the yoke of your own obfuscated understanding.

Speak not of righteousness until mine shines like the dawn—

And my justice like the noonday sun.

I was a child when my neighbor took us to church; away from the "house of desolation" and into the chambers of consolation. The church was cold, but the words were warm. I didn't think sex offenders went to church—my father didn't. I wasn't aware until my fourth decade that predators sat in the pews, much less in the pulpit. My abused body grew into adulthood. My trust remained a child. Children are inherently naive, long to be loved, and trust with ease. So it was with me. As I sought the Christ in adulthood, I was revictimized by clergy repeatedly. In 2017, I was sexually exploited by a powerful apologetic leader—a predator—whose motto was, "No question unasked." A private attempt to hold him to account ended in my and my family's public crucifixion. Christians led the way—*no questions asked.* As he died a hero, we lived in hell. Christians created my Saturday.

At the time of this writing, the proverbial stone has been rolled away from the tomb of my trauma. The truth has been revealed, the graveclothes have been set aside, I have even supped on the shores of my sorrow. Sunday has come with its resurrection and its restoration. I would be remiss if I did not say that this has mostly been despite the Christian community rather than because of it. An atheist led the way for the truth to be known about my abuser, but as too often happens, some Christians took the credit. Yes, I have much against you—and even so, I remain in your midst. Forgiveness is both a repeated choice and an iterative process. I will never be the same and you will never be the same to me. Love can build a bridge beyond brutality. If we are friends, if we love one another, we must be honest with each other. This is my love and my honesty.

WHAT THEN SHALL WE DO?

This is the question I hope is on your lips as you come to this book. There is much to say, but here are the first few steps.

Be Aware of Your Power

All abuse occurs in a power imbalance and a culture that cultivates it. A prerequisite for abuse of power is a dynamic and therefore a dialectic of dominance and submission; a power-holder and a powered-over.[1] You must have a measure of power to abuse it.

As men, you are present and historical power-holders due to the perpetuation of practices that are part of the patriarchy.[2] It can be uncomfortable to acknowledge that simply being born a biological male lends you power that biological females do not have—reality is indifferent to our discomfort. Most men are not offenders, yet overwhelmingly, most offenders are men.[3] Not all women are victims of sexual violence, yet overwhelmingly, most victims of interpersonal violence are women. It is always a red flag when power-holders blame those they hold power over for what they have done or failed to do. Jesus always bent to the powered-over and saved his harshest words for power-holders. Do likewise.

Be Aware of Your Culture

Christ elevated the status of women and children; Christendom does not. Christendom does not even pass the scratch and sniff test. Often women are not permitted to speak or lead or are relegated to lesser roles. Female staff report being repeatedly sexually harassed by their fellow male ministry staff.[4] Women in leadership are told to "go home" or asked to be silent; and if silence does not suit them, they are given little choice but to leave. When a religious male perpetrates abuse, invariably he is protected, applauded, and promoted, whereas the woman and her family are ostracized. It was in the beginning and remains to the end, "The woman you gave me" (Gen. 3:12). Ministry itself has become a machine that makes men into mass producers of a spirituality that is defined by professional productivity rather than personal piety. We do not have a bad apple; we have ourselves a bad barrel.

Be Aware of Your Privilege

Humans are inherently self-referencing. History has been kind to white, religious, heterosexual males and has been equally unkind to women and their children, as well as sexual, religious, and racial minorities. The story of humanity to the present moment is rife with a dialectic of domination and submission in which oppression, abuse, and tyranny have predictably played out in the public and private domains.

When asked what they do to ensure their personal safety from sexual violence, men typically have an abbreviated list. When women are asked what they do to protect themselves from sexual violence, the list is as long as it is detailed and complex. It's uncommon for a male to intuitively understand the lived experience of a female and invariably he forgets what it was like to be a child. Grateful are the women and children who interact with a man who wishes to be a student.

Be Aware of Your Language

Poet Joseph Brodsky famously said, "You ... are so naive. You think evil is going to come into your houses wearing big black boots. It doesn't come like that. Look at the language. It begins in the language." Language can betray your praxis (what you do) and your values (philosophy) as well as create incongruence between the two. Call a spade a spade. Keep abuse in the context in which it occurred: a power inequity. Hold the offender to the letter of the law and extend the gospel to victim(s).[5]

Be Aware of Your Praxis

Dictionary.com defines praxis as "practice, as distinguished from theory."[6] It is practical—the gap between practice and theory, between text and the world. *Oxford Learner's Dictionaries* defines praxis as "a way of doing something; the use of theory or belief in a practical way."[7] What you do is underpinned by your belief or philosophy. Our individual and institutional words and actions must be congruent with our purported philosophy. If our actions don't line up with our stated values, we cannot transform our own culture within our organizations, much less the broader culture. We simply must BE the change we wish to see.

Brazilian educator and philosopher Paulo Freire said,

> Those who authentically commit themselves to the people must re-examine themselves constantly. This conversion is so radical as not to allow for ambivalent behaviour ... Conversion to the people requires a profound rebirth. Those who undergo it must take on a new form of existence; they can no longer remain as they were.[8]

The Christ we purport to follow rightly called hypocrites those who were blind to their own immediate idiocy but quick to call out the perceived egregious offenses of others.

In practice, most sister survivors want to be heard. We know the past cannot be retracted but we would like the truth to be known in our own words. Listening, itself, is an intervention and a radical act of love.[9]

In practice, we also wish you would *ask*. Ask the very people who have been hurt what would help to make things right, or at least as right as possible. *Listen, really listen*, to the answers. Most sister survivors have very basic requests: public acknowledgment of truth as the beginning of justice. Telling the truth accurately and publicly is also an *initial* act of solidarity.[10] Importantly, abuse survivors also often benefit from assurance of safety for the survivor and accountability for the abuser. As basic as it sounds: *Do what you say you will do when you say you will do it*. Communicate. Listen. Check back. Repeat.

There is so much to mourn as we live in the reality of Saturday and all its harm. But holiness is only experienced by survivors through community when we acknowledge and embody Saturday. There are things that only suffering can instruct. There are treasures that only the darkness can expose. There is sacredness in solidarity with the suffering. The good news ceases to be good if we skip the dish of descending into the hell of Saturday, dwelling with those who despair, staying long enough for the light to do what it does best—illuminate.

16

DRESSING THE WOUNDS OF ABUSE

Angela Lam

is co-founder of Hagar's Voice, a nonprofit supporting survivors of clergy sexual abuse and offering training for religious organizations looking to prevent abuse. Angela has twenty years of experience as a pastor and works alongside licensed social workers and counselors who offer advocacy for survivors in religious whistleblowing and disclosure. As a pastor, she understands the dynamics and pressures of church leadership; as a woman, she knows the dynamics of abuse and the tensions of gender in religious spaces.

The steady stream of abuse disclosures in the North American church this past decade can leave leaders floundering as to how we might respond—overwhelmed; afraid to look, feel, or fully understand its presence, origin, or severity. We may even find ourselves frantically looking for an escape.

Approaching this topic, we might feel like a mother tensing in the face of labor pains—holding our breath as the triggers arise within us. But just as the laboring mother finds a way to manage, we can, too. And we must. It will require a similar "breathing through" that can ease childbirth (whereas tensing in the face of pain can create tearing), but we, too, can learn to attend to ourselves in such a way that we find the resilience to bear down and birth a new era of Christian communities.

So, friend, breathe deeply as you read this chapter. There is a spiritual "breathing through" that helps us manage the sensations of the moment. *Do not be afraid, the Lord Almighty is with us.*

> God is our refuge and strength,
> an ever-present help in trouble.
> Therefore we will not fear, though the earth give way
> and the mountains fall into the heart of the sea,
> though its waters roar and foam
> and the mountains quake with their surging.
>
> There is a river whose streams make glad the city of God,
> the holy place where the Most High dwells.
> God is within her, she will not fall;
> God will help her at break of day.
> Nations are in uproar, kingdoms fall . . .
>
> The Lord Almighty is with us;
> the God of Jacob is our fortress.
>
> PSALM 46:1–7

As we experience the discomfort of confronting the reality of abuse in religious spaces, let's hold to what we know to be true: that the God who designed this church we love with our whole heart, has the resources to carry us through the building and repair of her. The Master has tools for the Master's plan.

DEFINING ABUSE AND ABUSIVE SYSTEMS

In this moment of reckoning, it might seem as though we've looked the problem of abuse square in the eyes when we've acknowledged that religious establishments (churches, seminaries, schools, camps, missions organizations, etc.) are as capable of abuse—and just as likely to abuse—as non-religious organizations.[1] This acknowledgment is hard to make. Perhaps it's even more difficult to admit that our volunteer-based models are particularly ripe for the specific abuse of exploitation. This makes understanding how abuse works and lives and grows a lot more important than we have ever realized. The incongruity between what church is supposed to be and what we're discovering is happening in our midst is so hard to digest that we can distrust, minimize, or silence what we ourselves are hearing and seeing. Even when, year after year, fresh revelations surface that abuse of many kinds is happening in all corners of religious life, we still feel gob-smacked that this is real. That *Christian* organizations are capable of this. That *Christians* are capable of this. That *we* (you and I) are capable of this.

I believe *this* is the true wound that needs to be excised and healed: the reality of how our own actions, ignorance, and inaction has led to our involvement in the wounding. This is a hard pill to swallow, but it is the first step.

Our recoil from this reality can cause us to make too much of abuse or too little of it. Making "too much" of abuse can look like villainizing and excommunicating the offender instead of pastoring them to healthy discipleship and law-abiding behavior. It can also result in us creating a fear-filled environment around engaging in gendered relationships. Making "too little" of abuse can look like trusting our own assessment of situations rather than the voices of those who share their painful experiences, and/or failing to examine our everyday environments based on what's known about abusive dynamics. If we are to right size abuse and turn the tide against the onset of abuse in our settings, we need to understand what it is and reckon with its prevalence. To truly look the problem square in the eyes is to consider our responsibility for preventing and addressing abuse in our settings. Let's begin this work by setting some definitions and establishing a baseline of clarity together.

Abuse or harm is "defined within the Act."[2] Harmful conduct is behavior that causes physical or psychological harm (for example, harassment and intimidation; causing fear, alarm or distress; unlawful conduct which adversely affects property, rights, or interests.) It is important to name that intentions can be good even when behaviors are harmful. But our intentions do not mitigate our responsibility when it comes to behaviors that are harmful to others.

Furthermore, abuse within religious organizations is often addressed (or more likely dismissed) as one person's choice, moral failure, etc. However, we know from decades of observation of the Catholic church,[3] the Southern Baptist Convention,[4] and many other bodies, how these behaviors are allowed to exist within ecosystems that lack accountability, reinforce problematic narratives (including bad theology), and are otherwise askew in the care of the most vulnerable. The types of abuse we're seeing in our religious spaces do not live in a vacuum; they are the natural outpouring of specific conditions. These are not stand-alone assaults or missteps, but the culmination of narratives, experiences, and factors resulting in behavior—by individuals and their environments. Abuse lives in an ecosystem;[5] it is not just the actions of one "bad apple." Where you find someone abusing another, you will find other players, bystanders, systems, narratives, and/or agreements that have permissioned that behavior (perhaps even bred, perpetuated, and protected it). And, too often in religious spaces, mistreatment is normalized by bad theology.[6]

Abuse comes in many forms, but for our purposes, let's define some of the most frequent varieties of abuse found in our religious contexts.

Emotional abuse: using insults, humiliation, or intimidation to control or cause fear.[7] This can look like withholding affection, approval, and belonging, or applying psychological harm. In religious spaces it can be the silencing, cold-shoulder treatment of those who would question the spiritual authorities in that institution. Due to the power imbalances inherent in hierarchical settings, gaslighting is a prevalent form of emotional abuse. Gaslighting is the manipulation of someone into questioning their own story, sanity, or powers of reasoning. Gaslighting can consist of repeatedly challenging and questioning a victim's story of abuse, as if they made it up, or discounting their view when compared to that of a beloved leader.

Spiritual abuse: shaming or controlling someone from a position of spiritual authority, or using religious texts to minimize or rationalize abusive behaviors.[8] This can look like linking the love or wrath of God to the condition of one's behavior. Or using Scripture to diminish the experience of someone who is reporting harm in our religious space. Or using religious education to overpower someone's perspective.

Sexual abuse: making someone take part in sexual activities against their wishes.[9] This can look like the perversion of a platonic relationship or a perversion of the role of sex within a romantic relationship. In religious contexts, it includes everything from sexual harassment to unwanted sexual contact or threats, to the use of pornography. It also includes the grooming of someone under one's authority toward the sexualization of that relationship.

Abuse of power: the leveraging of power—intentionally or not—to prevail over others.[10] In religious spaces this can look like someone in spiritual authority using Scripture to quash dissent or a spiritual authority figure not realizing the power of their position and how it affects the people around them. Ignorance of power imbalances sets up all sorts of potential for abuse, and the abuse of power is often linked to other forms of abuse. For instance, welcomed persistence in pursuing a romantic relationship between peers can be harmless; but when someone with more power in a relationship persistently pursues a romance— or where the context of the relationship means meaningful consent can't be obtained—it is abusive. The power dynamics at play greatly affect the aspect of abuse in the situation. Abuse of power can also take the shape of bending those under our authority to our will based on the reality (overtly leveraged by the abuser or not) that the less powerful person could lose their job or standing in the organization or even be excommunicated from their spiritual community for falling from the leader's good graces.

Exploitation: the misuse of someone for profit or selfish gain.[11] This can look like pressure on community members to give time or resources beyond what they can afford. An example of exploitation in religious spaces is the justification of pushing volunteers beyond their means in the name of evangelism or mission when the true motivation is a leader's personal need for the validation that comes from having a growing ministry. Or when paid leaders abdicate their responsibilities and place them on volunteer workers instead. Or when a religious institution pays their interns minimum wage but then expects a lot of "off book" hours. Or when unmarried staff are paid an unlivable wage.

These descriptions of abuse might seem obvious, and it might feel unnecessary to cover the basics; but decision-makers in religious institutions are often people of privilege (those who hold the power and access),[12] and those with privilege often struggle to see the conditions of abuse, or the presence of intersectionality (dynamics that develop when multiple systems of inequality come to bear),[13] making them unaware of the impact of their behavior. It may be difficult to accept these statements about our unawareness of privilege, but the rampant abuse discovered in so many organizations stands as a witness.

We have a compelling second reason to cover the basics of what abuse is and how it takes shape in religious spaces: There is an alarming body of evidence that points to the propensity for organizational leadership to do everything in their power to minimize the disclosure of abuse. In our work at Hagar's Voice, we have found an overwhelming number of survivors who cite this secondary abuse as more hurtful than the original abuse they disclosed, because its ramifications on their life and faith are significantly more far-reaching and catastrophic. This clear pattern of abuse and the response of leadership to abuse is either blindness or evil intent (or both), but the evidence of this pattern in our organizations surely compels us to investigate.

For a broad swath of religious leaders, finding the resilience[14] to get curious about this discrepancy between intent and impact is the key to releasing us from the unintentional agreement we've had with evil. If this question gripped the hearts of paid and unpaid leaders, we would see wave after wave of a new kind of revelation in our religious spaces—one filled with confession, repentance, restitution, and hope. The gospel (good news) would be prolific in these spaces. Abuse would lose its grip. Systems of oppression and exploitation would be overturned, and revival would unfurl. Jesus-followers would find new levels of liberation and a new kind of discipleship marked by love, mutual submission, and tender care for each other. May it be so.

But this revival would quickly hit the reality that abuse lives in an ecosystem. The opening of our eyes to the layers of mistreatment of humans in our religious spaces[15] would compel us to disrupt the status quo of our institutions. And here is where the rubber often meets the road: It takes a lot of *personal* courage and spiritual maturity to face the reality that I may be complicit or even guilty of abuse; it takes *corporate* courage and *corporate* spiritual maturity to change the ecosystem that's built to reinforce the status quo.

Individual Jesus-followers find Jesus' liberation using spiritual tools such as:

- Prayer (intimacy with God that shapes our hearts)
- Confession (truth-telling that breaks the silence and shame)
- Repentance (intentionally altering my ways to reflect a new understanding)
- Forgiveness (first receiving it from God and then seeking it from others)
- Restitution ("first go and be reconciled to them" Matt. 5:24)

We know these tools well; they are basic principles of Christianity. But it may come as a shockingly simple revelation that the very same tools are needed in corporate discipleship!

Herein lies a painful reality: Too many of our organizations are religious-themed empires instead of kin*dom-bringing communities.† We see this in

---

† As Rev. Dr. Elizabeth Rios highlighted in chapter twelve, kin*dom has been used for decades by people who have wanted to get away from the imperialistic, patriarchal language of kingdom. Unlike a kingdom, a kin*dom is inclusive, non-hierarchical, relational, compassionate, justice-oriented, and anti-imperial. See Dr. Ada María Isasi-Díaz, *Mujerista Theology* (Orbis Books, 2005).

leadership's failure of nerve to apply these kin*dom principles to our religious institutions—we have failed to trust that God's kin*dom and church are built by God's ways. Instead, leadership too often defines its responsibility as the need to protect the institution (its momentum, its size, the demands of its budget, its reputation, the reputation of its leadership, etc.) in favor of its God-given responsibility to bring the kin*dom to earth. Let that soak in for a moment. The difference between these two things is astounding and speaks to so much in this moment of religious community life. What truly IS our responsibility as leaders in the church?

It can be staggering to consider the exodus from religious spaces in our current North American environment.[16] Amazingly, many of these exiles aren't leaving because they've lost faith in God; they're leaving in search of the "big C" Church—the one that looks like kin*dom-come! The exodus is of those who have lost faith in religious leadership and communities that protect and propagate mistreatment and marginalization of humans. For instance, one in six American women have experienced some form of sexual assault.[17] So many female spiritual exiles aren't done with God; they're done with being part of religious communities where they experience threats to their safety and threats to their children's and sisters' safety (not just emotional and spiritual, but literal physical safety). And many of us question which of our loved ones will be next to be harmed. The reality we often observe is that when survivors and advocates speak up to religious authority about these realities, they are gaslit, disbelieved, diminished, and dismissed (if not outright disgraced). Even if they haven't experienced this themselves, they've watched as others who look and sound like them have.

It really shouldn't surprise us that women are a huge part of the exodus from religious spaces.[18] Many women can draw a direct correlation between their own experiences/observations and those which other people groups in the margins are experiencing: people within the LGBTQ2SIA community, those who have been racialized, people under thirty, people who are neuro-divergent, etc. Their exodus is not their abandonment of the church; it is their loyalty *to* the church and the kin*dom that compels their actions.

Dissenters and whistleblowers have been perceived as unity-breakers, betrayers, and mutineers. But they are light-bringers. They're holding up a mirror to us. They offer us an opportunity to see ourselves truly and be liberated from this present darkness. These spiritual exiles are kin*dom-come.

There is an obvious need for change. But, friends, don't change just to keep _____ [people group] _____ in your organization.

Do it because you long to see the kin*dom come.

Do it because your discipleship and your organization's discipleship (the Body) deserve Jesus' liberation.

Do it because Jesus told you to (Matt. 28:16–20) and you love his ways.

Do it because you owe the world the kin*dom.

Do it because you deserve the kin*dom yourself.

Do it because the church isn't what she was meant to be without the very voices that are leaving our communities.

BARRIERS TO AND REASONS FOR PURSUING KIN*DOM HEALTH

Many leaders in religious organizations want to abuse-proof their environments and take Jesus-inspired action when abuse is discovered in their midst, but the organization's status quo is where they often get stuck. So, instead of taking action, they settle for longing and lament. They feel confined by the organization's systems that are built and reinforced in such a way that the concepts of corporate confession or repentance are so costly that it is impossible to get a quorum of leadership to sign off on the kin*dom's path to healing.

What we're discovering in this era of abuse disclosures is a theology that fuels colonizing[19] by growth-obsessed institutions that must be fed exploited labor to sustain their appetites. We've built this ecosystem with our own hands. Whatever the size or perceived "success" of the organization, models that feature solo-leaders have produced generations of leaders whose personal identities are enmeshed with their organization, leading to workaholism, burnout, isolation, pressure to be inhumanely perfect, addiction to production, and no time for personal discipleship.[20] Solo-leadership is not the only indicator of a religious-themed empire, but there seems an uncanny connection between the era of idealizing the solo-led megachurch model and the rash of narcissistic pastors we've seen in the last twenty-plus years of religious leadership.[21] And even when a religious-themed empire manages to avoid hiring leaders with narcissistic tendencies, there is still a bias toward hiring people who aren't in tune with their own humanity/needs—leaders who will run themselves ragged in service to the never-satiated institution. The natural ramification of these models is a high-pressured, inhumane environment in which there is no time for a leader to discover that they might hold gender bias, racist narratives, ableist assumptions, or a homophobic theology (all major causes for abuse in religious spaces).

In religious-themed empires, the appetite for growth—and mandate to protect the territory that has been "won"—leaves little room for its leadership's personal discipleship, let alone corporate discipleship. And so, people who are pushed to the margins continue to share their stories of harm and exclusion and are met by an institution unable to acknowledge the distance between its intent and its impact. Religious institutions mistakenly confuse their desire to grow their organization with their divine mandate to grow the kin*dom.

At first glance, in our North American conditions, it can seem normal to conflate the two; we'd like to think the growth of our local church *is* growth for the kin*dom. But in reality, a simple biblical assessment sheds abundant light on what the kin*dom is/isn't:

- The fruits of the Spirit (kin*dom symptoms) are love, joy, peace, patience, kindness, goodness, faithfulness, gentleness, and self-control (Gal. 5:22–23).
- The kin*dom is built to bless the poor in spirit, those who mourn, the meek, those who hunger and thirst for righteousness, the merciful, the pure in heart, the peacemakers, and those who are persecuted (Matt. 5:1–12).
- The kin*dom works like a hospital (Matt. 9:12).
- The kin*dom centers the least (Zech. 7:10), the last (1 Tim. 1:12–17), and the lost (Luke 19:10).

If you find yourself longing for a church/kin*dom that does these things and lamenting the obstacles between your organization's reality and the dream so vividly painted in those passages, well done. This is where it begins. The work of Jesus has always begun first in the heart. As we abandon ourselves to God's work there, Spirit is faithful to complete it (Phil. 1:3–6), bringing it to bear in actions, behaviors, narratives, systems, and values. This is the way of Jesus: "You have heard it said, 'Don't murder,' but I tell you, 'Don't be angry'" (see Matt. 5:21–22). This lamenting and longing are where discipleship begins. Jesus never settled for the performative (do not murder); Jesus' work has always started in the heart (do not be angry).

If you're committed to kin*dom discipleship both personally and corporately, the change is simple (not easy, but simple): Use every ounce of your influence to bring the kin*dom to your organization (guidance on that up next). If your response to that suggestion is that you can't because the cost of corporate discipleship is too high, then I suggest you commit whole-heartedly to your own personal discipleship and step out of that self-violating leadership role. Leadership is the natural outpouring of what's inside of us—and if you're in an environment where your personal discipleship cannot be reconciled to your corporate discipleship, you lose the authenticity and integrity of your leadership.

If you can't afford to slow down to do this type of discipleship work, you are part of an ecosystem that's exploiting and abusing people (and you're likely a victim yourself). The kin*dom has time and space to do the kin*dom's work. Period.

Let's sit with that a moment …

*God, grant me the courage to surrender to your ways. Ignite my imagination with a vision for the kin*dom. Forgive me for my fears and failures to act. Remind me of your goodness and everlasting love so that, from the safety of my identity as your child, I might walk into your light without fear (1 John 4:18). Guide me into the liberation only you can bring. Instruct me on your economy and how your kin*dom is built. Whisper to me about the power of vulnerability and the freedom of confession. Shine a light on those who have gone before me that I may take courage from that cloud of witnesses (Heb. 12:1–3). Right-size my role in this—protect me from overplaying my importance or diminishing my part to play. Right-size your role in this—remind me of who you are and how you redeem. But, ultimately, God, my prayer is "Your Kingdom come, your will be done, on earth as it is in heaven" (Luke 11:2, Matt. 6:10).*

BUILDING KIN*DOM ECOSYSTEMS

Each ecosystem has unique challenges and assets to do this anti-abuse work, but here are ten straightforward, actionable ways an organization can move the needle against abuse in their space.

Change Leadership Norms

Idea 1: Shift leadership dynamics. Most of our decision-making spaces in religious organizations have been populated by dominant cultures (white, able-bodied, cisgender, heterosexual males, often of middle-age). Bringing in a few women

or some younger leaders, etc., to our decision-making tables is not only ineffec-
tive against the status quo and power dynamics of a dominant-culture space, it is
unsafe for these diverse voices. So, move beyond the fantasy of the trickle-down
approach and choose to make the necessary changes that enable different conversations in these decision-making spaces. This may mean adding more voices to the
process than is "efficient." Or it may entail asking perfectly good candidates to step
aside to make room at the table so that status-quo voices no longer overwhelm the
conversations. This may call for acknowledging toxic/unsafe voices at the decision-making table and requiring their submission to mentorship/discipleship. It
may result in the mid-term removal of unyielding leaders (even if they are volunteers giving their time) in order to make it psychologically safe for voices on the
margins to offer their honest thoughts and/or for established teammates to participate safely in the changing culture. It might also look like committing to let the
voices of diversity be the first to speak—and the last to speak—in group discussions. It will definitely require a slower pace of conversation in order to prevent the
status quo and its assumptions from continuing to prevail.

Idea 2: Be prepared to break the org chart. Many organizations attempt
to take abuse disclosures seriously by running the process through their board
of directors, and yet most often board members in a religious organization
are not the folks best-gifted for victim work—even after becoming trauma-
informed (see Idea 6). It is vital to establish a path of safety for journeying *with*
survivors. Contracting a neutral third party for safe disclosures and victim
advocacy is a terrific first step. Second, establishing an empowered task force of
trained advocates and credentialed social workers and/or therapists brings the
expertise and safety-mindedness to a board that they likely do not have—nor
would they need under standard board-work conditions. Having these practitioners earmarked as consultants gives your organization the best shot at making
decisions that are healthy and safe for everyone in your midst. And having them
empowered in advance ensures the safety of survivors from the very moment
they approach your organization with a disclosure.

Idea 3: Commit to transparency, now. Practice transparency by making
your human resources policies public on your website. This indicates you have
a level of awareness about abuse and gives victims the information they need to
determine whether what they've experienced is something they can report and
expect your support in handling. It also signals to both potential abusers and
to survivors that you understand the dynamics of abuse and are committed to
preventing it and responding to it if/when it arises.

Idea 4: Stop letting abusers resign. When we allow abusers to resign (rather than be fired), we harm our own community in numerous ways:

- By covering up an unhealed wound.
- By abandoning and traumatizing the victim involved.
- By ignoring the reality that there are likely more victims than we know about.
- By failing to learn the lessons of how the ecosystem around the abuse impacted it.

When we allow abusers to resign, we also harm the broader church by sending an unhealed abuser on to the next unsuspecting community.

Instead, as scary as it may seem, be honest—full of grace and humility—as you go public with the need to remove people from positions of spiritual authority. Acknowledge that abuse is not a matter of a "bad apple," and speak about the situation in light of the ecosystem of abuse. Do not settle for scapegoating the abuser. Speak frankly of what you've discovered, speak humbly about what you've learned or need to learn, speak openly about the kin*dom's ways, and let Spirit's refining fire move through your midst. Trust God's narrative of truth (John 8:31–32), and be fully transparent.

Additionally, place a clause in your employment contract that notifies new hires from the very beginning that any investigation's findings of abuse in your organization will be dealt with as a whole body. This simple clause holds leadership accountable to the trauma-informed practice of transparency, but also prevents all future requests for silence from the abuser. This isn't just about holding an abuser accountable; oftentimes, the wider leadership also benefit from keeping abuse silent—or maintaining a tight narrative. This clause should be in place, and exercised when required, for *both* the perpetrator *and* the wider leadership, to ensure that abuse is brought into the open and dealt with publicly. While a commitment to transparency like this may feel uncomfortable, it is the only way in which the organization can become a space where everyone knows that abuse isn't tolerated and will be brought into the open to be appropriately dealt with.

Expand Community Capacity

Idea 5: Follow the law of the land. When abuse is reported to a religious institution, the leadership conversations are too often about what was theologically right and wrong in the situation or the "cost" of taking such a disclosure seriously.[22] Discussing what we are bound to do legally in these situations is all too infrequent and often not even on the radar of decision-makers. When sexual harassment, discrimination, exploitation, and/or any other human-rights violations are revealed in our religious spaces, taking these disclosures seriously is not optional. We are responsible to respond to these incidents as the law requires. As citizens and business managers, we have a responsibility to adhere to the law.

Furthermore, as Christians, we have a responsibility to go above and beyond what's required by law in consideration of our spiritual siblings. For instance, where the law might only apply to preventing your employees from abusing one another, our biblical mandate requires us to ensure that *all* humans in our midst are protected by the baseline standard of human rights.[23] There is something incredibly wrong with our idea of kin*dom if human rights seem like a luxury we cannot afford in our midst. So, before you're in a position to ask yourself if or how you'll respond to a disclosure, decide now to be a leader and an institution that abides by the law at a minimum. This means you must know what the law is in order to be prepared to act accordingly should you become aware of abuse in your environment.

Idea 6: Respond to victims of abuse well and with kindness. Invest in trauma-informed training for all leaders. This should be a minimum requirement for those in positions of spiritual authority in your organization (paid or unpaid). It is also worth opening the opportunity to anyone in your midst who wants to be equipped in this way. Whether they will deal directly with victims in the process of a disclosure or not, understanding trauma and its effects empowers your whole religious body to care for themselves and each other better. Having your organization's leadership team trauma-informed will equip them to understand what to expect and how to navigate the disclosure/decision process. Even an introductory level of trauma education will assist with policy-writing, decision-making about who's in which conversations, and deciding how things are communicated publicly or privately. Trauma-informed training is a must for leadership but is also a beautiful way to teach a faith community how to be a kin*dom hospital both inside and outside of your organization.

Idea 7: Outfit your toolbelt and choose wisely. As previously covered, there are spiritual tools useful for addressing the wounds of abuse in our midst (prayer, confession, repentance, etc.). There are also spiritual tools that are harmful when misapplied to abuse situations, such as making a survivor face their abuser (Matt. 18),[24] pressuring a survivor to forgive,[25] or weaponizing unity.[26] Also in your toolbelt are necessary non-spiritual tools like employment law and training in human resources. There are optional tools for these situations as well—things like consulting legal counsel to avoid making unnecessary mistakes, working with an employment lawyer to ensure your policies reflect human rights best practice, or carrying insurance as a protection against financial ruin if something horrible were to happen in your organization. But in using these non-religious tools, we must recognize they are not—by nature—designed to bring the kin*dom. For instance, no lawyer will ever guide you to the spiritual tool of repentance, nor will an insurance company ask the moral question of whether the costs of a credentialed investigation should be covered by your claim with their organization. So, knowing your toolbox and choosing your tools with intention is key to walking with Spirit in bringing the kin*dom to every corner of your organization.

Build Healthy Processes

Idea 8: Invest in people and policies for safety. You must know where safety comes from: Policies don't keep people safe; people keep people safe. But even though safety is a human responsibility, policies empower people to know the appropriate boundaries, to report abuse (because they can expect the outcomes of that report), and to hold accountability lines. But people are limited in their effectiveness if policies are out of date, so ensure your policies are up to code. If your organization's policies don't reflect the lessons learned from the #metoo movement or don't include clauses specifically about clergy sexual abuse, spiritual abuse, or abuse of power, then a Human Resource Audit is warranted.[27] Your organization definitely has loopholes that abuse can creep through that a function-specific audit can address. But because safety isn't found in policies, you can't stop there. Too many organizations fall short of empowering their people with the knowledge they need to recognize abuse, respond in real time to abuse happening in their presence, and/or get help from leadership in their organization. Build a baseline of safety with quality policies and then equip folks at every level of your organization as advocates and allies. You'll not only protect everyone in your midst, you'll be sending change agents out into the world who are creating safety wherever they go!

Idea 9: Accept the limitations of your expertise; ask for help. We are pastors, we are not psychologists, counselors, therapists, or social workers. Our expertise lies elsewhere, and we need to humbly accept this. This looks like:

- Deciding now that we will not give ourselves permission to label what experts say is abuse as "just sin" (and therefore assume our expertise will suffice in knowing how to heal the wounded psyche of either the abuser or the survivor). We can and should walk alongside these people as spiritual siblings—caring for the condition of their spiritual health and praying for God's redemptive work to be done—*and* lean on credentialed help to develop paths for healing and accountability.

- Deciding now that we are not qualified to investigate claims of abuse in our organization and committing to seeking outside, certified help. An appropriate investigation has three criteria: 1) independent (no relational connection to your organization or its people), 2) trauma-informed (practiced in the six principles of trauma-informed care), and 3) forensic (its conduct and reporting is evidence-based and not just a collection of interviews summarized with an opinion).

- Deciding now that we are not qualified to rehabilitate a sex offender or sexual predator; nor are we capable of policing their actions within community life. We can and should commit to walking with these offenders as spiritual siblings (leveraging our expertise), but we need to enlist the help of certified practitioners in the process of developing conditions for abusers when it comes to their access to groups of people who are under our responsibility of safety.

- Deciding now that we will refer people seeking our counsel for issues of abuse to trained professionals. Domestic abuse is too often "treated" with untrained pastoral counseling, causing even further harm (statistically most often harming women). Provide a safe space for someone to share their experiences, then walk with them in finding the qualified care they need to address their situation.

Idea 10: Make reporting accessible and easy. If you haven't already, establish a relationship with a neutral third party to receive disclosures on behalf of your organization. And then explain explicitly to everyone across your organization (both verbally more than once and on your website) what someone could expect if they came forward to your safe-disclosure spot. What will happen in that conversation? Is it a conversation or a written disclosure? How can someone be assured that this is a safe-disclosure place if your organization is paying to retain that service? What will happen to the story/information once a victim has disclosed it to the institution? What are your criteria for discerning if action will be taken? What level of detail do you require vs. what would eventually be shared with an investigator? Who will have access to what they've shared? What rights do they have to determine the next steps? Do they have the option of remaining anonymous? Becoming trauma-informed will help you understand some of the dynamics at play for a survivor during the process of disclosure, but there are also resources to help you establish an accessible path for disclosure to your organization.

CONCLUSION

The rampant abuse that's being revealed in North America's religious spaces did not grow overnight. While there are simple steps that will lead to improvement, there are no quick fixes. It takes resilience and tenacity to abuse-proof an organization. The older and larger the organization, the more the tale of the tortoise and the hare bears weight. But Jesus-followers are not discouraged or deterred—the church was always meant to be a safe place for injured humans to find solace, so we know we were made for this work.

However, be forewarned: To stand with the marginalized is to be marginalized. It is counter-intuitive to expect this from religious people or spaces, and yet it remains true. Jesus was killed by the religious leaders of his day. We may not face physical harm in following his footsteps to bring the kin*dom to the overlooked and oppressed, but we can be assured we will be ushered into the suffering of Christ in this work. But even as we may lose things we hold dear, where there is suffering with Christ, there is life (John 10:9–10). Whatever we lose in the work of kin*dom is a cost worth counting; as in its place, we will discover to new degrees our authentic selves, liberation, and pieces of heaven on earth. To enter into the self-sacrificing suffering of Christ is not a violation of ourselves, but an invitation into a freewill engagement with what it means to die to self out of love for others. This is work we are divinely made to do, and we will be super-humanly resourced to accomplish it. There is not an advocate on earth who is more invested in this than God. We must go forward, doggedly and faithfully co-creating the kin*dom with God so we may see the protection and flourishing of all the souls in our midst. And because we have been given a glimpse of the symptoms of kin*dom (Gal. 5:22), we can expect to receive the kin*dom-come ourselves (Matt. 5:1–12) and greater levels of love, joy, peace, patience, kindness, goodness, faithfulness, gentleness, and self-control.

This is what the LORD Almighty says:

"Consider now! Call for the wailing women to come;

send for the most skillful of them.

Let them come quickly

and wail over us

till our eyes overflow with tears

and water streams from our eyelids.

The sound of wailing is heard from Zion:

'How ruined we are!

How great is our shame!

We must leave our land

because our houses are in ruins.'"

Now, you women, hear the word of the LORD;

open your ears to the words of [God's] mouth.

Teach your daughters how to wail;

teach one another a lament.

Death has climbed in through our windows

and has entered our fortresses;

it has removed the children from the streets

and the young men from the public squares.

"Let not the wise boast of their wisdom

or the strong boast of their strength

or the rich boast of their riches,

but let the one who boasts boast about this:

that they have the understanding to know me,

that I am the LORD, who exercises kindness,

justice and righteousness on earth,

for in these I delight,"

declares the LORD.

JEREMIAH 9:17–24

RESOURCES

Practical Resources

- There is a terrific nine-session change-agent cohort called "GameChanger" that walks leadership teams through five key conversations and five shifts vital for reimagining and redefining religious leadership in the twenty-first century. For info: contact@boundlessenterprise.org.
- HagarsVoice.com offers a three-hour, online introductory course titled, "Becoming Trauma-Informed," as well as a how-to resource for setting up a safe-disclosure portal. For info: contact@hagarsvoice.com.

Third-Party Supports

- If you are looking to do a Human Resource Audit, consider engaging the services of a lawyer in human rights or someone in employment law. This article, "Conducting Human Resource Audits," is helpful in understanding the various types of audits available: https://www.shrm.org/resourcesandtools/tools-and-samples/toolkits/pages/humanresourceaudits.aspx.
- For help with policy writing, see NetGrace.org.
- AbuseResponseAndPrevention.ca has an incredible document called "Understanding Sexual Abuse by a Church Leader or Caregiver" that's a helpful overview tool to educate your teams on good policies.
- Contracting a neutral third party for processing disclosures can be done through organizations like HagarsVoice.com and IntoAccount.org.
- Examples of quality investigators are https://www.netgrace.org/; https://guidepostsolutions.com/; and https://veritassolutions.net/church-and-faith-based-organizations/.

Further Reading

- Pete Singer, Executive Director of G.R.A.C.E. (netgrace.org) has written a straight-forward and practical piece, "Toward a More Trauma-Informed Church: Equipping Faith Communities to Prevent and Respond to Abuse." It is a concise work filled with research statistics, helpful insights, and a wealth of practical explanations and examples of what being trauma-informed looks like in religious spaces. See https://currentsjournal.org/index.php/currents/article/view/444/483.

- *#MeToo Reckoning* is an enlightening book if you aren't confident about the lessons that should be learned from #metoo and #churchtoo. See Ruth Everhart, *The #MeToo Reckoning: Facing the Church's Complicity in Sexual Abuse and Misconduct* (IVP, 2020).

- Diane Langberg's book *Redeeming Power: Understanding Authority and Abuse in the Church* (Brazos Press, 2020), is a well-rounded and comprehensive look at the issues around and prevention of abuse.

- ClergySexualMisconduct.com is a worthy resource for gaining a clearer understanding of clergy sexual abuse.

- For a brief summary of how to respond to adult sex offenders, see Roger Przybylski, "Chapter 7: Effectiveness of Treatment for Adult Sex Offenders," *SMART*, https://smart.ojp.gov/somapi/chapter-7-effectiveness-treatment-adult-sex-offenders.

17

THE BIBLE AND ABUSE OF GIRLS AND WOMEN

Rev. Dr. Julie Faith Parker

is a Visiting Scholar at Union Theological Seminary and the Biblical Scholar in Residence at Marble Collegiate Church, both in New York City. She holds a PhD in Old Testament/Hebrew Bible from Yale University. An ordained minister in the United Methodist Church, she served as a congregational pastor then campus minister prior to doctoral studies. She has written or edited many scholarly articles and eight books, including, most recently, *Eve Isn't Evil: Feminist Readings of the Bible to Upend Our Assumptions* (Baker Academic, 2023).

Thank you for reading this chapter.

Thank you for caring about the abuse of girls and women.

Thank you for being brave enough to engage some of the most brutal, painful issues crippling people's lives.

My hope is to offer some ways that the Bible might be of help to you in addressing the life-shattering problem of abuse that silently rages on in our communities. Our active ignoring of this pernicious and pervasive predicament perpetuates the problem. We can—and as people of faith, we must—do better.

This chapter first reminds us why the work of countering abuse is critical to save lives. I then offer summaries of and responses to a few biblical texts that portray abuse of girls and women. How might these passages help us in this quest for the health and safety of the people in our communities? I have specifically chosen texts of violence against women and girls because most of the victims of abuse are female. Finally, I will add further practical suggestions and hermeneutical principles as to how these texts can help us serve the Christ who reminds us to treat other people as we would want to be treated ourselves (Matt. 7:12). If you were suffering from abuse, wouldn't you want people in your church to show they care by speaking up?

WHY WE NEED TO TALK ABOUT ABUSE IN CHURCH

The pervasiveness of domestic abuse is staggering. The National Center for Domestic Partner Violence reports that one-third of women and one-quarter of men have experienced abuse. One in seven women has felt threatened to the point of fearing for her life.[1] Physical abuse of women is not a niche issue, but a pervasive killer lurking in our pews as we politely sit in church each Sunday pretending this demon is not present. When is the last time you heard a preacher talk about the abuse of women? Have you ever preached such a sermon yourself?

And yet, abuse of women and girls surfaces repeatedly in biblical texts because the Bible is unafraid to grapple with the worst of human behavior. Reading its pages can lead us to witness appalling atrocities, including gang rape (Judg. 19:1–25); abduction of women (Judg. 21:1–23); incest (2 Sam. 13); stripping, shaming, and ostracizing of a woman (Hosea 2); and human trafficking of girls (Esther 2:1–14)—to cite a few of many examples.[2] Usually, our church readings omit these passages and others like them. Such texts do not feel appropriate for worship or even our spiritual lives. But they are part of sacred Scripture and so they deserve our attention as a vehicle to bring us in closer communion with God. How? Step one is to muster the courage to discuss them.

When we avoid biblical texts of sexual violence and other forms of abuse, we passively and irresponsibly contribute to the evil of the world. You may have heard people talk of "benign neglect"—leaving something alone and assuming that all is fine. But neglect is not benign. To be silent is to condone, which is the pervasive attitude in our churches regarding abuse. If we do look at these texts of terror, we may write them off as from another time and culture when norms were different and life was inherently harsh. But make no mistake: Life is brutal today, too, for the twenty thousand Americans who call the domestic violence hotline daily.

Also, people in our congregations read the Bible, as we encourage them to do. What if someone encounters one of these stories of women being abused in their own personal reading of Scripture and has no idea what to do with it? Worse, what if they interpret such stories as God's approval of any abuse that they may have endured themselves? Well-intentioned readers can be further damaged by controlling voices who essentially communicate that yes, such abuse is too bad—but if it's in the Bible, then it's not our place to question it. Such interpretations foster cruelty by suggesting that women should put up with violent behavior. Less directly, they encourage the general subjugation of women that enables abuse to thrive.

Subordination of women is a subtle, and therefore insidious, form of dehumanization. If you are a woman and I am a man, many people hold the belief (subconsciously or overtly) that you can/should/must serve me because such ways are "natural" or even "biblical." This patriarchal way of thinking has a powerful legacy stemming not from the Bible but from what we are told the Bible means. Such toxic thinking undermines the theological truth of women as fully human and equally created in God's image (Gen. 1:27), and therefore deserving of the same rights and privileges as men.

Women get all kinds of daily messages that they are inferior to men. In addition to appalling abuse statistics, less direct forces are at play. Language for men is often used to include everyone, erasing the presence of women. Wages for men are higher than the wages for women, even though women make up more than half of the national labor force.[3] In addition, women are expected to work in the household, supplying invisible labor (shopping, cooking, cleaning, child care, elder care, etc.) that is rarely acknowledged and almost never earns wages. The implications of subordinate views of women can extend beyond the expectation that women should freely and willingly supply free labor; these common societal expectations frequently fuel the notion that women's bodies are to serve men, who can treat them as they will, even when violence surfaces.

I know the work of countering abuse of women through the church is hard, awkward, and uncomfortable. I was ordained in the United Methodist Church when I was twenty-six years old and went on to serve a congregation as an associate pastor. I still remember the day that the church secretary came into work with a black eye. The most common way to get a black eye is a knock to the face. She was not a clumsy person. Her husband seemed surly, and I had my suspicions. Plus, I remember that she did not try to hide the black eye with makeup. Perhaps she was looking to me as a pastor, silently calling for help when she walked into the office that day. And what did I say or do? Absolutely nothing. Not even, "Are you okay?" or "What happened to your eye?" because I wasn't sure how I'd handle the answer if she had been abused—what would be the next steps? Sure, I can make excuses (I was only the associate pastor, I was young, etc.), but the bottom line is that I failed her. I can still picture her furtive, swollen eyes glancing at me with a questioning look. The image haunts me decades later.

Please do better than I did.

Look at the texts discussed below, learn how they reflect the realities of abuse, and be brave enough to talk about them to bring physical and sexual violence out into the light that points the way to safety.

BIBLICAL TEXTS RELATED TO ABUSE AND WHAT WE CAN DO WITH THEM

I have selected the following biblical texts because they highlight different forms of violence against women and girls and therefore might be helpful in calling attention to the range of forms that abuse takes. All of the passages are from the Hebrew Bible or Old Testament. This is *not* because the God of the Old Testament is a violent God and the God of the New Testament is a God of love, which is a common Christian assumption that veers dangerously anti-Jewish. Rather, I work with these texts because the Hebrew Bible is my area of expertise. Also, the Old Testament is a much larger corpus than the New Testament (the Old Testament has nearly a thousand chapters and the New Testament has about a quarter of that). The texts of the Old Testament were accordingly written over a much longer time period—about a thousand years (approximately from 1200 BCE to 167 BCE), compared with the New Testament's seventy years of composition (approximately from 50 CE to 120 CE). We might not then be surprised that the first part of the Christian Bible deals with a wide range of life situations, including incidents of abuse.

Judges 19–21

The story of the Levite's concubine in Judges 19–21 relays a shocking story of violent betrayal. The incident begins with a concubine, who was a secondary wife, leaving her husband, who is a Levite from the priestly tribe of Israelites. We don't know what drove her away from her home in the hill country of Ephraim, but it must have been bad because this is the only place in all of Scripture where a woman leaves a man. She returns to her father's house in Bethlehem (which means "house of bread" in Hebrew). After four months, the Levite sets out with a servant and some donkeys to bring her back. Once they arrive at his father-in-law's house, the Levite and the concubine's father eat and drink together for a few days; she is not included (no bread for her!). Then the entourage of the Levite, the concubine, and the servant start to head back home and eventually are taken in by a man in the town of Gibeah. That night, the men of Gibeah beat on the door seeking to rape (Hebrew: *yada* meaning "to know" or "to know sexually") the Levite (Judg. 19:22).[4] The host wants to save the man but has no regard for women. He makes the mob an offer: "Here are my virgin daughter and his concubine; let me bring them out now. Ravish them and do whatever you want to them; but against this man do not do such a vile thing" (Judg. 19:24).[†] When the men remain intent on raping the Levite, he (either the host or the Levite, the text is not clear) shoves the concubine out the door. Then "they wantonly raped her, and abused her all through the night until the morning" (Judg. 19:25). By the light of day, the rapists let her go.

But her horror story is not over. She lies at the threshold of the house where the Levite is, her hand on the door frame, perhaps using the last of her strength to seek safety. The next morning, the Levite leaves the house to go on his way, sees her there, and tells her to get up. No kindness, no help, no comfort—just a command. She says nothing. Is she dead? The Hebrew text does not specify.[5] The Levite puts her on a donkey, takes her home, and then cuts her body into twelve pieces to send to the tribes of Israel, seeking vengeance and claiming outrage (Judg. 19:28–30).

Even more violence follows. A war ensues that nearly wipes out the tribe of Benjamin (Judg. 20), so the people come up with a solution: abduct the girls who come to dance at the festival at Shiloh and take them to be wives for the remaining Benjaminites (Judg. 21:15–23). Girls who trustingly come to participate in a celebration are kidnapped, taken away from their families and home territory, and used sexually to perpetuate the tribe of those who raped the concubine. Violence against a woman begets more of the same.

What are we to do with such a shockingly awful Bible story?

---

† All verses in this chapter are from the New Revised Standard Version (NRSV), unless otherwise specified.

First, we can read this text in a congregational setting and talk about it, or even preach on it. I once preached a Good Friday sermon on the story of the Levite's concubine. Like Jesus, she is betrayed by those closest to her. Like Jesus, her body is broken and given to many.[6]

Speaking about the abuse of the Levite's concubine helps us to publicly recognize that rape is common. Gang rapes destroy lives. Giving voice to this lived reality in a church setting opens the door for people who may have been abused to come forward and seek help. Be ready to be confidential and compassionate. Be aware of organizations and resources in your community that have safe places and that help people who are abused. Know that you are serving the justice-seeking Christ who also knew betrayal and bodily abuse.

2 Samuel 13

Second Samuel 13 portrays another instance of abuse that also involves someone acquainted with the victim, as is the case in almost half of all rapes.[7] The rape of Tamar, daughter of King David and therefore a princess of Israel, reflects a common pattern in that the rapist is someone whom the young woman had reason to trust. In this story, he is her half-brother.

Both Tamar and Amnon are children of King David, by different mothers. Amnon lusts after Tamar and tells this to his friend, Jonadab, who coaches Amnon as to how to get Tamar. He suggests Amnon should pretend to be sick, then ask his father to send Tamar to him with some cakes. When she comes to deliver the cakes, he can seize her (2 Sam. 13:1–5). So, Amnon pretends to be sick before his father who then tells Tamar to go to Amnon. She does and makes him cakes; when Tamar gives the cakes to Amnon, he grabs her. But Tamar is a princess, and she speaks up. She begs her brother not to rape her and offers to marry him so both can retain their honor (vv. 6–13). "But he would not listen to her; and being stronger than she, he forced her and lay with her" (v. 14).

Then her story gets worse.

After raping her, Amnon, who had lusted after Tamar, now loathes her and wants her out of his sight. Again, she pleads with him not to treat her so treacherously, but he will have none of it. Amnon instructs his servant to put her out of the room, with the door bolted behind her, which he does. She weeps. "But Tamar put ashes on her head, and tore the long robe that she was wearing; she put her hand on her head, and went away, crying aloud as she went" (2 Sam. 13:19).

Yet, as a princess, Tamar is well-connected. Does no one help? Her full brother, Absalom, tells her not to worry about it. "Has Amnon your brother been with you? Be quiet for now, my sister; he is your brother; do not take this to heart" (2 Sam. 13:20a), as if the element of incest mitigates the violation! Her father, King David—the great warrior, father, poet, musician, and leader— does nothing to help Tamar. "When King David heard of all these things, he became very angry, but he would not punish his son Amnon, because he loved him, for he was his firstborn" (v. 21).[8] Does David have no love or concern for his daughter?

This story of violence also starts a trail of misery. Absalom arranges Amnon's murder and ends up as a fugitive himself (2 Sam. 13:23–30). Tamar— the beautiful, intelligent, articulate princess who had a promising life ahead of her—morphs into a portrait of sorrow after her rape: "So Tamar remained, a desolate woman, in her brother Absalom's house" (v. 20b). The Hebrew word that describes her condition, *shomemah*, means "desolate" and also "appalled," or "in a daze." The text does offer a small uplifting coda to her story, as Absalom names his daughter after his sister (2 Sam. 14:27). Still, incestuous rape has left Tamar a shell of her former self.

The story of Tamar sheds light on behavior around sexual violence. Notice the actions of Jonadab, Amnon's friend. Having someone to encourage or approve of cruel behavior plays a powerful role in promoting abuse. Groups or pairs of violators feel supported in abusing women when a single individual from that group or pair would not dare to initiate or execute the same abhorrent acts. We also see the need for care and support after violence has transpired. The mighty King David chooses to be powerless when it is time to stand up for his daughter. Absalom avenges Tamar's rape but shows no direct concern for her.

This text can also help us to recognize abuse. Is there someone in your congregation who seems like their demeanor has suddenly changed for the worse? Are they withdrawn and suffering from trauma? Ask to find out. Do better than famous King David by simply showing compassion. Offer support to someone who has been abused. Be ready to listen and believe someone's story, even if you do not want it to be true.

Hosea 2

Hosea 2 is a shocking poetic metaphor that breaks on the bodies of women. The book of Hosea comes from the eighth century BCE when the people of Israel were facing an ominous threat from the powerful empire of Assyria. To frighten the people into changing their ways, Hosea tells the story of his wife, Gomer. Since she has worshiped another god (Baal) who is not the God of the Hebrews, she will pay with shame, humiliation, and degradation. Even though Gomer is the mother of Hosea's three children, the prophet tells their children to issue a threat to their own mother, graphically describing her sexually abusive punishment.

> Plead with your mother, plead—
>> for she is not my wife,
>> and I am not her husband—
> that she put away her whoring from her face,
>> and her adultery from between her breasts,
> or I will strip her naked
>> and expose her as in the day she was born,
> and make her like a wilderness,
>> and turn her into a parched land,
>> and kill her with thirst.
> Upon her children also I will have no pity,
>> because they are children of whoredom.
>
> HOSEA 2:2–4

Then after describing more abuse that he will heap upon her (Hosea 2:5–13), Hosea's tone radically changes. Hosea 2:14–15 offers words of tenderness:

> Therefore, I will now allure her,
>> and bring her into the wilderness,
>> and speak tenderly to her.
> From there I will give her her vineyards,
>> and make the Valley of Achor a door of hope.
> There she shall respond as in the days of her youth,
>> as at the time when she came out of the land of Egypt.

While such a shift might seem like a hopeful reversal, it also fits the pattern of intimate partner violence. Abusers will harm their partner and then act like nothing happened, gaslighting the victim to doubt their own painful experience. Abuse establishes power over another person and uses that power to control, manipulate, and harm, as we see in this text. The cycle of tension leading to an incident followed by reconciliation and a period of calm is common in domestic abuse and reflected in the first two chapters of Hosea. An abuser's words of reconciliation do not erase the abuse. Rather, they set it up for the cycle to begin again. Sometimes preachers use this text from Hosea, raising him up as an example of faithfulness who justifiably punishes his wayward wife, Gomer. Hosea speaks with the voice of God and Gomer represents sinful Israel, therefore his treatment of her, some maintain, is justified. Such thinking is deeply dangerous for it portrays God as an abuser. Know also that the audience of this prophecy was Israelite men, whom Hosea shames. To use the Bible to shame anyone is its own form of abuse.

So much of the Bible reveals how ancient people tried to understand their relationship with God, here seeking fidelity to Yahweh over the Canaanite god, Baal. The text does not mandate what we should do today, shaming ourselves or others with holier-than-thou authority. Sometimes our testimony to a text needs to come from resistance. Jesus, quoting the Torah, offers the interpretative framework needed for our understanding of Scripture: "Love your neighbor as yourself" (Lev. 19:18; Matt. 22:39).

Esther 2

Esther is an orphan whose story we celebrate: She is a Jewish teenage girl who becomes queen and saves her people when they are about to perish. Mordecai, the uncle who had adopted her, challenges Esther to intercede with the king when the Jews are about to be killed. Perhaps she has been brought to greatness, Mordecai tells her, "for such a time as this" (Esther 4:14). Indeed, her intervention is what saves her people. At the end of the book, she writes letters confirming the peace and security of the Jews.

But in our telling of Esther's tale, we often gloss over how she got to the palace. Esther 2:3 tells of all the "beautiful young virgins" from around the kingdom who are to be gathered as possible brides for the king. They are then brought to the palace where they remain in his harem. While the English tells us the captured girls were given "cosmetic treatments" (v. 12), the Hebrew is harsher, suggesting the girls were scrubbed (coming from the word *maraq*, meaning "to scour" or "to polish"). The king has a night sleeping with each one of them (vv. 13–14). The girls are young, before the age of marriage, which was in the early or mid-teenage years. No one consulted them when they were taken from their homes to be kept as sexual slaves.[9]

This part of Esther's story conveys a scene of human trafficking: recruiting, transporting, and harboring someone for the purpose of exploitation. The girls are gathered, brought to the palace, and kept in the harem to be sexually used (raped?) by the king, as he decides which virgin he likes best. We need to pause before we get to the happy ending of Esther, as there is a lot that should trouble us for this girl and the others like her, used for sex.[10] While Esther rises to be queen, the other "candidates" remain in such a *bind* as this: girls who have been trafficked and know sexual abuse. What future exists for them?

Esther's story is often lifted as a model for young women as a fairy tale with a happily-ever-after ending. A girl becomes a queen then risks her own safety for the good of her people and saves them. Yet we shouldn't ignore all the difficulties, and even abuse, that occurs prior to the satisfying conclusion. And look closely at chapter 9 of Esther: After the Jews slaughter those who hate them (v. 5), Queen Esther orders that they be allowed to do so again, and that the ten sons of Haman be hanged on the gallows (v.13). Without intervention, cycles of abuse continue. Are Esther's violent orders tied to the sexual trauma she experienced herself? Violence, in any form, must never be valorized. When it is extolled or excused, abuse thrives.

HOW CAN THESE TEXTS HELP US FIGHT ABUSE?

We need to talk about abuse and the Bible can help us. Let your church be known as a place where people can be their honest, full selves—including the parts that have been battered. Help to erase the stigma of abuse and combat the shame by letting these passages and others like them lead your congregation to care about those who suffer from violence.

Some practical suggestions for using these texts have already been alluded to above: Preach and teach texts related to abuse. Know and recognize the signs of abuse. Have resources ready when survivors come forward. Here are a few more: Place notices in bathroom stalls with phone numbers for hotlines that people can call for resources to help. Form support groups. Listen to and believe the people who muster the courage to break their silence. Let the Bible help erase the stigma of abuse by showing how God's word reflects these painful realities.

And as you interpret biblical texts, these three hermeneutical guidelines are critical:[11]

1. The Bible is usually descriptive, not prescriptive. It describes a time and place very different from our own that still speaks to shared realities.

The people in its pages yearn to make sense of their relationship with God, which does not mean that we are to do everything they did. Our job is to learn from them thoughtfully, not imitate them recklessly. To navigate away from the violence in some biblical texts is part of experiencing the continuous unfolding of God's grace.

2. There is no one right way to interpret the Bible. Different passages will yield a range of meanings—not only to various people, but also to the same person at different times in their life. How could it be otherwise? But there *is* a wrong way to interpret the Bible, and that is any way that is harmful to someone, including yourself. Never weaponize sacred Scripture.

3. The power is not in the text; the power is in the interpretation. This is joyous news, for it means we can use God's word to promote love in God's world. Even texts that portray violence and abuse can be read, discussed, and offered for shared reflection and action as vehicles for countering and preventing harm.

If you are still with me at the end of this chapter, I want to thank you again. The good that can come from addressing abuse directly and biblically will yield health and safety—but the laborers are few (see Matt. 9:37). If we see Jesus in those who are hungry, thirsty, strangers, naked, or in prison, should we not also see Christ in the faces of abused women and girls?

Perhaps you, too, have been called for such a time as this.

SECTION FIVE

THE FUTURE
CHURCH

If we are to move away from the systems that have steeped the church in inequality for so long, we must consider what new structures to strive for. In this section, five women share their experiences and expertise that point to a brighter, more equitable church.

Dr. Tammy Dunahoo shares her experiences of pursuing God's call on her life, despite the barriers she has had to overcome. She calls us forward to a more unified church that can better represent Christ to the world. As Carolyn Whatley details, the emotional health of our spaces will determine how well people flourish within them. Shifting away from male-dominated, functional approaches to leadership will allow us to pursue healthier ways of being. Mariah Humphries highlights that our spaces need to not only be equitable for women, but also for those who are Black and brown. She details the challenges of creating multicultural environments and reveals the importance of first combatting a lack of diversity and unity in our own lives before pursuing truly equitable integrated spaces. Meghann Jaeger points to the importance of the poor and how our ecosystems of inequality and injustice render us all responsible for elevating the voices of the oppressed and allowing them to lead the way in combatting poverty and marginalization in our local communities and the wider world. And finally, Lisa Rodriguez-Watson calls us to the holy work of resistance, expounding the ways we can work against the systems that quash the contribution so many women want to make.

The authors of this section point us toward a more hopeful future for the church—one that doesn't solely focus on equality for equality's sake but pursues a kingdom mandate that we are all called to and that can only be realized when everyone is involved.

18

WHAT I NEED YOU TO KNOW

Dr. Tammy Dunahoo

is an ordained minister with more than forty years of ministry, church, and denominational leadership experience. She is the executive dean of Portland Seminary of George Fox University, where she also earned her doctorate.

Tammy has spent twenty years leading in various capacities at the International Church of the Foursquare Gospel based in Los Angeles, overseeing numerous teams and ministries, church planting, and serving the network across all fifty states. She is passionate about investing in the spiritual formation of leaders and helping them to navigate an ever-changing culture in the church and the world.

On a beautiful Sunday morning in 1998, some one hundred eager seekers and followers of Jesus gathered as part of our new church plant. Because new faces were joining each week, no one thought it unusual when an unknown gentleman walked to the third row and sat on the end seat on the center aisle—though he was hard to miss given his six foot, five inch, three-hundred-pound presence! As the speaker that morning, I walked to the podium, opened my Bible, and asked everyone to join me in Ephesians chapter 3. Suddenly, our new NFL-linebacker-sized friend showed his obvious disdain for my presence as the preacher and chose to protest by turning around in his chair and placing his back toward me. He crossed his legs and put his head down for the remainder of the message. In a room that size, it was obvious to everyone what was happening. As my mind raced, wondering how to handle the situation, my insecurities and inner critical voices had a heyday. But in that moment, I sensed the gentle question of the Holy Spirit that settled my heart, "Who called you?"

And so, I preached. My objector waited until my closing prayer to walk out.

That day marked decision day and the beginning of many such encounters for me as a woman in church leadership, often being the first woman in an assignment. The big man of strong conviction became a catalyzing figure for my future: I grew in biblical understanding and leadership skills and made the decision to follow God above all, and lead others with wisdom, grit, and grace. My story is similar to thousands of women with a desire to do God's will but who face systemic barriers and debilitating biases. I have heard many of these pose the same frustrated question I have asked, "Why is this painful struggle necessary simply because of who God made me to be?" The answer is clear: patriarchy.

The *Oxford English Dictionary* defines "patriarchy" as a system of or government in which the father or eldest male is head of the family; a system of society or government in which men hold the power and women are largely excluded from it; a society or community organized on patriarchal lines.[1] This is the arc of the narrative of humanity in Scripture since the fall. Yet, throughout the Bible, we find many examples of God entering the story to show a different way—one that reveals God's kingdom relationships and overturns patriarchy. Carolyn Custis James, in her breakthrough book, *Malestrom*, recounts many such stories from Genesis to Revelation while describing what patriarchy has cost men as well as women. In the forward, Frank A. James III, president and professor of historical theology at Missio Seminary, states,

> The overwhelming emotion in reading this book was a mixture of sadness and apprehension. My sadness is that the life and teachings of Jesus seem to have been missed for so long. Part of the power of the malestrom is that it obscures our reading of the biblical text and so our pulpits promulgate unhealthy notions of manhood. My apprehension is derived from the anxiety that escape from this cultural captivity of manhood will not come easily. Jesus' own disciples demonstrate the difficulty. Blinded by the malestrom, they failed to grasp that Rabbi Jesus was inaugurating a new kingdom—not of this world.[2]

I share Frank's sadness and apprehension as we often read the teachings of Jesus through our cultural lenses. When questioned by an expert of the law in Luke 10, Jesus asks a poignant question, "What is in the Law and *how do you read it*?" (vv. 25–27, my paraphrase). He knew the power of interpreting Scripture through humankind's broken lens rather than what he was teaching and enacting.

The high cost of patriarchy is not only to women and men, but to the witness of the church, as the good news is tainted by this fractured system. We sometimes seem more comfortable steeped in this culture that surrounds us, rather than showing the more excellent way as we are transformed within by the Spirit. We are citizens of a different kingdom—one of love, grace, mercy, justice, and shalom. As citizens of this kingdom, we should live right-side-up as the faithful presence of God in the middle of this upside-down world. Instead, we tend to promote the message of the world—often subconsciously. This causes us to miss obvious bias, obvious systemic barriers, and even obvious misinterpretation of Scripture. For example, women are often told we can teach women and children and can be missionaries in other nations; we can even teach mixed groups in homes—but we cannot teach behind the pulpit on Sunday morning, and we certainly cannot serve as elders. The glass ceiling is real—even in the church.

The other phenomenon, the glass cliff, is where women are only given the opportunity to lead in crisis situations where the church or organization is already on a downward trajectory. According to a survey by the *Harvard Business Review*, women leaders are seen as a good option in a crisis situation.[3] But, if the situation ends in failure, the blame is placed on the leadership of the woman, rather than the unraveling situation she was handed. The rationale is women do not have the experience to be assigned to something more "successful." We also discover in the same survey that people tend to prefer men's traits over women's in companies that are solid. The same is most often true in the church.

Women struggle to gain the requisite experience for more significant assignments when these kinds of systemic barriers are in place. Alongside this, how many leadership development opportunities—including mentoring, experiential learning, and informal peer mentoring gatherings—are male-dominated, leaving less opportunity for women to grow?

Patriarchy over the centuries has always fostered a deeply biased view about women's very nature, capabilities, and characteristics that has become entrenched in our culture.[4] Equally powerful are the biased views of what defines a leader that are inherently masculine characteristics. These biases are so normalized, no one even notices. Except the women.

The few women who do break through the barriers become anomalies and are often compared to the biblical character Deborah of Judges 4–5. Anomalies become a token for churches and organizations to argue that they do believe in and promote women in ministry. This mindset keeps the broader collective of women from being developed and assigned to senior leadership.

With all the sadness and apprehension, I am still hopeful. This hope does not spring from overwhelming evidence around me, but from early signs of transformation we are seeing. A few churches and networks are being intentional to make theological statements and develop strategies to change their posture regarding women in leadership. Men, such as Rick Warren, who have changed their positions, have made public statements describing their change.[5] More books, addressing difficult scriptural passages, have recently been written by respected scholars.[6] Men have been doing research on what predicates a change of mind and heart on the subject. My hope also comes from the confidence that the work of the cross that reversed the curse will be fully realized here in this "already-not-yet" world and that the Holy Spirit will fill and form God's people into the new-creation community God ordained when we surrender to the Spirit's work. This kingdom community, Jesus' church, will be a place where he is leader and Lord, and his people minister as members of his body according to our gifts and graces. It will be a community of women and men, and boys and girls, of every ethnicity, generation, and social strata who hold to Jesus as our elder brother and link arm-in-arm as sisters and brothers in this beautiful household of faith. The apostle Paul, in training young Timothy to pastor, gave these clear instructions for church relationships: "Do not rebuke an older man harshly, but exhort him as if he were your father. Treat younger men as brothers, older women as mothers, and younger women as sisters, with absolute purity" (1 Tim. 5:1–2).

My hope and prayer is that a new creation community is standing up to say, "We believe that God is making all things new. We are reimagining how women and men can serve side by side as sisters and brothers, respecting and honoring one another with 'absolute purity' to fulfill God's original design. We believe Jesus' life, death, and resurrection make this a reality for us to live into for the sake of the world!"

19

PAIN IS AN INVITATION

Carolyn Whatley

is a marriage and family therapist working in an addiction recovery center and is the Team Lead for Activism of Hagar's Voice, an organization that strategically supports people impacted by clergy sexual abuse. As part of her work, Carolyn seeks to integrate spiritual transformation, trauma recovery, and healing of grief and loss with those impacted by and recovering from addiction, abuse, and oppression in all its forms. She also engages in community justice initiatives through a decolonizing, anti-racist lens in hopes of cultivating spaces that are trauma-informed and safe for everyone. Her clinical practice, research, and interests are deeply seated in the awareness that each person embodies the image of the Holy Mystery and is worthy of honor and dignity.

One of my most transformative experiences as a church leader took place behind a pastor's closed door.

Headed into its second decade, our church was recovering from the recent departure of its founding pastor: a charismatic, autocratic, and complicated man. Several people from the inner circle of leadership were in the process of deconstructing and healing from years of emotional and spiritual highs and lows. This felt very far from the excitement of those early days when a handful of like-minded friends met in living rooms and dreamt of doing church differently.

Standing in the doorway of our new pastor's office, I knew there was a strong likelihood that yet another season of tarrying with an emotionally unhealthy, privileged, unaware male leader lay ahead. A familiar sense of dread arose in me: how to be a woman entering her third decade as an oft-labeled "intense," "strong," "intimidating" leader who regularly had to muzzle herself and diminish her presence to help insecure male counterparts maintain their sense of power and dominance, and stay out of the firing line when it erupted. I recognized the growing tension in my nervous system as I prepared to navigate one of the many gender-charged sites in church spaces: *door open or door closed?*[1]

I entered the room, and my new pastor remained at his desk, relaxed and welcoming. After greetings, I paused, projected an aura of calm, and asked if he wanted the door open or closed.

In the time it took for him to respond, a reservoir of charged, oppressive somatic memories sent lightning bolts through my nervous system. Decades of experience and training kept these jolts at bay and helped me remain externally at ease while my internal system braced. I waited as this man, this leader, this person with spiritual power and authority over me, determined the trajectory of the next epoch of my leadership journey.

He looked up casually and said, "Whichever you prefer."

My nervous system released and my tear ducts filled—threatening to spill down my cheeks. I turned and made the choice to close the door.

Over the next five years working alongside this pastor, I experienced more spiritual growth and leadership development than in any previous ministry season. This transformation occurred through relational, psychological, and emotional healing and a significant increase in my capacity to trust male leaders and experience safe spaces in which I could be more at ease in evangelical leadership roles amongst male colleagues. I learned to stop disclaiming my thoughts and ideas before expressing them in mixed company and started to believe my suspicion that I had unique attributes, skills, and gifts to offer the church. It was apparent that this pastor was doing leadership differently as he consistently opened space for others to have choice, welcomed differing voices, demonstrated and maintained trust and transparency, cultivated peer support and mutuality, empowered those often pushed to the margins, and began the long, slow process of cultivating safety through decolonizing and anti-racism work—first in himself, then in the wider church community. As he embodied and expressed emotional and spiritual vulnerability and maturity amongst church leadership, and invited church leaders to heal from various wounds related to historic abuses of power, he was disappointingly more often met with resistance than embraced by other leaders, unwilling to engage with the legacy of abuse of power.

A number of years later, after this pastor was called to a different ministry, I tried to remain in the church and serve in various capacities, but it soon became obvious that unhealthy, immature, unsafe patterns within leadership were reemerging. I engaged in a long discernment process with trusted spiritual friends and mentors and reached the decision to leave the church, becoming one of many exiled women leaders who longed to stay, yet could not do so without fearing for the loss of their souls.

THE COST OF FUNCTIONALISM

The experience of exile is all too familiar to many women and people who are deeply committed to pursuing the kingdom of God and who experience marginalization in church spaces. The leadership team I was a part of consisted of those who had spent the early 2000s riding the wave of "missional" and "emerging" church planting and all the crests and crashes along the way. Back then, every time a new church-planting book, video series, or podcast was released, our restless, evangelical energy would erupt into a flurry of meetings and vision-casting sessions intended to improve on previous strategies and practices. It was an exciting time to be a church planter and many leaders with integrity and wisdom—Frost, Hirsch, Kriminski, Rios, Searcy, Strickland, to name a few—were sharing profound and prophetic insights gained through devotion to Jesus' mission and their extensive church and ministry experience.

Sadly, in recent years, the tone and content of books, blogs, documentaries, and podcasts released by church-planting leaders in exile seem more mournful than hopeful. Painful and tragic stories from wounded church leaders abound, particularly from women and the marginalized. Each time I engage in sacred witnessing of these stories, I imagine friends and former colleagues as walking wounded—burdened by injustice and oppression perpetrated by male Christian pastors and leaders who did not steward their power and positions well. Too often, zeal and fervor for church planting and other ministry initiatives far outpaced the cultivation of emotional and spiritual health in pastors and lay ministers, and those they were entrusted to shepherd became collateral damage. I don't believe this is the "battle" the apostle Paul was calling us to (Eph. 6:12).

Instead, the pursuit of success has become a major factor that has led to emotional and spiritual repression in ministry leadership. Adrian van Kaam, a Dutch priest and existentialist psychologist, wrote extensively about "formation theology." His work focused on the importance of spiritual formation for the flourishing of faith in individuals and spiritual communities. One of the keys to transformation in van Kaam's theory is differentiating *functionalism* from *inspired functioning*. Susan Muto, esteemed author and teacher and dean of the Epiphany Academy of Spiritual Formation, offers this description:

> Functionalism should not be confused with enlightened functioning [any] more than activism should be confused with right action. Functionalism, like all "isms," is the absolutizing of a practical truth, in this case that the main value of life is measurable success, mass production and achievement, even at the expense of personal relationships. The effectiveness, not the goodness, truth and beauty of things, persons, deeds and encounters, is what counts. The key questions in a functionalistic society are: Is my life productive? profitable? practically relevant? These criteria become for many the guidelines for living.[2]

Male leadership seems particularly prone to functionalism. I am convinced that the $1.2 trillion industrial engine that is the church (worth more than Google and Apple combined)[3] is fueled by functionalism, and it is sucking the life out of pastors and those they lead with and serve. When we become driven by measurable "success" at the expense of spiritual and emotional health, we have fallen into functionalism and miss the transformative power of the gospel that we are called to.

A DIFFERENT WAY

One of the greatest blessings I received under my new pastor was the invitation to explore the spiritual formation practices he had integrated into his personal and ministry life. This eventually led me to attend a school of spiritual formation which helped me cultivate ongoing transformation, a process I hope to continue for the rest of my life. Through my time at the Epiphany Association in Pittsburgh, I had space to start integrating my theological, biopsychosocial, and justice education with van Kaam's sweeping formation science. This process of integration was like nothing I had ever encountered—despite having completed an undergraduate degree, two master's degrees, several certifications, and a seminary degree. Even with all this educational success, it turns out I was a virtual ignoramus in the ways of spiritual transformation and maintaining a consistent disposition of awe toward God, the Holy Mystery.

Through the support and shepherding of a mature pastor who intentionally and consistently attended to his mental, emotional, and spiritual health, I experienced significant healing in myself, my relationships within church leadership, and my capacity to engage with Christian ministry. My experience leads me to question why so many evangelical spaces continue to perpetuate functionalism at the neglect of spiritual formation, which can bring the kind of transformation Jesus promoted in the Gospels. From contemporary sages like Peter Scazzero, David Benner, and Thomas Merton all the way back to John Calvin, Socrates, and Lao Tzu, the wisest men throughout history asserted that true wisdom, maturity, and knowledge of God flows from knowing self. Yet today we are more often than not faced with emotional suppression in male leaders in evangelical spaces, and arguably see women excluded from these spaces because of perceived "emotionalism." But engaging with our emotions can bring exactly the kind of freedom Jesus promoted.

As a therapist, one of the experiences I treasure most is the sacred witnessing of the birth of emotional self-awareness in clients. This seems even more sacred when supporting trauma recovery with those who have been emotionally suppressed by years of spiritually abusive, coercive, and oppressive patterns of authority. I have occasionally considered removing my sandals on account of the holy energy in the room. As I witness the transformation in someone as they travel the long journey of recovery from painful experiences of discrimination, dehumanization, sexism, and other abuses of power that have mutilated their bodies, hearts, and souls, I have come to realize that it is not only those on the receiving end of coercive spiritual practices who suffer from emotional exile, but also those committing or complicit in these practices. When oppressors create emotional prisons for others, they always get trapped in a prison of their own. What I have recognized is that the process of recovering emotional awareness and expression is vital for both the wounder-oppressor and the wounded-oppressed.

The process begins when they feel safe enough (this can take anywhere from months to years) to share a story of abuse, and dissociation, distraction, or deflection arises. I invite them to notice these responses with me and encourage their interest and curiosity in this emergence. Eventually I ask what is happening in their body, and they often describe growing tension in their chest, or an emerging pain behind their eyes, or nausea flickering in their gut. I gently ask what their body might be saying to them, and they almost always look at me with heartbreaking sadness in their eyes and say, "I don't know." At this point, I invite them to listen to some words and see if any of them resonate with what is happening in their body. I start with "sad," "angry," "fearful," "surprised" … and each time they connect with an emotion, I invite them deeper in with more words: "envy," "irritation," "disgust," "rage." We keep going until we both sense their arrival at the truest and best description of what they are feeling, and this moment is often met with tears and always with overwhelming relief. Their system has remembered how to feel pain after a lifelong battle to keep these threatening feelings far, far, away. Each time we practice this exercise, the words come more easily until they are emerging spontaneously throughout each session. This is the process of reclaiming emotional literacy, and each time I witness it I am reminded that it is *for freedom Christ has set us free* (Gal. 5:1 NRSVUE). This freedom invites us to renew our relationship with pain, fear, shame, and other tender emotions and receive these experiences and related feelings as information for the life journey, rather than things that bind us.

Male pastors would do well to commit to emotional maturity rather than functionality. In doing so, they might encounter some of what I see as my clients find healing from wounds via connection with emotional awareness.

But in order to do this, male leaders must be willing to identify, name, and face the pitfalls of functionalism in themselves and the institution they lead. They might start this work by interrogating their capacity to listen for God's voice and distinguish it from the need, pressure, and compulsion to be useful and efficient. Not that these characteristics do not have value, they are simply not preeminent in Jesus' ways of doing things. Muto highlights the need for pastors and other leaders to be committed to love if they are to go on the journey of transforming from functionalism toward inspired functioning:

> Chaste, non-violating love means that we respect our own and the other's integrity not only physically but also psychologically and spiritually. We venerate the mystery of each person's being, everyone's inalienable right to privacy and community in Spirit.[4]

When we commit to emotional maturity rather than functionality, we no longer see people as vehicles for our own aims and successes. The way we relate to one another and the way we lead others is dramatically changed.

THE WAY OF JESUS

Emotionally mature leadership is how Jesus modeled ministry to the disciples and how he set up life for the early church. We need to go back to the original intentions of Christ in order to recapture a healthy form of leadership.

Jesus Resisted Efficiency

One of the temptations of functionalism is efficiency. And yet when we look at Jesus' ministry, we do not see a particularly efficient type of leadership.

One example is that Jesus walked everywhere. While other people of power would use more efficient ways to get around such as chariots, horses, or being carried by slaves, Jesus chose to walk the dusty roads with his disciples. Perhaps this very inefficient way to travel offered abundant opportunities to connect with himself, others, creation, and his holy Father. Through this lens, inefficiency offers space for engagement of that which at first glance might appear *unuseful*. Conversely, it offers an abundance of riches if one's purpose is to bring light and love to those in the world who need it most. This "inefficiency" is an invitation to see other people and creation not as opportunities in a perpetual pursuit of useful mutuality, but as co-committed sojourners on the road toward God's kingdom manifested on earth as it is in heaven.

Furthermore, we see in the essence of Jesus' call and ministry a "less efficient" way of doing things. He resists using the power available to him to rule by calling upon an army of angels; he fails to position himself as the chief priest or a king using earthly power; and he even invests in a core group of disciples, rather than solely focusing on equipping the large crowds.

Lest the Western tendency toward binaries interject, as it so often does when taking in new, possibly unsettling information, I caution readers to resist an *all or nothing* position toward inspired functioning. It does not imply needlessly doing things the hard, slow way at the altar of scarcity and dejection. Rather, it subordinates efficiency and prosperity to mutual, committed love in the image of Jesus, and positions respectful service, holistic health, equity, and non-violence (mind, heart, body), and other loving characteristics as preeminent.

Jesus Resisted Control

Embracing Jesus' teaching about what it means to be poor in spirit is a gateway to freedom from the shackles of functionalism. Pastor Aaron White, who lives and ministers with those who would be considered economically poor by North American standards, describes being "poor in spirit" as being "free from the enslaving fear of having to be in control of everything inside and outside of us. It is to humbly acknowledge there are some things we cannot control, and to confess that our attempts at wresting control have led to greater harm to ourselves and others."[5] Where functionality encourages us to continue to hold onto control and pursue success, inspired functioning allows us to embrace Jesus' priority of poverty and simplicity. Choosing to embrace this form of poverty opens space for pastors and other leaders to feast on the richness of stillness, simplicity, appreciation of creation, silence, and slowness; it also cultivates a new apprecia-tion for the daily gifts God provides, which are so easily taken for granted. So much becomes dear to us which we barely noticed before.

Jesus' teaching on being poor in spirit seems anathema to running church like a business with pastors positioned as front men and executive pastors as CEOs, because businesses require profitability. Profitability necessitates ever-increasing activity, content, processing, and high production values to constantly draw more bodies to consume the business's product. If this process slows or falters, the engine—in this case the institutional church—will run out of fuel and cease to produce enough cash flow in the form of tithes and offerings. Is it any wonder so many contemporary churches, which were molded on the industrial forge, are running out of gas and emptying out? Is it any wonder pastors who started out with zeal and fervor to expand the kingdom of God are being worn down and worn out by functionalism?

This also relates to Jesus' invitation to play. All too often, pastors and other ministry leaders forget how to play as they become consumed with function-alism and all the duties it entails. Muto wisely observes, "Play and celebration liberate us from worry and preoccupation ... Having fun makes the world of play relaxed, free, and exciting. Stress and tension are kept at a minimum ... Compulsion and pragmatism are the opposite of play and celebration."[6] Jesus' admonishment to "become like little children" instantly comes to mind (Matt. 18:2–5 NRSVUE). I imagine Jesus holding a bouncy ball and skipping rope and wandering the offices and boardrooms of so many of our churches looking for someone to play with.

Pastors might ask themselves: "What does play look like for me?" If you are struggling to find answers, float back to your earliest years and consider what forms of play brought joy. What made you laugh—a great belly laugh, that left you feeling emptied out in the best possible way and came at no cost to your dignity or that of anyone else? Embark on a journey to restore play in your work, your ministry, your mind and imagination, your relationships, and your roles. If the "art of play"[7] were to permeate mission and ministry, I suspect individual pastors and leaders would not take themselves so seriously and would have the capacity to be much gentler on themselves as well as those they lead and shepherd. This is not possible if pastors and leaders are enamored by consumerist, colonizing models of ministry which confuse functionalism with inspired functioning, buying into the partial truth that, "the main value in life is measurable success, mass production and achievement, even at the expense of personal relationships."[8] We are our relationships: relationship with the Creator, with the self we were knit together to be, and with others made in the image of God.

Jesus Faced Pain

In my work with people who are recovering from residential school abuses, clergy sexual abuse, and other forms of abuse and oppression stemming from power disparities—once they have recovered a sense of safety and begun noticing and exercising their emotional range—I invite them to consider giving themselves permission to notice their pain. This may seem like a needless or ridiculous step for those whose hurts and sufferings are easily seen and tended to in our society, or those whose inconveniences are centered and soothed. However, for those forced to walk in the margins of our society and who struggle to access triage, let alone binding and rehabilitation of wounds, pain is not often acknowledged; more often it is safer to pretend it does not exist and keep moving forward. Only when it is noticed, acknowledged, and named does it manifest in a way that allows it to be tended and eased. This can be a very difficult and complex process in a society which exerts inordinate pressure and invests incalculable resources in camouflaging pain.

Once again, as we look at Jesus' life and ministry, we see a different approach to pain and grief. Rather than avoiding the pain of others, Jesus chose to be among those who were suffering. He didn't encourage those among whom he ministered to suppress or numb their pain, but instead he helped them to express their difficulties, he had compassion for them, and he brought healing and transformation. This is sadly the antithesis to what many who are suffering experience in the church today.

Hugh Walker, an esteemed reverend and clinical supervisor, identified patterns of pain, deafness, and blindness, which many of us encounter at an early age.[9] He was inspired to refer to them as the "sinister six" adult reactions to childhood manifestations of pain, which emerge in the face of suffering and make it difficult to honor our pain, let alone name and attend to it.

The first of the sinister six responses to pain is to *punish the pain out of the child*. At first glance, this sounds horrible and none of us can imagine punishing someone, let alone a child, simply because they are expressing their pain. This pain response is easier to identify when we hear the familiar phrase, "Quit your crying or I will give you something to cry about." I can hear the sudden recognition—"Oh, *that* response!"—and I am always fascinated by the shift in energy in a room full of adults when the light bulbs of awareness suddenly switch on. We may assume we are immune from complicity with this damaging pain-denial pattern until we hear it phrased, "Quit whining or I will take away your phone." Suddenly we not only recognize this tactic but recall making similar threats. We didn't realize it stemmed from our own pain intolerance and we are both wounded and wounder all at once.

Patterns of punishing the pain out of the person extend beyond caregiver and child relationships and into church spaces. Consider what happens in Sunday School or at youth group when the children's ministry worker or youth pastor gets overwhelmed. There is often a turning to some form of withdrawal of attention, affection, grace, benefits, or the limiting or cut-off of privileges. Consider how church pastors and leaders respond when volunteers try to call in sick, or when women leaders show indications of physical ailment or emotional distress. How often have women been removed from valuable roles in church and other ministries because the male leaders around them could not tolerate feminine expressions of pain and suffering? This is the slippery use of punishment as a coercive tool to diminish expressions of suffering and instead reinforcing preferred behavior through responses such as "power through," "perseverance makes your faith stronger," or "He will never give you more than you can handle." Those who dare to draw attention to the natural toll of overwork and inhuman performance expectations gradually move to the margins of Christian leadership and often join the exiled wounded.

The second of the sinister six is to *blame the pain out of the child*. Again, it may seem impossible for a loving caregiver or committed pastor to blame a person for their own suffering. However, this is one of the patterns which is most often used in church spaces, and it has a particularly gendered edge. One very familiar example is demonstrated when wives attempt to bring their broken-heartedness over their husband's abuse to the attention of their pastor and other leaders. Too often, they are met with interrogating questions about their own behavior which precipitated the abuse. Other examples fall under the category of spiritual bypassing in which experiences of suffering are attributed to a lack of transcendence.[10] This may sound something like, "Perhaps you should pray about that"; or "You really need to lay that at the foot of the cross"; or "It sounds like you haven't forgiven that person." Those who seek counsel and comfort from pastoral authorities are sent away condemned and guilty and still very much in pain. This is the tragic legacy of pain intolerance, and many pastors ignorantly perpetuate this legacy under the guise of spiritual strength and perseverance.

The pattern of society's response to pain is evident: Those with power offload their pain intolerance to those with less or little power. Rather than having their pain and suffering identified, named, honored, and salved, wounded people are directed to search for its source within themselves, which exacerbates the pattern of pushing the pain away and further inside where it can no longer be seen.

The remaining four patterns are *humiliating* ("How could you let that happen?"); *neglecting* ("I know you have gone through a lot, but we really need a volunteer for PowerPoint this Sunday"); *distracting* ("That sounds awful; maybe you should come to our fall kick-off event?"); and *moralizing* ("That's tough, but a lot of people have it worse"). Each time women leaders and those belonging to marginalized groups gather the courage to express their pain and suffering, only to be met with pain intolerance, the armor around their pain grows just a bit thicker. Eventually, they can no longer reach it even though its symptoms spread like a cancer impacting their mental, emotional, and spiritual health and development in powerful ways.

Having been trained to punish, blame, humiliate, neglect, distract, and moralize their own and others' pain and suffering, men with power in church and ministry exile their most vulnerable, generous, and compassionate parts. I am convinced the inability to contend with pain and suffering is one of the core challenges to emotional maturity in church leaders. Walker states:

> Finally, it is essential to consciously return to Jesus' own self-description as
> He inaugurated His public ministry in Nazareth; the location of His family

of origins. This is not simply a coincidental detail cited by Luke. "The spirit of the Lord is upon Me to proclaim Good News to the poor, to heal the broken-hearted, to give recovery of sight to the blind (we can include deaf), and to set at liberty those who are captive ... ." Moreover, there is a dire need for the expansion of consciousness regarding what constitutes heartbreak, blindness, deafness, and captivity. Otherwise, pain deafness and [the] death it eventually deals to all systems will continue to be perpetrated.[11]

THE FUTURE-INSPIRED FUNCTIONING CHURCH

I often facilitate group formation through practices of *lectio, audio,* or *visio divina.* I have witnessed some of the most profound, emotionally connected, and Holy Spirit-infused experiences in these spaces. Restoration, reconciliation, and freedom from sin and shame are just a few of the realized outcomes when people bravely enter and engage their senses and encounter the Holy Mystery together. Sadly, there are usually one or two people who feel the need to demonstrate or express their intolerance of communal emotional experiences in these spaces. They maintain an erect or hardened posture, or fidget—perhaps sighing or refusing to respond to invitations to share an inspired thought or word. Occasionally, after most of the group has left the space, one of these resistors burdens themselves with the responsibility of being God's personal spokesperson and approaches me to declare all the ways I am not following Scripture, being spiritually manipulative, or stirring deceptive emotions. On rare occasions, I am accused of "engaging in New Age practices"! In response, I look into their eyes, speak in a soft and gentle tone, and let them know how much I appreciate their concern. I thank them for having the courage to speak up and reassure them that I will take their words to heart. And I do.

When met with the hard shell of resistance to emotional expression and connection, I really do give prayerful thought and consideration to what the person said and how they said it. I consider the rigidity and tension in their body and wonder when it began. I reflect on their words, often filled with fear, protectiveness, and coercive energy. I wonder about the sorts of spiritual spaces and practices they experienced that cultivated an image of a non-emotive God who is unyielding and incapable of tolerating expressions of human pain, suffering, and collective joy; I pray for the burden of coercive, corrective energy they seem compelled to carry and wield toward people with good hearts who love God; and I wonder when coercive spirituality was first wielded upon them. I reflect on the Beatitudes and pray these folks will be drawn to the truth of Jesus' teachings and learn to walk in a good way. Most of all, I allow sadness and mercy to well up inside of me and flow out in an expression of hope for healing. This is how I lean into my developing emotional maturity and spiritual health to navigate what could be a tense or uncomfortable exchange. I relinquish any grasping for power or control and trust the Holy Spirit to touch this dear wounded soul in the ways my soul has been touched and healed from pride, coercive practices, and spiritual abuse and oppression. This is what emotional maturity and spiritual health can look like. It does not always look like this every time someone comes at me in a flurry of corrective and coercive passion, but this posture is gradually becoming more natural and immediate. As a natural-born challenger, this has been a profound transformation in me.

As I near the end of my third decade of Christian ministry and church engagement, I am so thankful to be growing in emotional health and maturity. Awareness of my need to attend to my spiritual and emotional health becomes so apparent when I pay attention to my emotions and attend to any pain and suffering that is arising. Being intentional and engaging in practices that cultivate awareness and maturity help me shift toward inspired functioning and away from compulsive functionalism. A rhythm of daily, weekly, and monthly spiritual and wellness practices helps me restore balance and return to health. I have learned not to hide, deflect, or press on through my pain, but to let it be seen by trusted others, especially my male colleagues. I am so grateful for the healing this brings after so many years of suffering in silence and shame. The safety I find in these relationships continues to heal me on the long, hard journey of identifying and addressing historic weeping wounds inflicted by immature and emotionally underdeveloped male leaders. When compassionate and supportive male colleagues invite me to engage in their grief and loss recovery, I sometimes wonder if this is what Jesus envisioned when he repeatedly engaged women in ministry when it was not culturally normative to do so (John 4:7–26; John 8:10–11; Luke 7:12–13; Luke 7:44–50; Luke 8:48, NRSVUE). He demonstrated a companionship and demeanor unique to being completely comfortable in intimate groupings of mixed genders. Together, in our differences, I think we beautifully reflect the wholeness and vitality of the *imago Dei* within us, individually and communally. In contrast, when I recognize a male colleague who holds power and influence is intolerant of emotional expression and unable to engage in grief and loss work for themselves and others, I steer away from working with them. It just is not safe and not worth the risk. Too much time has been lost to navigating fragile egos and recovering from hurtful encounters. Too many opportunities have been withheld or threatened, and I recognize it is not my calling to point out compulsive pain avoidance and coercive pain infliction patterns to unhealthy leaders.

I will close with a call to male pastors and leaders to identify sites of functionalism and address them before they cause further harm to you and those entrusted to your care. Bravely face the challenge of living as one poor in spirit and resist the messages of toxic masculinity both within and beyond church spaces. If this courageous work is met with private or public rebuke or dressing down in front of peers, know you are in good company as Jesus faced the same attempts to shame and disown him. These humiliating experiences are intended to resound in the male psyche as a cry to storm the church, and this has resulted in the "extreme patriarchal construction of Christianity" through the ages![12] Instead, accept the invitation to choose the path of inspired functioning and all the playful, joy-filled opportunities for connection with your Creator, with your truest self as intended from creation, and with beloved others who long for authenticity, meaning, and safe spaces to minister with you. Trust that you will discover a depth of meaning and purpose in life and become who you were always intended to be. This will truly draw those around you to join the journey into realizing the kingdom coming on earth as it is in heaven.

20

EQUITABLE MULTICULTURAL SPACES

Mariah Humphries (MTS)

is a Mvskoke Nation citizen, writer, and speaker. Through her experience navigating the tension between Native and white American culture, she writes and speaks on the intersections of Christianity and racialized identities. With more than twenty-five years of vocational ministry service and a master's degree in theology, she is focused on using her theological education and lived experience to challenge and encourage the American church to lead the conversation around racial literacy and cultural humility.

During the COVID-19 pandemic, I was invited to a youth conference to lead some sessions on diversity. Concluding my last session, I had some very pointed questions directed toward me. Even though Scripture had been my foundational text, speaking on racial diversity ruffled some feathers—namely with some white attendees. During the Q&A, the attendees expressed some overtly racist ideology, and I debated cutting them off and walking away. But I decided to let them reveal who they really were, and what they thought of me and people who look like me. One person said that my topic on diversity was today's "problem" in the church. Another person said the current climate of society had given me a false sense of empowerment to challenge the status quo; there are reasons we have "our own" churches. When I inquired more about these statements, they continued to share that they felt brown and Black people seeking diversity and justice were the main problems in Christianity today. This group felt diversity was distracting people from the gospel and promoting an anti-Christian social justice agenda. It was clear to them that the gospel does not include diversity, justice, or equity. For them, diversity was causing disruption and division in the church. Considering how they spoke about leaders of color, past and present, and the familiar terminology used, it was clear to me that these attendees were coming from a particular political stance, and they had allowed those political talking points to reduce the words of Jesus to an anemic level in their lives. However, some of their concerns were not unfounded; anyone coming from any political view or orthodoxy can perpetuate a divisive mindset, even when pursuing racial equity in our churches.

Diversity *is* causing issues in the church, but not in the way these attendees believed. Diversity is an all-inclusive view; everyone and every group should be included and valued. I cannot think of a more Christlike perspective than that. And yet this inclusiveness is precisely what scares so many Christians. As I debriefed the interaction with these attendees, I was reminded of things I have witnessed regarding the rejection of diversity in churches.

This youth conference came during the height of the pushback against racial injustice. During the racial awakening the country faced in the summer of 2020, while some church leaders' eyes were opened to diversity and equity, we watched other leaders resist racial equality and equity. That summer came on the heels of a heated political presidential campaign where we witnessed the rise of White Christian Nationalism,[1] and it was during this time that the topic of race became extremely divisive in the American church—and continues to be today.

We saw people of color leaving predominantly white and even multiethnic churches. Racialized events became a topic for political pundits to exploit and sway the American public away from racial justice and conciliation. Those filling pulpits were filled with angst about whether to step into this conversation or defiance against the view that racism had any place in preaching and teaching. From a woman of color's eyes, this rejection and ambivalence is deeply rooted in white supremacy and fear. Fear of difference, fear of unassimilated diversity, and fear of being uncomfortable. This fear is backed by misinterpretation and weaponization of Scripture.

At that youth conference, something larger was revealed about the conference's leadership, which can be applied to church leadership. They simply were not ready to deal with the repercussions of offering sessions in which leaders of color talked about racial and cultural humility. You may desire diversity in thought and representation, but are you ready for it? Is your church ready? Readiness is important. If you have done the work ahead of time, staff and congregants of color will feel seen and heard. Conversely, staff and congregants of color will be harmed if your leadership is unprepared for a diverse congregation. If you merely look for diversity, it quickly becomes tokenism—the performative action of bringing on a person of diversity as a symbol rather than as a full participant in leadership. When your view of diversity aligns with tokenism, it reflects sameness of thought, not the beauty of oneness in unity through diversity.

PURSUING EQUITY, NOT INTEGRATION

To pursue true diversity, we must recognize that integration is not equity. Integration in today's church leans toward the assimilation of others, and it does not represent true diversity. As writer Adrian Pei says, "When we approach diversity in this pragmatic way, we make the mistake of treating minorities as a means to an end. They help us achieve our goals and visions instead of shaping the vision and process themselves."[2]

Although there is the perception that "all are equal" in America, we should know by now that this is not true. History has proven that our society was intentionally unequal from day one and remains this way. Plantations and colonization serve as examples of how this mindset has plagued the church, even in diverse spaces.

On a plantation and during colonization, brown and Black women held no power; they had no voice. How does this play out in today's cross-racial churches? Women of color are often used for music entertainment, support staff, and maintenance, but with no voice when decisions are made. Their perspective, experience, and knowledge are often devalued in these cases. They are merely physical representations of diversity.

Plantation and colonized mindsets in churches today are overlooked or ignored because the majority of the culture views American history through the lens of whiteness or, to be more accurate, through the lens of white maleness.[3] Whiteness is the dominant cultural construct that historically has kept Indigenous, Black, Asian, and Latine people on the margins. Whiteness is often assumed to be a label and critique of white people, but whiteness is not reserved for white people; we can see Indigenous, Black, Asian, and Latine people display or support whiteness, even when they are the ones who are marginalized. Upholding whiteness often comes from the desire to fit in or as an attempt to avoid prejudice and racism from white counterparts. Diversity and equity flourish when the dominance of whiteness is no longer upheld, and the beauty of experience, existence, culture, and giftedness can work in tandem.

Along this white-male-dominated timeline of history, there are only glimpses of the experiences of Indigenous, Black, Asian, and Latina women. When the focus is on the white male existence and experience, brown and Black women become sub-narratives rather than an accurate representation of how the supremacy of whiteness has shaped and damaged our collective health. Women, and especially women of color, have become optional stories in our collective history, often assimilated into the "greater" white-male-dominated narrative. Our history is a collection of diverse stories and events, and to withhold its totality only handicaps the future of the church and the need for diversity and equity. Adrian Pei describes, "In the most blunt and pragmatic sense, diversity is optional to many White organizations because their historical success has not relied on it."[4] This is imperative to grasp, not only in creating a culture of diversity and equity, but also in retaining it.

When true diversity and equity devolve into integration and assimilation, it reveals a deeper reality. Women, specifically women of color, are viewed as less qualified in leadership positions and as problematic in the workplace. There is a mindset that we have a human hierarchy. This not only negatively affects the church, but it goes against Scripture. Genesis 1:26–31 reminds us:

> Then God said, "Let us make humankind in our image, according to our likeness; and let them have dominion over the fish of the sea, and over the birds of the air, and over the cattle, and over all the wild animals of the earth, and over every creeping thing that creeps upon the earth." So God created humankind in his image, in the image of God he created them; male and female he created them. … God saw everything that he had made, and indeed, it was very good. (NRSV)

God calls us good. In Christianity, we often skip over the first two chapters of Genesis and dive right into the fall of Adam and Eve. I get it; it is not as much of a draw to focus on the order of creation, except there is one thing we miss when we skip to the dramatics of the garden and sin: We forget where humanity is created and called *good*. There is no hierarchy mentioned. If we are honest about the American church, we have historically viewed and treated people of color as less than "good." We were missional objects to be assimilated rather than humans created in the image of God. White saviors rush to communities of color with little regard for how God has already been there, working. Yet history, and how it plays out in our current culture, is in the mind of women of color today who work in predominantly white spaces, and it is reflected in how little equity women of color have in our churches. When you consider creating and sustaining a diverse and equitable space, one's racial identity must be navigated with intentionality and care. Women of all identities will face patriarchy on staff, but brown and Black women also face racism in all its forms—from both white men and women. Ultimately, when voices are suppressed, it is due to the desire for homogenous thought.

UNITY IN DIVERSITY, NOT UNITY IN CONFORMITY

Homogenous unity can be a comfortable environment for white spaces. Of course, there are areas of division that can arise, but, at its foundation, it is a safe way to do ministry when considering the complexity of developing a multicultural space. Multicultural churches are hard work; when they are created with equity as a goal, they are some of the most accepting faith spaces I have encountered. But when homogenous thought is considered unity, we have gone off track.

In *Disunity in Christ*, Christena Cleveland writes about cultural conflict vs. realistic conflict. In the church today, we have many monocultural and monoracial "traditions" that have become unwritten doctrines for congregations and denominations. When people of different cultures and racialized identities enter, they also have traditions they hold to. Although the collaboration of cultures and traditions can be beautiful, unfamiliar views can be perceived as threats and become a point of division. We often set our own experience as the standard, rather than one part of a larger, diverse Christian culture.[5]

Forming a staff that represents a "good old boys' club," rather than the church of the New Testament, does not benefit our churches. Such staffs confirm patriarchy as the dominant culture of the church. Patriarchy is not how the gospel leads us to worship with one another. Seeking diversity in both representation and thought is worth the work. It is *not* easy, but the most precious things in my life have been revealed from the hard work of moving past my comfort and considering my neighbor as I want to be considered. Women bring a totality to a staff that a male-only staff cannot provide.

In addition to patriarchy, a significant hurdle to cross in unity is our racialized society. The church has long struggled with racial dynamics and racism in our congregations. We have shouted or we have been silent, and both reactions are significant to a current dilemma in the church: Why should we focus on diversity if it causes division? We need to talk about race because, in America, our churches reflect historic and current stances on race, whether we acknowledge it or not.

Often, when people of color enter a space as their whole cultural selves, they are viewed as divisive and not on board with the current homogenous thought. So, Christians of color sacrifice their culture to be peacekeepers and keep employment. Instead of requiring assimilation and conformity, this is an excellent opportunity to build a culture that is true to Scripture and that values and honors many cultures, traditions, and ways to represent the larger body of Christ.

In their book *Divided by Faith*, Michael O. Emerson and Christian Smith write about the issue of monoracial churches upholding systemic racism more than other social institutions.[6] I know the term "systemic racism" may stop you in your tracks but keep reading and consider what it means. Their research provides a reason for this statement: Most churches are not only monoracial, but most Christian social circles are formed from their congregational relationships. If we attend churches that look like us and our friendships come from those same demographics, we sustain division, not diversity. Church leaders are guilty of this as well. Pastor, do you seek out fellow leaders with diverse thoughts and racial and gender diversity, or are you satisfied and comfortable in a monoracial and homogenous life? What does your bookshelf look like? Do you seek out authors of color and female authors in order to have a broader education? This is not to say every church is promoting systemic racism, but the church should be leading in diversity, not ignoring or fighting it at every turn.

Do multicultural churches solve the issue of diversity and racial disunity in our churches? No, but it would be great if they did! Why are multicultural churches not the solution? Many leaders of "multi-" churches (racial, ethnic, cultural) believe visual diversity and representation is enough. If we can get brown and Black bodies in the church and on stage, and women in leadership, then we can breathe easier and separate ourselves from those other churches that are taking the heat in our society. But diversity for the sake of diversity only leads to failure. When we need to label a church as multiethnic, multiracial, or multicultural so people know who attends, we still have a race problem.

So, what is the goal? Christian unity is the goal. But without diversity, unity cannot be achieved. True Christian unity reflects the kingdom of God, not the empire of an American church. When we learn how to grow in diverse communities as the body of Christ, we gain the strength to be unified. Diversity is a significant step in achieving true unity. We cannot reach true Christian unity if we are siloed with people who look like us and who experience life as we do.

We see this in the New Testament as churches struggled with this very issue of unity and equity. The early church found themselves searching for unity amid societal division—Jew and Gentile—and for equity in God's eyes at a time of cultural opposition. Their unity, through diversity, became essential for the future of the church—a church filled with every people group. It is hard to imagine what might have happened if Paul had not proclaimed those infamous words: "There is no longer Jew or Greek, there is no longer slave or free, there is no longer male and female; for all of you are one in Christ Jesus" (Gal. 3:28).

When we talk about equitable spaces, it is essential to know that Scripture is the foundation for the affirmation of both women in general and women of color. That is important to recognize and talk about because if you cannot acknowledge and accept that racial conciliation is biblical, then it becomes optional. When our role as women of color in society and the church is optional, our identities can become topical, divisive, and political—which is what we are experiencing in congregations today. If women of color are not viewed through a biblical lens, the church can ignore their needs and their qualifications as leaders. The whole topic will come and go as a passing moment in Christian history instead of being a challenging but necessary Christian conversation.

START WITH YOURSELF

What keeps leadership from engaging and creating multicultural spaces? Fear and discomfort. Fear of losing control, fear of making mistakes, and fear of causing harm. When discomfort happens, patriarchy and whiteness can rear its head, and the issue dies. Attendance numbers and money also prevent multicultural spaces from happening. As we saw in 2020 and 2021, the work of racial unity became a secondary or even tertiary issue in many churches in America. Congregants became uncomfortable with the topic of race, and the threat of financial support being withheld by congregations was a reality pastors had to navigate. The body was fractured, and the church was ignoring the wounds by focusing on comfort and allowing fear to prevail.

Diversity should not be created out of societal pressure or internal desire; it should be Spirit-led and pursued out of biblical conviction. When we seek diversity out of pressure, it can quickly be halted to maintain white male comfort. When it is Spirit-led, we know there will be work ahead, and discomfort can be expected; but some of the most rewarding parts of the work grow out of discomfort. You should only promote diversity or recruit diverse voices if you are ready to navigate the intersections of identity and culture. Even when you are ready, patriarchy can still have an effect as you lead. Patriarchy will keep you from building a strong, empathetic, genuinely diverse leadership and congregation.

So how do we overcome fear and discomfort? Some time ago, I participated in a panel session where the topic was our work experience as persons of color in a predominantly white Christian environment. I was asked, "What is one thing you would tell a white supervisor who wants to pursue diversity with their staff?" My answer then is my answer today: Sustain racial diversity in your personal life before taking steps toward diversity on your staff. This is not to say there cannot be a healthy cross-racial staff without first having personal relationships with people of other races. Those staff relationships may be healthy, but they still reflect power dynamics, and those dynamics can heighten the acts and reactions to patriarchy, microaggressions, gaslighting, and prejudice. Your work environment will suffer when you have not personally done cultural-humility and racial-literacy work.

Building relationships outside of your identity should bring you to a state of empathy for what someone else faces, whether your experiences mirror one another or not. Although you cannot embody their experience, you should come to the point of listening to and learning from people of color. In their book *Faithful Anti-Racism*, Christina Edmondson and Chad Brennan share about white Christians and the need to understand a person of color's past, present, and racial trauma.[7] The more you know about what your friends of color face regarding racialized experiences, the more you will recognize those experiences in your staff of color and your congregation. This will lead to a more equitable and unifying space.

Being racially aware will help white leaders establish an environment where staff of color feel seen and heard. This not only applies to current awareness of our racialized society, but to history as well. How can you possibly grasp current racial experiences if you ignore or dismiss the historical atrocities done to people of color, especially where the church and self-proclaimed Christians have been active participants?

Dr. Twyla Baker, citizen of the Mandan, Hidatsa, and Arikara Nation, and some of her colleagues coined a phrase that describes the need for historical knowledge in order to grasp today's experiences: translation exhaustion. Translation exhaustion refers to the situation where "Indigenous people (or any marginalized person/group) engaging with the larger population on a given subject or topic related to bias," have to "first set the stage in terms of historical context ... before even addressing said topic of bias—over and over again—due to the lack of education/background the listener has."[8] Marginalized people are often the educators in their work environments due to the lack of knowledge or historical foundation of white colleagues.

As a woman of color, navigating a white-dominated space—more specifically, a white-*male*-dominated space—can be exhausting. No matter how equitable the work environment is perceived to be, too often there is a moment when white comfort depletes its vitality. When that happens, the woman of color will ultimately pay the price. When there is a crack in the working relationship, the person of color will usually walk away wounded while their white counterpart "learns a lesson." Learning from an error, as valuable and needed as this might be, can come at a cost. In a white-dominated space, the lesson allows the mistake to turn into an opportunity for growth as the "learners" enter the next cross-cultural or cross-racial interaction. Still, the woman of color remains harmed, rarely with an acknowledgment, apology, or reconciliation taking place. To transition white male spaces into diverse and equitable spaces, it is imperative for white leaders to take the initiative and personally educate themselves, rather than simply expecting to be educated by marginalized people.

EQUITY THROUGH DIVERSE REPRESENTATION

Some years ago, I was listening to a sermon given by two pastors: one white male and one Latina. They were preaching from the same passage and unified in purpose, yet the way they presented the passage was different; one, but not the same. The Latina's interpretation of the passage brought a profoundly relevant and applicable point to women in the congregation. Both took an accurate view of Scripture, but their diversity allowed them to provide a deeper glimpse into how the Holy Spirit works in each person.

The senior pastor of this church recognized the need for diversity in church leadership—in gender and racial identity. He had realized the congregation needed to reflect more oneness than sameness—kingdom more than empire. It meant leadership needed to be diverse and have equity. This diversity and equity was reflected in racial and gender representation on stage and in thought. A diverse and equitable staff space was created. A male pastor may not have the same effect a female pastor, or a female pastor of color, can have. Diversity in representation and thought does not diminish one person's impact or influence. Diversity and equity are not a see-saw mechanism where one must be suppressed or lowered for the other to thrive. Everyone can thrive when this is done correctly.

Representation matters. It makes an immediate connection when we see ourselves represented in a leadership position. This matters for under-represented individuals, but seeing diverse representation is essential for all of us. We become a fuller individual and society when we all experience diversity and equity. The church has failed to embody the beauty of diversity in its pursuit of sameness, not oneness. Engaging in diverse thought opens our faith communities to be equitable and more reflective of the kingdom rather than remaining limited to the view of a patriarchal church.

To create a space that is both inclusive and equitable, you must be ready to listen and learn from diverse voices. It will be uncomfortable to decenter yourself and begin to view the whole body. Romans 12:4–5 (NRSV) reminds us, "For as in one body we have many members, and not all the members have the same function, so we, who are many, are one body in Christ, and individually we are members of one another."

When you are growing from a male-dominated space into a diverse environment, it will be women who are harmed if you are not ready. As someone who has been harmed by leaders who were not ready for diversity of thought or women in leadership, and one who has caused harm to another woman of color, I can testify that it was not due to a lack of desire for diversity. Instead, it was due to the lack of readiness and care taken. Lack of *desire* will be evident to women and women of color—they can see it and feel it. Lack of *readiness* for diversity will take some time to reveal itself, often bringing longterm harm to women. For the majority in leadership, it will be a learning opportunity, and yes, it will teach you what not to do in the future, but at the immediate expense of the safety and positive experiences of brown and Black women.

Multicultural spaces sometimes happen by accident, but it takes intentionality and humility from all parties to create and enter a diverse space that will sustain longevity. For leaders in a majority white space, here are some steps to consider as you lead toward equitable multicultural spaces:

Ask yourself some questions.

- Do I want to create a diverse space, or do I want to grow in an equitable space? Why or why not?
- As the leader, am I ready for diversity? Am I prepared for equity in my ministry? Why or why not?
- Is the congregation ready for this shift? Why or why not?

Explore a fuller history. To know what women and women of color face, you must know more about the historical system that led to their experiences today. Here are some recommended resources.

- *An Indigenous Peoples' History of the United States*, Roxanne Dunbar-Ortiz
- *The Color of Law*, Richard Rothstein
- *Unsettling Truths*, Mark Charles and Soong-Chan Rah
- *Stamped from the Beginning*, Ibram X. Kendi
- *Voices of Lament*, Natasha Sistrunk Robinson
- *Indigenous Children's Survivance in Public Schools*, Leilani Sabzalian
- *The Minority Experience*, Adrian Pei

If you are prepared and have done your homework, provide space for women of color on committees and pastoral staff. Here are some ways that move away from tokenism and toward the practice of diversity.

- Humbly solicit feedback from women about ideas you have that will impact a specific group or the broader community. When you ask for feedback, be willing to listen to learn from them and not just listen to justify or defend your work.

- Ask a woman of color to take the lead on projects outside of typical diversity/equity/inclusion (DEI) initiatives. For example, do not ask women of color to only lead in remembrance holidays, history programs, and heritage months.
- Trust the experience of women. Women and women of color provide unique perspectives in ministry and lead in ways that can strengthen the ministry, but we often face disbelief when we share our experiences. Our experiences will be contrary to what you, as a male, have experienced; and that is okay. Stop and take in what we are sharing without immediately questioning the validity of our message.

When we lack knowledge or understanding of the historical experiences of Indigenous, Black, Asian, and Latina women, assumptions, biases, and prejudices easily creep into work interactions. The history of brown and Black people with the church is complex and painful, so we need to talk about women's historical and current experiences. When you do have women on staff, project their voices. Women are often suppressed even though they have a seat at the table. When a woman's perspective is pursued and respected as a voice of authority, everyone can experience an equitable space. Creating equitable multicultural space means women's perspectives are an equal priority for the staff and the congregation. When churches represent equity, not just equality, we are actively being the body of Christ and the church. Each church may look different, based on your community and need, but when we pursue an equitable multicultural space, our congregations are more representative of the church.

21

FROM "THEM" TO "US"

Meghann Jaeger

is an entrepreneur, business owner, wife, mother of two, and voice for the exploited. She is based out of Vancouver, Canada, where she works in fund development for a global charity that works with survivors of human trafficking, and runs her own businesses—The Intersection: Fair Trade and Your Story Coffee. Meghann loves good coffee, good books, weekend adventures, gourmet donuts, beating her sons at Mario Kart, and hipster tacos. She is passionate about seeing women who have been exploited and trafficked brought into freedom and wholeness, and also about ethical businesses as a means to combat poverty.

At some point in our lives, we all encounter poverty. Maybe we grew up living in poverty; maybe we've been involved with ministry to the poor, or have at least been invited to partake in serving or giving to the poor; maybe we've had friends or family members living in poverty. Our experiences will have shaped our ideas about what "poverty" is and who "the poor" are.

When I was growing up, I would define a "poor person" as someone who was homeless or asking for a dollar in a grocery store parking lot. I was aware of the reality of these people's existence and had a certain amount of compassion for their situation, but there was also a sense of "us" and "them." I learned to keep my distance, to dismiss them, and to compartmentalize in a way that allowed me to ignore them as people. I was taught to see what the person looked like and how they behaved, but not the person themselves.

In my teen years, I was introduced to Jesus and the calling of being on mission with God here on earth. At this point, my understanding of poverty began to shift. Between what I read in Scripture and the influence of a new group of friends who frequently talked about the poor, my ideas about "poor people" were challenged. Where I once thought I needed to keep my distance and focus on my own safety, I now responded with an eagerness to be involved. I participated in various expressions of service to the disadvantaged in my community—including feeding programs, home building in Mexico, and children's programs.

There were some really great things about being involved in this ministry: It helped me get over my fear of people who were living on the streets and who had less than me, and it helped me feel good and like I was doing something meaningful in the world. But there were also harmful things about this ministry: It reinforced my view of "us" and "them." The way we prepared to go out and serve people made serving the poor into something that we did—a specific action—not something that we lived as part of God's calling for us to love and care for one another. It was a program, a checked box. It was something that I was *supposed* to do because I was a Christian.

You may be wondering why a chapter on serving the poor has been included in a book about equality. We cannot address the issues of inequality within our Christian spaces while simultaneously failing to bring transformation to the world around us—working to give women equal status to men in every sphere of society. And combatting issues of poverty, slavery, and injustice in our world is very much about women. Poverty and human trafficking adversely affect women and girls.[1] When we fail to address these issues as the church, we are failing to value females. Arguably, this also works the other way: When we fail to value females—when the church treats women and girls as less than their male counterparts—we fail to be able to truly care for the poor and oppressed in our world.

We must work on our hearts to recognize that *every* person is created in the image of God, and *every* person is worthy of freedom and dignity. The call of Jesus is to join him in his work in the world, restoring all things, and all people. There is no *them* and *us* … there is just *us*.

WHO ARE THE "LEAST OF THESE"?

Jesus put the poor front and center in his life and ministry: He proclaimed the good news to the poor (Matt. 11:4-6), he preached about the importance of the poor (Luke 6:20–21), he honored the poor (Mark 12:43–44), and he even identified himself with the poor, saying, "Whatever you did for one of the least of these ... you did for me" (Matt. 25:40). In his example and call to those who chose to follow him, he made it abundantly clear that caring for the poor should be a key priority (Matt. 19:21).

According to the World Bank, about 9.2 percent of the world (719 million people) live on less than $2.15 a day (absolute poverty).[2] The United Nations' definition of absolute poverty is "a condition characterized by severe deprivation of basic human needs, including food, safe drinking water, sanitation facilities, health, shelter, education and information. It depends not only on income but also on access to social services."[3] While we might think of poverty existing only in certain nations or on certain continents, poverty is present in every country and region of the world.[4] Children and youth account for two-thirds of the world's poor, and women represent the majority of poor adults in most regions. Root causes of poverty include economic inequality; lack of access to education, healthcare, and infrastructure; and discrimination.[5] Arguably, poverty can become a cycle of these issues, as many experience these elements as effects of their poverty, as well as root causes. We may believe that we are playing our part to alleviate poverty through charitable giving and volunteering. We certainly wouldn't want to think that we are doing anything to directly *cause* the oppression and suffering of the poor. Yet there is another side to poverty that we must face if we are to be part of the kingdom redemption for the poor that Jesus spoke about, and that is the oppression of those who are already marginalized and vulnerable.

My work for the last twelve years has been in Fair Trade and ethical business. My husband and I started our business, The Intersection, with the hope of supporting communities in the developing world through ethical practices. We truly believe that ethical business is one of many ways to see the cycles of systemic poverty broken. Throughout the course of this work over the last ten years, we have learned about human trafficking and "modern-day slavery" and the disproportionate way the vulnerable and poor are being exploited. This has helped to shift our focus toward this important issue.

Modern-day slavery is one of the most horrific crimes in the world. It includes human trafficking, sex trafficking, forced labor (including domestic labor), sweat shops, online exploitation, and forced marriages. In a 2017 report from the International Labour Office, it was estimated that there were more than 40 million enslaved peoples in the world. Women and girls accounted for 71 percent of all modern-slavery victims and 25 percent of all slavery victims were children.[6] Today, the trafficking of human beings is the second largest grossing criminal enterprise in the world after drug trafficking.[7] People, especially women and children, are being enslaved all over the world. You might not see it, but it exists in your community, as well. Trafficking happens everywhere, and because we purchase products and services in our local, national, and even global economies, we are all participating in the system that allows human trafficking to occur—even if we would never want to knowingly support such atrocities.

When I became aware of this, I began to do more research and discovered small enterprises all over the world that were employing survivors of exploitation. As a household and a business, we expanded our buying of ethical goods to include products from these businesses. We quickly realized the impact that meaningful employment had in the lives of survivors of exploitation as they sought safety and healing.

These complex issues can be overwhelming and can leave us feeling inadequate to do anything. It can seem as if poverty, trafficking, and oppression are issues that are impossible to solve, so why bother? The answer, of course, is because Jesus has called us to care for the least of these among us. This is what he declared about his own ministry and purpose on earth: "The Spirit of the Lord is on me, because he has anointed me to proclaim good news to the poor. He has sent me to proclaim freedom for the prisoners and recovery of sight for the blind, to set the oppressed free, to proclaim the year of the Lord's favor" (Luke 4:18–19). His whole purpose on earth was to bring freedom and dignity to those who were oppressed, broken, and forgotten; and he has entrusted to us, as his people, the same ministry of restoration.

Deuteronomy 15:7–11 says,

> "If anyone is poor among your fellow Israelites in any of the towns of the land the LORD your God is giving you, do not be hardhearted or tightfisted toward them. Rather, be openhanded and freely lend them whatever they need. ... There will always be poor people in the land. Therefore I command you to be openhanded toward your fellow Israelites who are poor and needy in your land."

We are in a time in our world where we need to confront our understanding and our response as Christians to the poverty and oppression that so many people are living in and suffering under—particularly women and girls. Considering the revolutionary actions of Jesus in his defense, championing, and liberation of women during his time on earth gives us cause to act on the inequalities women face today. It gives us the opportunity to look beyond our current responses to local and global poverty and oppression and to engage with new solutions. We need to embrace the example and teachings of Jesus in order to address the needs in our world.

HOW WE CARE FOR THE POOR

We need to move beyond caring for the poor being an afterthought or one of a number of programs we are involved with, rather than a key priority in our lives, as was the way of Jesus. At times, we have taken the idea of caring for the poor and turned it into something that we can track, advertise, and feel good about. None of those things is wrong, but the heart of caring for the poor needs to come from a space of empathy, understanding, and compassion. As the church, we think a lot about bringing people to Jesus, but we fall short when we focus solely on their spiritual health and fail to be the hands and feet of Jesus—meeting their very real and felt physical, emotional, and mental health needs. Sometimes the downtrodden are better able to understand God's love for them once they have experienced it by being fed, clothed, and housed, or once they have received counseling, medical care, crisis intervention, or access to resources. The whole gospel is that God values them and cares about their freedom and wholeness and wellness (see 1 Thess. 5:23 MSG).

As followers of Jesus, we should want to see people freed from exploitation, freed from abuse, freed from addiction, and freed from the systemic oppression that is both causing poverty and causing people to remain in poverty. And I truly believe that we can do this if we work together. Below are just a few ways that we can begin.

Offer Holistic Care

When we started working with businesses that employed those who had been exploited, I did not have a full understanding of what trauma does to a person because of my lack of lived experience. In my mind, women who had suffered years of abuse and trauma were now working in a safe space, and that meant they were okay. I have come to know that there is much more to healing and restoration than a physically safe space. Once I became trauma informed, my understanding of poverty shifted from physical needs alone to include a person's unmet emotional, mental, and community needs. This has enabled me to see the fullness of who each person is made to be. As Jesus said, "I have come that they may have life and have it to the full" (John 10:10). As the body of Christ, we must see each person as the whole person God created them to be, and we must look for ways to equip every person to have fullness in their lives.

Along with physical poverty, many are facing psychological poverty—which can look like mental illness, PTSD, or struggling through issues and trauma from their past. Those who are struggling in this way are not always accepted by or easily integrated into society. Even once their situation has improved, a person who has faced extreme trauma, exploitation, or generational poverty often does not have the same education, skills, or mental coping mechanisms to face pressures and challenges as does someone who has lived without trauma. Their poverty is not simply physical, and its complexity requires a more holistic and trauma-informed approach.

We must be mindful that in our churches we are more likely to see people living in psychological poverty than someone who is homeless or living with an addiction. Within our pews, our youth programs, and our outreach work, we are likely to encounter those living with this type of poverty. It is easy to identify those who are physically poor, but not nearly as easy to identify those who are facing other kinds of poverty. All forms of poverty are intertwined and linked and our approach to caring for all people needs to take their whole person into consideration and not just what we can see.

Work *With*, Not *For*

In 2017 and 2018, my family and I were living in Eastern Europe and working with a church plant, where we participated in hosting missions teams. Groups of people would come to us with funds they had raised and a willingness to serve. Often, however, they were lacking in understanding of the culture or what was already happening within the church and community. They would arrive with their own agendas and the church would end up serving them and what they wanted to do in the community, rather than the teams serving the ministry happening there already.

This wasn't just about how they worked with us as the church plant. I would sit and watch the moms in the community, who had become my friends, as their kids were being fed and entertained by foreigners, and I knew what the look on their faces meant. It was hard for them to see others who didn't know their children feeding them and giving them treats and gifts. Those moms had hopes and longings for their children, and they deeply desired to give them what they really needed. It was uncomfortable for them to see other people providing for their children, assuming that they knew what those children needed. The visitors from other countries saw poverty and they wanted to do something about it. Their hearts were in the right place, but the outworking wasn't equipping the local community in the best way.

What I learned from that experience was that we need to make the effort to know those we are serving and understand their wants and needs first, and then we can work alongside them to accomplish their goals. Sometimes this approach means putting aside our desire to do something seemingly "bigger and better." But when we take this different approach, we empower the ones we serve.

There is sadly a disconnect in our Western society from what we know of Jesus and the way we operate as the church. Jesus spent time with the poor—he led a physically poor life—so he truly understood the needs of those around him. The church has an immediate need to re-engage with our communities, and to understand the unique needs that are present and the unique solutions that are required. What's more, we need to do this in partnership with other churches and denominations around us. No one person, church, denomination, organization, or business can serve their entire community alone. If we don't work together—if we don't support work that is already being done and instead choose to come up with our own thing—we are missing what Jesus calls us to.

Listen to Those with Lived Experience

If we are to fully understand how we can best serve the poor, those with lived experience need to be leading us. Who better to lead us in combatting exploitation—systemic issues creating cycles of poverty, homelessness, and addictions; mental health issues; and broken justice systems—than those who have lived through them? Some of the most bold, courageous, and tenacious leaders I know are women who I would call survivors. Not only have they survived exploitation and trauma, but they have also worked hard on their personal healing and gained the tools they need to thrive in this world. They have taken all of their experiences and are now leading social justice initiatives to help more women find freedom and Jesus.

Unfortunately, people who have survived exploitation are frequently sidelined and further oppressed, because they aren't deemed "appropriate"—they have some "rough edges" or don't talk the same way as others. More and more we are seeing women with lived experience who have been working to see people freed from cycles of oppression taking a step back because of the prevalence of "performative activism"—involvement for the purpose of increasing one's social capital rather than out of devotion to a cause.[8] The result is that those with lived experience are not being invited into the same spaces as those who have influence or who are part of organizations with curated social media feeds and big budgets. It is the latter who are offered speaking engagements and given opportunities. Most organizations led by those with lived experience are not invited into those in the same way. This impacts funding and grant opportunities which further widens the gap.

So, how can the church help them as they lead us through impacting change? We can take a step back and allow their voices, insights, and wisdom to come through. We can provide finances, resources, and people to join and support them. We can work together—collaborating and collectively supporting people with lived experience within our churches and communities. We can amplify the voices of those who have survived and overcome. We can create equal opportunities for sharing, speaking, and teaching.

The issue of making space for the voices and leadership of survivors is intrinsically linked to the problem we have in so many Christian organizations where women's voices in general are pushed to the margins. We need male leaders to intentionally create room for women to be able to lead in these spaces in order that those with lived experience can be heard, learned from, and followed into new ways of serving.

Share Stories Appropriately

One of the benefits of having those with lived experience lead us in these spaces is that they understand the impact that can be made both positively and negatively, often in ways those of us without their experience can't. Within nonprofit and social-impact spaces, a well-told or well-written story can have significant impact and value. Stories are currency. Bringing in eloquent speakers is currency: "We tell stories to amplify awareness and to raise money—to do the good we want to do. And when we've done that good, we tell more stories so donors, volunteers, and supporters can participate in the good their gifts make possible. We tell stories to invite others in."[9] At times, however, telling someone's life story to leverage involvement, support, or donations can be a form of exploitation. We need to be very cautious that we do not sensationalize the poverty and oppression people have gone through for our own purposes. There are many reasons I value leadership from those with lived experience, but one of the top reasons is that they carry understanding of ethical storytelling. They know what exploiting someone else's story means and the harm that it can cause.

Give Women a Place at the Table

If we are to follow in Jesus' footsteps and care for the poor, it is clear we need to listen to women's voices and welcome and champion them to lead within our churches and social justice initiatives. Women need a seat at the table. When we look at the statistics surrounding abuse, slavery, exploitation, poverty, and lack of education in the world today, these numbers convey the reality of women being affected at a much higher rate than men. In order to serve the oppressed, we need to draw from the lived experiences of these women.

Additionally, the majority of workers in anti-trafficking, rehabilitation programs, workplace training, and domestic abuse support are women. In my twelve years of running a social justice initiative, it has been young women who have continued to come through the door to help, volunteer, learn, replicate, and get involved. They are on the front lines of battling injustice and are uniquely suited to do so because they can provide safety for women where men can't, particularly when the women they are helping have been abused by men. There are so many women leading the way, and we need to support and resource them instead of taking over from them or creating new programs that compete with the work they are doing.

Walking alongside those in situations of poverty is where we as followers of Jesus need to be. The question is, how can we do this differently from the way it has been done in the past? How can we collaborate instead of keeping ourselves insulated? How can we learn from survivors instead of causing harm to those we are wanting to support? How can we include women with lived experience in the leadership of social justice initiatives? How can we treat eliminating poverty as a main focus of our lives as citizens of earth and participants in the kingdom of God?

As human beings, and members of the body of Christ, we need to grow in our understanding of what poverty looks like. We need to open our eyes to what is happening around us and we need to work together to serve. We need to let go of the programs, checked boxes, and canned ministries to the poor and seek fullness of life for survivors of these injustices. We must recognize that *every* person is created in the image of God, and *every* person is worthy of freedom and dignity.

Jesus said where much has been given, much will be required (Luke 12:48), or, as Uncle Ben tells Peter Parker, "With great power comes great responsibility." Once we know about the issues and the oppression and the poverty and the abuse of people in our world, we cannot turn our backs. We must join together as men and women in leadership in the church to address these issues in our world—including our own backyards—and work together to be part of the solution. We must become more informed about the issues and be open to being taught and led by those with lived experience. We can't bury our heads in the sand. We need the church to be on the forefront of teaching and understanding the issues of poverty, trafficking, and modern-day slavery so we can inform the culture and enact change. And we must continue to consider what Jesus is calling us to, as collaborators on his mission of restoring hope, dignity, and worth to all people in all places.

22

THE HOLY WORK OF RESISTANCE

Lisa Rodriguez-Watson

is the national director for Missio Alliance and serves as associate pastor at Christ City Church. Her heart to see people reconciled to God and one another has led her to invest her life, family, and ministry in places and people that have often been overlooked by the world. Lisa has served as an urban church planter, collegiate minister, seminary professor, international missionary, and community development practitioner for the last twenty years. She was the co-founder of a grassroots organization in Memphis, TN, that was committed to mobilizing Christians to love their undocumented neighbors and consider an appropriate Christian response to the nation's immigration crisis. Lisa lives in Washington, DC, where she is a mom to three fantastic children, and wife to her best friend, Matthew.

The work of resistance is a holy work. It requires imagination that sees beyond what is to what can be. It requires courage to reject the status quo and accept that another more beautiful and just way is possible. Resistance is the path that leads to the promised land of equity and justice.

The Bible offers us numerous examples of women who resisted in the face of opposition. Esther, Ruth, Miriam and Jochebed, and Mary the mother of Jesus, are just a few. But two women who exemplify the strengths of the feminine, the beauty of God, and what it means to be obedient in the face of opposition are those whose names may not be familiar. They didn't get a book of the Bible named after them. They're not mentioned in the lineage of anyone significant. They don't even have a chapter heading to recognize their valiant efforts. Rather, their story is only told once over the course of six verses in the first chapter of Exodus. They are the midwives named Shiphrah and Puah who are the very first women in the Bible to give us a vision for, and example of, civil disobedience and holy resistance.

Why were they heroes? After Joseph and his family died, another Pharaoh rose up in Egypt. He felt threatened by the ever-growing population of Hebrews in his land. Nervous that they would soon outnumber the Egyptians and possibly join the enemies of Egypt to overthrow him, the Pharaoh gave diabolical orders to Shiphrah and Puah. Exodus 1:16 relates the grisly details of his command: "When you are helping the Hebrew women during childbirth on the delivery stool, if you see that the baby is a boy, kill him; but if it is a girl, let her live." Upon receiving this clear and horrific order, the Scripture records, "The midwives, however, feared God and did not do what the king of Egypt had told them to do; they let the boys live" (Ex. 1:17).

Shiphrah and Puah resisted in the face of blatant evil. When opposition grew toward the Hebrew people, these two midwives acted in obedience to God, and saved countless generations of Israelites. They quite literally brought forth life in resistance to an edict of death. This is the aim of resistance work—to usher in the fullness of life as God intends.

Perhaps it's no coincidence that these earliest resisters were midwives; those who set the scene for liberation. What better occupation than a midwife could there be for those whose calling is to deliver new life into the world? It was the midwives who saw what had been conceived and nurtured that potential into full existence. Midwives knew the right times for resting and breathing, and the right times for pushing and delivering. Midwives were central in the lives and stories of women. They didn't simply show up at the moment of delivery, rushing in to catch a baby. Instead, they were present amidst the pain, confronting despair and audaciously cultivating courage and persistence when women were weary and wanted to give up. They were spiritual leaders and healers.[1] They dwelled and worked in the margins among the laboring women who were systematically oppressed. Shiphrah and Puah represent the feminine strength of God's presence and power. God dwells with the brokenhearted. God dwells with those who long for justice and labor for righteousness, who seek liberation from the limitations of broken systems. God accompanies women who are relegated to the margins of male-dominated Christian culture, whispering words of strength and resistance, signaling when to breathe and, guiding us toward the right times to push so that, in the end, new and fuller life can be experienced by the church.

WHY WE RESIST

The work of resistance is necessary in our day because we as women are so often systematically kept from opportunities to lead and flourish. Not only are we not invited to lead, we're also limited in our chance to influence and, unfortunately, oftentimes we don't even have the space to contribute to important matters facing our churches.[2] The structures are so rigid and narrow that our gifts, passions, and skills are constricted to the point of asphyxiation, or are simply pushed out of the church.

Years ago, I was part of a church that held a complementarian view of women in ministry leadership. Prior to my husband taking a pastoral position on the staff, we inquired about their approach toward women in leadership and preaching. Being a young church at the time, we were told that they hadn't fully settled on their position. Women were allowed to speak on Sunday mornings, and the children's pastor was given the title of pastor. I was hopeful that there would be space for my gifts of preaching and leadership, even as someone who was not on staff.

Soon after moving, I was given the opportunity to speak to the women of the church at a day-long retreat. I was so grateful for the opportunity early on to connect with the women of the church and use the gifts God had given me. But after a couple of years had gone by, I hadn't had another invitation to share or speak—and certainly not to preach on a Sunday morning. At this point, I had a conversation with my friend Gia, who'd been part of the ministry I led prior to making the move to this new town and church. She was very familiar with my leadership and teaching gifts. She asked me, "How are you using your gifts of speaking and leading in church?" I explained that I had hoped there would be more room for me to do that. I was certainly welcome to teach the children, and I had been faithfully serving in the four-year-old class that my son was part of.

Much beyond that, there wasn't space for me to lead or teach. Astounded, Gia responded with a Holy Spirit challenge and said, "I think it might almost be a sin that you're not using your gifts!" I had to reckon with the power of her words and the reality of my situation. What was I to do, as a woman called into ministry, but in a system and church that had solidified their theological position and disallowed women to preach and lead at the highest levels of our congregation? It felt like my legs had been cut out from under me. I was unable to walk in my God-given calling and leading in that context.

Like many other women, unable to use their gifts in their congregation, I found ways to use them elsewhere. I resisted the system that hemmed me in, and I moved out from under it. I was no longer content to have my gifts sitting idly on a shelf, gathering dust like useless trinkets. Taking Gia's words to heart, and recognizing that obedience to God superseded whatever barrier I was up against, I began mobilizing and training churches in my city to coalesce around immigration issues. Dozens of churches and scores of pastors joined events I hosted throughout the city. I taught about God's love for justice and for the immigrant, guiding men and women through Scripture passages that dealt with our response as Jesus-followers to newcomers in our city and country. It was a tragedy that my gifts were unwelcome in my church, but my refusal to accept the status quo led me to have greater influence across the city. It was obedience in the face of opposition that helped create more Jesus-shaped followers in my city, and more kingdom-like hospitality for the immigrant communities in that place.

While these kinds of restrictions that leave women unable to use their gifts can feel galling, holy resistance doesn't come from a place of vengeance, bitterness, or power-mongering. Like Shiphrah and Puah who resisted the Pharaoh's orders because they feared God, the starting point for our resistance is always our reverence for God. A male-dominated church is an incomplete representation of the fullness of God, who is not male. When we revere the fullness of who God is, it's unacceptable to continue to proliferate a truncated and stunted view of God. It will take men and women operating in the fullest capacity of their giftedness across all levels of leadership in the church for us to bear witness to the extraordinary grandeur of our God.

Furthermore, reverence for God invites us to divine defiance so that someday all women can be unleashed to live wholly into their God-given callings for the sake of the kingdom. This embodied obedience allows for wholehearted and integrated lives that result in flourishing for women as well as men. Finally,

THE HOLY WORK OF RESISTANCE | 259

by God's grace, the world will see a more accurate representation of God and can more easily take hold of fullness of life. Whatever resistance costs us, this vision is worth it!

THE CALL FOR GREAT LEADERS

In 1956, Dr. Martin Luther King Jr. gave a clarion call for leaders. In his speech he wisely declared, "We need leaders not in love with money but in love with justice. Not in love with publicity but in love with humanity. Leaders who can subject their particular egos to the pressing urgencies of the great cause of freedom ... a time like this demands great leaders."[3]

Just a few years after Dr. King spoke these powerful words, a group of *abuelas* (grandmas) from Sepur Zarco in Guatemala became victims of unfathomable suffering during the civil war that broke out in 1960 and lasted for more than thirty years. The United States government backed the Guatemalan federal government in this "armed conflict" during which the soldiers of the federal army massacred nearly 200,000 people—most of whom were poor, illiterate, indigenous, and living in rural communities. After executing their husbands and sons, the soldiers subjected the women to sexual assault—including rape and sexual slavery.[4]

In the early- to mid-2010s, the *abuelas* took their case to the highest court in Guatemala to seek justice for the abuse they experienced. Elderly, frail, and filled with courage, these fifteen women testified about their suffering. They were the kind of great leaders Dr. King described in his speech. They were great leaders, not because they were popular. To the contrary, they had become outcasts in their community and were called prostitutes because of what had been done to them. They were great leaders because they were in love with justice and humanity.

They testified because they were determined that the terrible exploitation they endured would be prosecuted. Thankfully, they won their case for justice—which was significant because it marked the first time in history that a tribunal found its own citizens guilty of sexual enslavement.[5] In the process of sentencing, eighteen measures of reparation the *abuelas* requested were granted. Among these measures were a health center and primary schools in Sepur Zarco; reopening cases regarding land claims the *abuelas'* husbands had died defending; publishing a children's book recounting *las abuelas'* history; and translating the text of the judge's sentence into all indigenous languages spoken throughout Guatemala.[6]

The *abuelas* were great leaders. They were resisters. They exemplified what the prophet Isaiah described in chapter 58 verse 12, "You'll use the old rubble of past lives to build anew, rebuild the foundations from out of your past. You'll be known as those who can fix anything, restore old ruins, rebuild and renovate, make the community livable again" (MSG).

TOKENISM OR EXCLUSION

The *abuelas* are exemplars for those of us wanting to resist injustice. Women facing opposition in the church have much to resist and restore. The hurt of being refused the right to express who God has made us to be and serve with our giftings runs deep—not to mention the victim-blaming, demeaning, and misogyny so many women have had to endure within the church. And while there has been recent progress in our struggle for equity and representation, the issue of tokenism remains a challenge.

Women continue to be underrepresented in positions of power. Decisions are made about things that affect us without our input or inclusion. Recent progress aside, the change is painfully slow. Additionally, though invitations to influential and leadership spaces are becoming more common, true shared power remains elusive. Women are asked to be present for the sake of optics more than the genuine desire for our leadership. This is the epitome of tokenism.

Certainly, being invited to leadership conversations is good! However, it's simply insufficient to have a presence in the room. In addition to being present, it's essential that we be heard and that our input is taken into consideration. Many women have the experience of sharing thoughtful and strategic suggestions, only to have them dismissed or ignored. Equally frustrating is the experience of making insightful and forward-thinking suggestions and having them not be recognized until the same idea is articulated by a male counterpart. This type of treatment is tremendously disempowering. When our input isn't taken into consideration, we lack adequate representation in the decision-making process, and the outcomes will be weaker without our influence. We can and must do better. Tokenism falls woefully short of, and is an affront to, the mutuality that kingdom living calls us to. The flourishing that can result from sincere efforts to work side by side, with shared authority, is completely undermined by mere tokenism. Not surprisingly, tokenism is more indicative of empty virtue-signaling than a genuine movement toward inclusion and mutual belonging.

Because of the resistance we experience in places of leadership, we respond with our own forms of resistance. We use our positions to create space for women coming behind us, ensuring that influence and leadership doesn't terminate with our position, but is instead multiplied for future generations. We boldly and tenderly challenge assumptions of women who can't see themselves in leadership because, unfortunately, female leadership representation has been lacking in their world. This is part of the call we have on our lives. We get to join in with what God is doing in repairing the broken systems that keep some people in power and others in places of marginalization. God is too great and too beautiful and too vast to be represented by men alone. It takes the leadership, influence, and authority of men *and* women, working side by side, in order to be an accurate signpost to the marvelous nature of God.

While tokenism is one example of a way that women are kept at the margins, we also experience exclusion in environments that uphold "the Billy Graham Rule." This rule has its origins in the late 1940s as Rev. Dr. Billy Graham, the famous evangelist, gathered with his team in Modesto, California, to construct a set of resolutions to uphold the highest standards of biblical morality and integrity. One of the resolutions dealt with sexual immorality, and together this group of men determined to "avoid any situation that would have even the appearance of compromise or suspicion."[7] From that day on, Billy Graham did not meet alone, travel alone with, or eat alone with any woman other than his wife. Inspired by Paul's mandate to Timothy, to "flee from youthful lusts" (2 Tim. 2:22 NASB) these sets of rigid boundaries have been adhered to and have shaped the thinking and behavior of many men in ministry. The repercussions of this Billy Graham Rule were huge—generations of men have viewed women as objects of youthful lusts who must be kept at a safe, non-threatening distance.

Rather than viewing women as capable ministry partners and sisters in a common faith, all too often we have been viewed as a sexualized temptation and a threat. That—combined with these types of sweeping, absolute boundaries being tied to having the "highest standards of biblical morality and integrity"—have naturally resulted in women being excluded from places of influence and leadership, which in the Christian landscape are primarily held by men.

Rob Dixon, in his book *Together in Ministry,* bravely and necessarily interrogates the Billy Graham Rule. His research names several unintended consequences. First, it can be impossible for people to do their jobs if they are unable to be physically present with members of the opposite sex. Second, it can perpetuate the narrative that men and women are unable to control themselves sexually. Finally, it can "systematically deprive women of access, power, and agency."[8]

The best intentions sometimes have unfortunate effects. Rob Dixon also highlights the related research of Halee Gray Scott, which found that men "didn't intend to exclude women or sexualize them. Instead, they wanted to ensure their actions were always above board."[9] Wanting to take the moral high ground and be above reproach are good things, to be sure. The last thing the church needs is another sex scandal that sullies the reputation of the Christian faith. However, after decades of adherence to the Billy Graham Rule, two things have become abundantly clear. First, it doesn't always prevent lapses of judgment or moral failure. Second, because of its exclusionary and disempowering outcomes, it falls woefully short of the flourishing that is possible when men and women partner together in ministry.

I recently heard a story of a pastor who had spent his early years of ministry being formed in a thoroughly complementarian church. Over the years, his theology shifted to one that incorporated women at all levels of leadership within the church. Naturally, he left the complementarian church, and began leading one that upheld egalitarian values. He empowered women to preach and pastor. Yet, the women on his team had a growing concern that they eventually raised with him.

The issue was that they were not being mentored by him in the same way that he was mentoring the men on the team. He was intentional about meeting with each man on his team over lunch once a month. Because of his apprehensions about meeting with women one on one, he never initiated these same kinds of mentoring/discipleship sessions with them. This was to everyone's detriment. The women did not receive the professional and ministerial coaching they deserved, and he missed out on learning from the women on his team, as well. Thankfully, when they brought this to his attention, he was responsive and willing to shift his thinking and behavior.

This is an example of the challenges women must overcome in Christian contexts, even those that say they value women at all levels of leadership. If men are unwilling to invest in women in the same ways that they are willing to invest in men, the result is the propping up of systematic inequity that propagates the marginalization of women.

Another barely noticeable way that gender norms play themselves out to the detriment of women happens in meetings. Consider for a moment, who takes the notes in your meetings? Have you ever tried to take notes and meaningfully participate in the conversation during a work meeting? It's a challenging task! Research has shown that women are asked to take notes more often than their male counterparts, and Adam Grant and Sheryl Sandberg noted in their editorial in *The New York Times* that, "The person taking diligent notes in the meeting almost never makes the killer point."[10] If women on your team are continually relegated to note-taking responsibilities, it is very possible you will miss out on their incredibly valuable contributions regarding the conversation at hand.

As women, we're already given more than our fair share of "office housework."[11] These tasks are not necessarily the best gifts we have to offer. But what further complicates this reality is that when we say "no" to office housework requests, we are perceived as not being team players, leaving us vulnerable to missing out on promotion or pay raises—when we're already inequitably compensated. When we advocate for ourselves because we sense God inviting us to higher levels of leadership, we are deemed to be power-hungry. When we assert ourselves and request an increase in compensation, we are labeled as "only in it for the money." At every turn, we shoulder the load of numerous, layered gender biases. It requires a tremendous amount of strength and resistance to stand in the wake of these challenging forces.

And yet, it is here, in the confluence of the raging waters of opposition, that I believe we garner and display the strength and power of God. We know that God is at work in and through us in our places of ministry. It is by God's grace that we are called and equipped and sustained to withstand the oppositional pressures we face. What else but the crystal-clear calling of God on our lives and the compelling summons of the kingdom would hold us in the wake of all this hardship?

A FEW GOOD MEN

Edward Burke is often erroneously quoted as saying, "The only thing necessary for the triumph of evil is that good men do nothing." Despite the misattribution, the meaning of the statement holds true.

Systematic oppression and opposition are evil. Relegating women who are capable and called to anything less than full participation in the kingdom of God distorts the beauty of God's grand design and perpetuates evil. The only thing needed for evil to continue to prevail is for us to remain content with the status quo. The only thing needed is for you, kind readers of this book, to determine that we cannot live kingdom-oriented, counter-cultural lives. The enemy of our souls would deceive us into believing that even simple steps forward would be too costly and too complex to achieve. They are not. We serve a mighty God, and we are empowered by the boundless Holy Spirit to do exceedingly and abundantly more than we can imagine (Eph. 3:20). So what is the work? How do we move ahead?

There are a few practical ways to disrupt the status quo and join us, your sisters, in the resistance. You're headed in the right direction by reading this book. The next step is to read other women. Buy books written by women leaders in the church and in the academy. There are remarkable, brilliant female theologians who will help us and you gain a clearer vision of God and God's kingdom. Read their books, listen to their podcasts, find their articles on the web. You've already begun. Keep going!

Another step is to ask women about their experiences in the church and believe what they tell you. Again, you've taken a good first step with "listening" to women's stories being shared here. Take courage and devote more time to building the kind of relationships that foster an honest and humble learning posture on your part. I imagine God taking great delight in his daughters and sons telling stories of hurt and hope as God fortifies us as a body and fashions us toward the new creation.

Perhaps one of the most counter-cultural ways to be part of God's work is in the sacrificial task of making space for women. It is a work of *kenosis* or emptying. The apostle Paul, when writing to the church in Philippi, instructed them to have the same attitude of mind Christ Jesus had (Phil. 2:5–8). Even though he was God, Jesus did not consider equality with God something to strive for; instead, he emptied himself. Making space for women in the context of the dominant, Christian male landscape will require you to relinquish some aspects of control and privilege. Consider inviting a woman into places you've easily had access to that include very few, and possibly no women. Make it a point to not merely tokenize, but champion her, and help her succeed. Give up leadership opportunities in favor of women. Give up speaking and preaching opportunities to allow women to take your place. Help us not to just enter the space, but build the bridges to help us cross the chasm that exists.

These practical steps toward dismantling the status quo are not just effective disruptions and necessary agitations to the power structures that oppose God's dream for women and men in the church; they are beautiful evidences of God's grace that serve as signposts to the glorious kingdom and our matchless worth of our Creator. With every effort of resistance, we forge a path for those behind us and beside us that is a clearer image of the kingdom that has come and is coming. Since Shiphrah and Puah, women have been doing this work of resistance. It's time for men to come join us.

CONCLUSION

Danielle Strickland

I honestly don't know how to conclude this book.

These holy prophetic voices have left me overwhelmed with gratitude, weeping with remorse, inspired at the possibilities of the future, broken-hearted with the pain of the present, amazed at the depth of their biblical insight, thankful for their detailed and intricate research, hopeful at their vision of godly leadership, awed at the practical steps laid out for change, and gobsmacked that everyone in this diverse chorus is unified in their vision of an equitable shared future. That last part is mind-blowing.

Take a minute to think it through. Despite the years of abuse, oppression, and marginalization that so many women have faced, they have remained faithful to the callings and purposes God has spoken into and over their lives. And yet, at great cost to themselves and those who stand with them, many endure the sting of rejection and ongoing marginalization from board rooms, pulpits, theological discussions, mission fields, and leadership positions in their areas of expertise.

Here is how I know this book is a holy prophetic call: if it were anything else, it would demand that male leaders be pulled down. You would hear a resounding call to topple the power structures that have represented and continue to tolerate injustice toward women at the expense of the whole body of Christ. These pages would have been filled with appeals for the resignation of those male leaders who have demonstrated callous indecision, who have repeatedly supported the intolerable status quo, and who remain complicit in upholding corrupt power structures that promote male dominance at the expense of anyone outside of their patriarchal circles. You would have been asked to silence those who have benefited from and continue to enjoy platform, position, and control—all the while being propped up and supported by women. Certainly, at the very least, there would have been a well-deserved naming and shaming of all who know the truth yet remain silent.

But the sheer miracle is that's not what you've heard in this book. The prophetic call here is in keeping with the biblical witness. Like any good prophetic word, it deals with the truth. It's far too late for kid gloves or dancing around the issues to protect fragile egos or raw feelings. We had to be bluntly honest about the cost of male primacy in the current leadership structure of the church because that cost is surely being felt in the mass exodus from the institutional church that is happening now. It can be no coincidence that the exposure of patriarchy's influence in the church has coincided with unprecedented numbers of women leaving the church—or no longer engaging with church.[1]

The truth of a distorted view and practice of power has come out and is as evident as the sun. Male-centered, positional-based, and controlling leadership has marred the gospel, crippled the body of Christ, limited the witness of Jesus, and made room for the principalities and powers of darkness. But that's not the final word. Nope. Because the beauty of God is revealed in the HOLY prophetic call of these witnesses.

The prophet speaks truth to power to offer something else—a different future. A path to repentance. A *metanoia*. An awakening. A way to deal with our sin and move toward the ways of God with a pure heart and clean hands (Ps. 24:4). It's a restoration that's on offer here—a vision, not of female power that uses the very same demonic strategies to wield control and authority, but of shared leadership. There are no usurpers longing to "take over" and subjugate men, reversing the oppression—as we've seen some fear-dealing misogynists warn. What's on offer here is a prophetic imagination: an ancient, holy vision of a power that is not like any other. A holy power. A force for change. Love expressing itself through a mutuality that celebrates diversity. What's on offer is a never-ending source of dynamic energy and creative possibilities. What we are invited into, by this beautiful chorus of voices, is a fundamental shift in the way we are the church. We're being challenged to exemplify the countercultural way of Jesus—to demonstrate the trinitarian relationship of self-giving and co-suffering Love; to use our power to empower; to access capacities that can save us from ourselves and change our entire orientation from upward mobility and centrality to downwards and out; to immerse ourselves in the flow of God's power; to reverse the prevailing systems, inverting them with joy.

So, what does this mean? Well, it's up to you. First, open your heart. (Your mind can come too, eventually, but please don't start there.) The kind of change being called for here will require us all to lead from our hearts. We will need to feel. Remorse is a great first step. Forgiveness and confession are all signs of a changed heart. We need those; and only God can help us there. We also need a spiritual revelation to get to the place of change—not just belief in Jesus, but nothing short of a complete and utter conversion to the *ways of Jesus*. And surely, our head and our hands must follow.

We will all need a reordering and reshaping—internally, externally, structurally, and systemically—that must be thorough, intentional, and timely. There will be apologies, wrongs made right, solidarity, allyship, and strategic decisions that include real changes to our current culture, along with an intolerance of the status quo. This will most likely be uncomfortable. As Franklin Leonard said, "When you're accustomed to privilege, equality feels like oppression. (It's not)."[2] The "normal" must be disrupted and in its place there needs to be determined, rugged, persistent, measurable, specific, and hopeful action to make a "new normal" that is inclusive and empowering for everyone.

So, what will that look like?

Because God is ever creative and always contextual—willing, and able to meet us right where we are—I'm reluctant to specify how this will play out. I don't want you to miss what the Spirit is saying to you, specifically. But here are some principles I'll humbly offer, that might help guide us to move toward a shared future of mutual flourishing:

- Embrace disruption. Reread the chapters that disturbed your heart and mind. Let this disruption be an invitation instead of a threat. Get curious instead of defensive and ask God for revelation and insight.
- Lean into the tension. Most of our contributors have published works on the area of expertise they've written about. Read more from them. Keep learning.

- Cultivate curiosity. Consider some further exploration with your team/church/board/family. This book could be an excellent group study for staff members or future leaders.
- Learn how change can happen. As a helpful next step, we've put together a guided coaching cohort (Changing the Game) to help leadership teams develop strategic paths to genuine equity.
- Get honest. Do an equity and diversity assessment: Look at your theological library, your podcasts, and your go-to teachers and preachers, and notice who is shaping you. This self-assessment might be enough to convince you to start listening and learning more intentionally.
- Ask for help. There is a reason we chose the contributors to this book. Many of them are experts and have all kinds of resources that could help you. Reach out. Keep asking for help. Find some diverse voices around you and start asking them, too. You can't do this work alone. That's kind of the point.

This is not an exhaustive list, but one of these ideas might lead you to the next important step on your journey. Our deepest hope is that the truths shared in this book from our hearts to yours might lead toward discovering the way of Jesus, the healing of the church, the equipping of the saints, and the advance of the Good News and Good Ways of Jesus. Our world desperately needs to see a demonstration of what we so often and so easily proclaim.

Our dream for the outcome of this book is to see a lived reality of God's work and reign through the empowerment of the whole church. We hope to see a fulfillment of Joel's prophetic vision: God's Spirit poured out on men and women, young and old (Joel 2:28). We breathe an apostolic prayer that we all would discover the depth of God's love and test how far it can go (Eph. 3:14–21). We yearn for the Spirit-infused witness of Jesus' resurrection power that Mary was first encouraged to tell. We seek the revelatory teaching of ancient Scriptures that continue to blow our minds and expand our hearts to understand the mystery of Christ, revealed through the radical inclusion of those who "used to be outsiders" (Eph. 2:11). We envision shepherds who lead the sheep in safe passage and lay down their lives to keep the wolves at bay (John 10:11). We hope for a mutually thriving diverse people, who spend their lives demonstrating the love of God by the way they treat each other. For, as Jesus told us, this is how the world will know him.

God help us live this together.

NOTES

INTRODUCTION

1   Diana Chandler, "EC removes six churches from cooperation including Saddleback Church," *Biblical Recorder*, February 21, 2023, https://www.brnow.org/news/ec-removes-six-churches-from-cooperation-including-saddleback-church/.

2   See Simon & Schuster, "About the Author: Rick Warren," https://www.simonandschuster.com/authors/Rick-Warren/39904606.

3   Rick Warren (@rickwarren), "My biggest regret in 53 years of ministry is that I didn't do my own personal exegesis sooner on the 4 passages used to restrict women. Shame on me. I wasted those 4 yrs of Greek in college & seminary" X (formerly known as Twitter), June 10, 2023, 8:49 pm, https://twitter.com/RickWarren/status/1667620086251925505?lang=en.

4   See Barna, "Five Factors Changing Women's Relationship with Churches," June 25, 2015, https://www.barna.com/research/five-factors-changing-womens-relationship-with-churches/; Ryan P. Burge, "With Gen Z, Women Are No Longer More Religious Than Men," *Christianity Today*, July 26, 2022, https://www.christianitytoday.com/news/2022/july/young-women-not-more-religious-than-men-gender-gap-gen-z.html.

5   For example see Jack Zenger and Joseph Folkman, "Women Are Better Leaders During a Crisis," *Harvard Business Review*, December 30, 2020, https://hbr.org/2020/12/research-women-are-better-leaders-during-a-crisis; Jack Zenger and Joseph Folkman, "Women Score Higher Than Men in Most Leadership Skills," *Harvard Business Review*, June 25, 2019, https://hbr.org/2019/06/research-women-score-higher-than-men-in-most-leadership-skills; Carles Muntaner and Edwin Ng, "Here's why having more women in government is good for your health," *World Economic Forum*, January 16, 2019, https://www.weforum.org/agenda/2019/01/the-more-women-in-government-the-healthier-a-population/; and Kevin Kruse, "New Research: Women More Effective Than Men In All Leadership Measures," *Forbes*, March 31, 2023, https://www.forbes.com/sites/kevinkruse/2023/03/31/new-research-women-more-effective-than-men-in-all-leadership-measures.

2 OTHERING

1   *The Office*, season 7, episode 25, "Search Committee Part 1," written by Paul Lieberstein, directed by Jeffrey Blitz, aired May 19, 2011 on NBC.

2   Albert Sydney Hornby, *Oxford Advanced Learner's Dictionary of Current English,* 5th ed., Jonathan Crowther, ed. (Oxford University Press, 1995), s.v. "othering."

3   Fred Dervin, "Cultural Identity, Representation and Othering," *The Routledge Handbook of Language and Intercultural Communication* 1, (2012).

4   Simone de Beauvoir, *The Second Sex*, translated and edited by H. M. Parshley (Vintage Books, 1989), xxii.

5   Caroline Criado Perez, *Invisible Women: Data Bias in a World Designed for Men* (Abrams Press, 2019).

6   John W. Rettig, Transl., *The Fathers of the Church: St. Augustine Tractates on the Gospel of John 55–111* (The Catholic University of America Press, 1994), 289.

7   Pinchas Stolper, "The Man-Woman Dynamic of Ha-Adam: A Jewish Paradigm of Marriage," *Tradition: A Journal of Orthodox Jewish Thought* 27, 1 (1992): 34–41.

8   Benjamin R. Knoll and Cammie Jo Bolin, *She Preached the Word: Women's Ordination in Modern America* (Oxford University Press, 2018).

9   See Conrad Hackett, *The Gender Gap in Religion Around the World* (Pew Research Center, 2016).

10 See Katie Lauve-Moon, *Preacher Woman: A Critical Look at Sexism without Sexists* (Oxford University Press, 2021).

11 Lisa Weaver Swartz, "Wesleyan (Anti)Feminism: A Religious Construction of Gender Equality," *Religions* 9, no. 4 (2018): 97.

12 See Alan Hirsch and Jessie Cruickshank, *Activating 5Q: Understanding and Applying 5Q in Your Church Or Organization: A User's Guide* (100 Movements Publishing, 2018).

13 Cecilia L. Ridgeway, "Why Status Matters for Inequality," *American Sociological Review* 79, no. 1 (2013): 1–16.

14 "Percentage of the U.S. population who have completed four years of college or more from 1940 to 2022, by gender," *Statista Research Department*, July 21, 2023, https://www.statista.com/statistics/184272/educational-attainment-of-college-diploma-or-higher-by-gender.

15 AJ Willingham, "More women are aiming to become church leaders. Together, they could change American Christianity," *CNN*, July 30, 2023, https://edition.cnn.com/2023/07/30/us/women-church-leadership-united-states-cec/index.html.

16 Gail Murphy-Geiss, "Married to the Minister: The Status of the Clergy Spouse as Part of a Single Two-Person Career," *Journal of Family Issues* 32, no. 7 (2011): 932–55.

17 Shelley J. Correll, Katherine R. Weisshaar, Alison T. Wynn, and JoAnne Delfino Wehner, "Inside the Black Box of Organizational Life: The Gendered Language of Performance Assessment," *American Sociological Review* 85, no. 6 (2020):1022–50.

18 bell hooks, *Black Looks: Race and Representation* (South End Press, 1992), 71.

19 Albert O. Hirschman, *Exit, Voice, and Loyalty: Responses to Decline in Firms, Organizations, and States* (Harvard University Press, 1972).

3 THE BLESSED ALLIANCE

1   Emily Field, Alexis Krivkovich, Sandra Kügele, Nicole Robinson, and Lareina Yee, "Women in the Workplace 2023," *McKinsey & Company*, October 5, 2023, https://www.mckinsey.com/featured-insights/diversity-and-inclusion/women-in-the-workplace.

2   Ivor J. Davidson, *A Public Faith: From Constantine to the Medieval World AD 312–600*, vol. 2 (BakerBooks, 2005), 98.

3   Carolyn Custis James, *Lost Women of the Bible: The Women We Thought We Knew* (Zondervan, 2008), 37.

4   Anthony A. Hoekema, *Created in God's Image* (William B. Eerdmans Publishing Company, 1986), 12.

5   Hoekema, *Created in God's Image*, 12

6   Hoekema, *Created in God's Image*, 13.

7   Hoekema, *Created in God's Image*, 14.

8   Natasha Sistrunk Robinson, *Hope for Us: Knowing God through the Nicene Creed* (Credo House Publishers, 2017), vii.

9   Hoekema, *Created in God's Image*, 14.

10 Hoekema, *Created in God's Image*, 14.

11 Hoekema, *Created in God's Image*, 14.

12 Kat Armas, *Sacred Belonging: A 40-Day Devotional on the Liberating Heart of Scripture* (Brazos Press, 2023), 9.

13 Hoekema, *Created in God's Image*, 67.

14 Carolyn Custis James, *When Life and Beliefs Collide: How Knowing God Makes a Difference* (Zondervan, 2002), 181. References for "Yahweh": Ex. 18:4; Deut. 33:7, 26, 29; Ps. 20:2; 33:20; 70:5; 89:19 (translated "strength" in the NIV); 115:9, 10, 11; 121:1, 2; 124:8; 146:5; and Hos. 13:9; references for "prophet": Isa. 30:5; Ezek. 12:14; Dan. 11:34.

15 See https://www.ebonyvisions.com.

16 Carla D. Sunberg, Jamie Wright, and Suzanne Burden, *Reclaiming Eve: The Identity & Calling of Women in the Kingdom of God* (Beacon Hill Press, 2014), 53–54.

17 Sunberg, *Reclaiming Eve*, 55–56.

18 Timothy S. Laniak, *Shame and Honor in the Book of Esther* (Scholars Press, 1998), 150–151.

19 Laniak, *Shame and Honor*, 156.

20 Kat Armas, *Abuelita Faith: What Women on the Margins Teach Us about Wisdom, Persistence, and Strength* (Brazos Press, 2021), 172.

21 Armas, *Abuelita Faith*, 155.

22 Armas, *Abuelita Faith*, 172.

23 Armas, *Abuelita Faith*, 155.

24 Nell Irvin Painter, *Sojourner Truth: A Life, A Symbol* (W.W. Norton & Company, 1996), 125.

25 Painter, *Sojourner Truth*, 126.

26 See Cathy Pieters, "Empower a Woman and a Whole Community Will Thrive," *Business Fights Poverty*, August 11, 2016, https://businessfightspoverty.org/empower-a-woman-and-a-whole-cocoa-community-will-thrive/.

27   Stanley J. Grenz, David Guretzki, and Cherith Fee Nordling, *Pocket Dictionary of Theological Terms* (IVP, 1999), 100–101, s.v. "redemption."

28   Elyse M. Fitzpatrick, *Found in Him: The Joy of the Incarnation and Our Union with Christ* (Crossway, 2013), 147.

29   Patricia S. Parker, *Race, Gender, and Leadership: Re-Envisioning Organizational Leadership from the Perspectives of African American Women Executives* (Psychology Press, 2005), 24.

30   Sandra Maria Van Opstal, *The Next Worship: Glorifying God in a Diverse World* (IVP Books, 2015), 79–80.

4   IN MEMORY OF HER

1   See W. Baxendal, "The Early Christian Women," *Bible Hub*, https://biblehub.com/sermons/auth/baxendale/the_early_christian_women.htm.

2   Elizabeth Lesser, *Cassandra Speaks: When Women Are the Storytellers, the Human Story Changes* (HarperCollins, 2020), 15.

3   Deborah F. Sawyer, *The Blackwell Companion to The Bible and Culture*, edited by John F. A. Sawyer (Blackwell Publishing, 2006), s.v. "gender."

4   See for example Rom. 16:1–7 and Acts 18:1–3.

5   Karen Jo Torjesen, *When Women Were Priests: Women's Leadership in the Early Church and the Scandal of Their Subordination in the Rise of Christianity* (HarperSanFrancisco, 1995), 33.

6   Elizabeth Gillan Muir, *A Women's History of the Christian Church: Two Thousand Years of Female Leadership* (University of Toronto Press, 2019), 10.

7   Catherine Kroeger, "The Neglected History of Women in the Early Church," *Christian History*, accessed March 23, 2019, https://www.christianitytoday.com/history/issues/issue-17/neglected-history-of-women-in-early-church.html.

8   Patricia Gundry, "The Problem with Special Women's Issues," *Christian History: Women in the Early Church*, no. 17 (1988), and Muir, *A Women's History of the Christian Church*.

9   Megan Brenan, "In-Person Religious Service Attendance is Rebounding," Gallup, June 2, 2021, https://news.gallup.com/poll/350462/person-religious-service-attendance-rebounding.aspx.

10   Torjesen, *When Women Were Priests*, 82.

11   Torjesen, *When Women Were Priests*, 37.

12   Torjesen, *When Women Were Priests*, 40.

13   Torjesen, *When Women Were Priests*, 37.

14   Torjesen, *When Women Were Priests*, 33.

15   Muir, *A Women's History of the Christian Church*, 2.

16   Torjesen, *When Women Were Priests*, 33.

17   Muir, *A Women's History of the Christian Church*, 3.

18   Rena Pederson, *The Lost Apostle: Searching for the Truth About Junia* (Jossey-Bass, 2008), Kindle loc. 1392–1394.

19   Muir, *A Women's History of the Christian Church*, 3.

20   Torjesen, *When Women Were Priests*, 20.

21   Muir, *A Women's History of the Christian Church*, 7.

22   Mimi Haddad, "Women Leaders in the Early Church," *Sojourners*, February 16, 2009, https://sojo.net/articles/women-leaders-early-church.

23   Pederson, *The Lost Apostle*, and Muir, *A Women's History of the Christian Church*, 7.

24   Haddad, "Women Leaders in the Early Church."

25   Muir, *A Women's History of the Christian Church*, 7.

26   Muir, *A Women's History of the Christian Church*, 5–6.

27   Muir, *A Women's History of the Christian Church*, 5–6.

28   Muir, *A Women's History of the Christian Church*, 5–6.

29   Muir, *A Women's History of the Christian Church*, 5.

30   Torjesen, *When Women Were Priests*, 15.

31   Torjesen, *When Women Were Priests*, 15.

32   Torjesen, *When Women Were Priests*, 15.

33   Torjesen, *When Women Were Priests*, 15.

34   "Lydia of Thyatira," *Wikipedia*, October 25, 2023, https://en.wikipedia.org/wiki/Lydia_of_Thyatira.

35   Carla D. Sunberg, *The Cappadocian Mothers: Deification Exemplified in the Writings of Basil, Gregory, and Gregoy* (Pickwick Publications, 2017), 1.

36   Sunberg, *The Cappadocian Mothers*, ix.

37   W. K. Lowther Clarke, ed., "Medieval Sourcebook: Gregory of Nyssa (c.335–d.c.395): Life of Macrina," *Fordham University*, accessed April 4, 2021, https://sourcebooks.fordham.edu/basis/macrina.asp.

38   Sunberg, *The Cappadocian Mothers*, 137.

39   Clarke, "Medieval Sourcebook."

40   Clarke, "Medieval Sourcebook."

41   Lynn H. Cohick and Amy Brown Hughes, *Christian Women in the Patristic World: Their Influence, Authority, and Legacy in the Second through Fifth Centuries* (Baker Academic, 2017), 20–21. See also Schaff, Philip, ed., *The Complete Works of St. Augustine* (Patristic Publishing, 2019), Kindle location 4760-4761.

42   Edward Smither, "Pastoral Lessons from Augustine's Theological Correspondence with Women," *HTS Teologiese Studies/Theological Studies* 72, no. 4 (August 2016): 2.

43   Schaff, *The Complete Works*, 120.

44   Smither, "Pastoral Lessons," 2.

45   Smither, "Pastoral Lessons," 2, 5.

SECTION TWO: ALL ARE MADE IN THE *IMAGO DEI*

1   Jeff Miller, "7 Places Where Gender-Inclusive Bible Translation Really Matters: Part 1," *CBE International*, April 25, 2016, https://www.cbeinternational.org/resource/7-places-where-gender-inclusive-bible-translation-really-matters-part-1.

6 WOMEN WERE MADE STRONG

1   Danielle Strickland, "Women Were Made Strong w/ Jo Saxton," March 10, 2021, in *Right Side Up podcast with Danielle Strickland*, https://daniellestrickland.substack.com/p/women-were-made-strong-w-jo-saxton-077.

2   See R. David Freedman, "Woman, a Power Equal to Man," available at https://temple.splendidsun.com/PDF/equalto.pdf.

3   Michele Guinness, "Can women have it all?" *Church Times*, April 30, 2021, https://www.churchtimes.co.uk/articles/2021/30-april/faith/faith-features/can-women-have-it-all.

7 GOD IS NOT A MAN

1   Other examples of Renaissance painters' depictions of God as an elderly white male include Vittore Carpaccio's *Glorification of St. Ursula and Her Companions* (1491), Raphael's *Ezekiel's Vision* (1518), the anonymous painter from Westphalia's *God the Father on a throne, with the Virgin Mary and Jesus* (late 15th century), Cima da Conegliano's *God the Father* (1510–1517), Peter Paul Rubens, *God the Father* (1628), or Pieter de Grebber's *God Inviting Christ to Sit on the Throne at His Right Hand* (1645). Later depictions of God the Father as a white male include William Blake's *The Ancient of Days* (1794) and Victor Mikhailovich Vasnetsov's *Savaoph, God the Father* (1885–96).

2   Explanations include the early church's understanding that God is speaking as Father, Son, and Holy Spirit, though this is more a theological interpretation than exegetical. God speaking on behalf of the Divine Council has support.

3   In the Septuagint Version of the Old Testament, the Scriptures most cited by New Testament writers, the Greek translators used the proper name *Adam* much earlier, beginning in Genesis 2:16, when God first speaks to the human being.

4   The divine name YHWH reflects the Hebrew consonants, which in the Masoretic Text are marked with the vowels of *Adonai*, Lord. From now on I will use "Lord" in deference to the Jewish tradition and Septuagint's *kurios*.

5   The Greek Version of Genesis 1:26-28 uses the non-gendered term *anthropos*, which could be translated "humankind," as in the NETS translation of the Septuagint.

6   Robert Alter, ed., *Genesis: Translation and Commentary* (W. W. Norton and Company, 1996), 5.

7   Writes Alter, "In the middle clause of this verse, "him," as in the Hebrew, is grammatically but not anatomically masculine." *Genesis*, 5.

8   Francis Brown, S. R. Driver, and Charles A. Briggs, *A Hebrew and English Lexicon of the Old Testament*, abridged (Clarendon Press, 1907), 9–10.

9   Phyllis Trible, "Depatriarchalizing in Biblical Interpretation," *Journal of the American Academy of Religion* 41, no. 1 (March 1973): 35.

10   These Hebrew terms for male and female humans are used consistently for male and female animals (Gen. 6:19; 7:3, 9, 16). In contrast, Genesis 2:23 uses the gender terms woman (*ešâ*) and man (*'îš*).

11   Johannes P. Louw and Eugene Albert Nida, eds., *Greek-English Lexicon of the New Testament*, Accordance electronic edition, 59.62.

12   See also 1 Cor. 3:6; 2 Cor. 9:10, 10:15; Eph. 4:15; Col. 1:10; 1 Pet. 2:2; 2 Pet 3:18.

13   Louw and Nida, *Greek-English Lexicon of the New Testament*, 59.68.

14   Mark S. Smith, *The Priestly Vision of Genesis 1* (Fortress Press, 2010), 134–35.

15   The Lord God here translates the divine name YHWH together with *Elohim*.

16   The Hebrew pronouns are only male or female. However, since the human is not inherently "male" until the woman is fashioned and differentiated from him, "a helper opposite it" is a possible translation.

17   Going with this translation, Phyllis Trible writes: "Corresponding to it" *kenegdo*, "tempers this connotation of superiority to specify identity, mutuality, and equality," Phyllis Trible, *God and the Rhetoric of Sexuality: Overtures to Biblical Theology* (Fortress Press, 1978), 90.

18   The Septuagint of Genesis 2:18's *boethon kata auto*—"I will make for it helper corresponding to him" (NET)—is followed by Genesis 2:20's *boethos homoios auto*—"a helper like him" (NET). The Hebrew can be translated "But as for 'adama,' it did not find a companion corresponding to itself." See Phyllis Trible, *God and the Rhetoric of Sexuality*, 90.

19   Trible, *God and the Rhetoric of Sexuality*, 90.

20   Trible, "Depatriarchalizing in Biblical Interpretation," 36.

21   See also Deut. 33:7, 26; Isa. 49:8; 50:7, 9; 63:5; Hos. 13:9; Ps. 10:14; 20:2; 28:7; 37:40; 46:5; 54:4; 70:5; 72:12; 79:9; 86:17; 89:19; 109:26; 115:9, 10, 11; 118:7, 13; 119:86, 173, 175; 121:1, 2; 124:8; 146:5; Job 26:2; 29:12; 1 Chron. 5:20; 15:26; 2 Chron. 14:11; 18:31; 25:8; 26:7; 32:8.

22   The Hebrew terms *ish* and *isha* can signify "man, husband, or biological male," and "woman, wife, or biological female." See Brown, Driver, and Briggs, *A Hebrew and English Lexicon of the Old Testament*, 35.

23   Trible, *God and the Rhetoric of Sexuality*, 99.

24   The dual form of the Hebrew term for breasts, *shad*, is used (see Brown, Driver, and Briggs, *A Hebrew and English Lexicon of the Old Testament*, abridged, 7699), excluding the mistaken translation of "many breasted God." *El Shaddai* occurs in Gen. 17:1; 28:3; 35:11; 43:14; 48:3; Exod. 6:3; 10:5).

25   See R. Chris Fraley, "A Brief Overview of Adult Attachment Theory and Research" (University of Illinois), http://labs.psychology.illinois.edu/~rcfraley/attachment.htm. See also John Bowlby, *A Secure Base: Parent-Child Attachment and Healthy Human Development* (Basic Books, 1988) and Mary D. Salter Ainsworth, "Object Relations, Dependency, and Attachment: A Theoretical Review of the Infant-Mother Relationship," *Child Development*, 40 (1969): 969–1025.

26   Bruce Fink, *An Introduction to Lacanian Psychoanalysis* (NYU Press, 1997), n.

27   In Luke's Gospel, "women who had come with Him [Jesus] out of Galilee" are identified as the first witnesses to his resurrection and told these things to the eleven male disciples. They are identified as Mary Magdalene, Joanna, Mary the mother of James, and "other women with them" (Luke 23:55; 24:10). See also Matthew 28:1–10 and Mark 16:9–11.

8   THE HAND THAT ROCKED THE MESSIAH'S CRADLE

1   William Ross Wallace, "The Hand That Rocks the Cradle (1865)," *Wikisource*, May 28, 2020, https://en.wikisource.org/wiki/The_Hand_That_Rocks_the_Cradle.

2   On Mary, see my book *The Real Mary: Why Evangelical Christians Can Embrace the Mother of Jesus* (Paraclete, 2016).

3   Scot McKnight, *The Second Testament: A New Translation* (IVP Academic, 2023).

4   In Mark 6:3, Jesus is mentioned as only being the son of Mary and the sibling of James, Joses, Judas, and Simon. There is no mention of his father, Joseph. Given individuals at the time were primarily associated with their paternal lineage, it seems likely that Joseph was no longer alive at this point.

5   On kingdom, as sketched here, see my book *Kingdom Conspiracy: Returning to the Radical Mission of the Local Church* (Baker Academic, 2016).

9   WHAT DO WE DO WITH PAUL?

1   Lucy Peppiatt suggests that the small minority who argue that head coverings are still an applicable apostolic tradition "are more faithful to the text if we believe this to be Paul's view." See Lucy Peppiatt, *Women and Worship at Corinth: Paul's Rhetorical Arguments in 1 Corinthians* (Cascade Books, 2015), 59.

2   Peppiatt, *Women and Worship*, 42–43.

3   Peppiatt, *Women and Worship*, 43.

4   Peppiatt, *Women and Worship*.

5   Peppiatt, *Women and Worship*, 133.

6   Ben Witherington, cited in Peppiatt, *Women and Worship*, 79.

7   Peppiatt, *Women and Worship*, 133.

8   Peppiatt, *Women and Worship*, 81.

9   Peppiatt, *Women and Worship*, 62–63.

10 There are *all kinds* of problems and questions associated with this hierarchical descent, not the least of which is the apparent subordination of Christ in the Godhead, and the equating of the Father's relationship with Christ to men's relationship with women. Suffice it to say, no one is really sure what is going on here and the stakes are high, which further illustrates my overall point.

11 Lucy Peppiatt, "Man as the Image and Glory of God, and Woman as the Glory of Man: Perspicuity or Ambiguity?" *Priscilla Papers* 33, no. 3 (July 2019): 16.

12 N. M. Flanagan and E. H. Snyder, cited in Peppiatt, *Women and Worship*, 110–111.

13 Douglas A. Campbell, cited in Peppiatt, *Women and Worship*, 84.

14 Peppiatt cites Douglas A. Campbell on this form of "diatribal discussion" in *Women and Worship*, 83.

10   CRUCIAL CONVERSATIONS BETWEEN EGALITARIANS AND COMPLEMENTARIANS

1   For an expanded exploration of this content see "History Matters: Evangelicals and Women" and "Human Flourishing: Global Perspectives" in the 3rd edition of *Discovering Biblical Equality: Biblical, Theological, Cultural & Practical Perspectives*, Ronald Pierce and Cynthia Long Westfall, eds. (InterVarsity Press, 2021).

2   See Bob Allen, "Pastor says male/female roles will continue in heaven," *Baptist News Global*, March 19, 2014, https://baptistnews.com/article/pastor-says-male-female-roles-will-continue-in-heaven/.

3   Jamin Hübner documents the varied ways prominent complementarians limit or permit women's leadership. Jamin Hübner, "Revisiting the Clarity of Scripture in 1 Timothy 2:12," *Journal of the Evangelical Theological Society* 59, no. 1 (2016): 99–117, https://www.cbe.org.au/wp-content/uploads/2021/01/Hubner_1Tim2.pdf.

4   Dana L. Robert, *American Women in Mission: A Social History of Their Thought and Practice* (Mercer University Press, 1997), ix.

5   See "History," *International Mission Board*, accessed December 2, 2023, https://www.imb.org/history/.

6   "Lottie Moon," *International Mission Board*, accessed September 28, 2023, https://www.imb.org/about/lottie-moon/.

7   "Lottie Moon," *International Mission Board*.

8   "Lottie Moon," *International Mission Board*.

9   "Lottie Moon Christmas Offering," *International Mission Board*, accessed December 2, 2023, https://www.imb.org/generosity/lottie-moon-christmas-offering/.

10 Ruth Tucker, "Lottie Moon: 'Saint' of the Southern Baptists," *Mission Frontiers*, January 1, 1999, https://www.missionfrontiers.org/issue/article/lottie-moon-saint-of-the-southern-baptists.

11 "Lottie Moon Christmas Offering," *International Mission Board*.

12 "Lottie Moon Christmas Offering," *International Mission Board*.

13 "VI. The Church," *Baptist Faith & Message 2000*, https://bfm.sbc.net/bfm2000/#vi. See also Mark Wingfield, "13 Southern Baptist Missionaries Fired for Refusal to Affirm Faith Statement," *Good Faith Media*, May 12, 2003, https://goodfaithmedia.org/13-southern-baptist-missionaries-fired-for-refusal-to-affirm-faith-statement-cms-2546/.

14 CBE honored SBC missionaries who refused to sign the Baptist Faith and Message 2000 with the Priscilla and Aquila Award that recognizes those who have made sacrifices for the sake of biblical equality for women, just as Priscilla and Aquila "risked their lives" (Rom. 16:4) for the sake of the gospel. The first Priscilla and Aquila Award was awarded at CBE's first conference in 1989. See "Priscilla and Aquila Award Recipients," *Christians for Biblical Equality*, https://www.cbeinternational.org/primary_page/priscilla-and-aquila-award-recipients.

15 See Wayne Grudem, *Evangelical Feminism: A New Path to Liberalism?* (Crossway, 2006).

16 See Ruth A. Tucker and Walter Liefeld, *Daughters of the Church: Women and Ministry from New Testament Times to the Present.* (Zondervan Publishing, 1987).

17 K. Kris Hurst, "'Who Controls the Past Controls the Future' Quote Meaning: What George Orwell Meant and How That Applies Today," *ThoughtCo.*, June 11, 2019, https://www.thoughtco.com/what-does-that-quote-mean-archaeology-172300.

18 Bruce Ware, "Could Our Savior Have Been a Woman? The Relevance of Jesus' Gender for His Incarnational Mission," *Journal for Biblical Manhood and Womanhood* 8, no. 1 (Spring 2003): 31–38, https://cbmw.org/wp-content/uploads/2013/05/8-1.pdf.

19 Denny Burk, "Mark Driscoll on Women in Ministry," *Denny Burk*, July 5, 2007, https://www.dennyburk.com/mark-driscoll-on-women-in-ministry-2.

20 John Piper, "'The Frank and Manly Mr. Ryle'—The Value of a Masculine Ministry,"

from the *Desiring God* 2012 Conference for Pastors, January 31, 2012, http://www. desiringgod.org/resource-library/biographies/the-frank-and-manly-mr-ryle-the-value-of-a-masculine-ministry.

21 Owen Strachan (@ostrachan), Twitter post, August 14, 2014, https://twitter.com/ ostrachan/status/499933939767574529.

22 David Mathis, "Why Jesus Was Not a Woman," *Desiring God*, October 11, 2020, https:// www.desiringgod.org/articles/why-jesus-was-not-a-woman.

23 Mathis, "Why Jesus Was Not a Woman."

24 Outlined in Rom. 12:6–8; 1 Cor. 12:8–10, 28–30; and Eph. 4:11.

25 See *"To Gar Aprosleptom atherapeuton"* Gregory of Nazianzus, "Epistle 101," in Hardy, *Christology of the Later Fathers* (Westminster John Knox Press, 1954), 218.

26 Num. 23:19 reads, "God is not a man...." The Hebrew for "man" is a masculine noun.

27 Ps. 22:9; Luke 13:20–21, 15:9.

28 Clement of Alexandria, *Christ the Educator*, translated by Simon P. Wood (Catholic University of America, 1954), 41, 43. Much of chapter 6 engages the God-as-mother metaphor.

29 Anselm of Aosta, *The Prayers and Meditations of St. Anselm with the Proslogion*, quoted by Jennifer P. Heimmel, *"God is our Mother": Julian of Norwich and the Medieval Image of Christian Feminine Divinity* (Institut für Anglistik und Amerikanistik Universitat, 1982), 153–154.

30 Edmund Colledge and James Walsh, translators, *Julian of Norwich: Showings* (Paulist Press, 1978), 293.

31 Teresa of Avila, *The Interior Castle*, translated by Kieran Kavanaugh and Otilio Rodriquez (Paulist Press, 1979), 179–80.

32 Søren Kierkegaard, *Christian Discourses*, translated by Walter Lowrie (Oxford University Press, 1939), 298–300.

33 See Evangelical Theological Society sessions: Wayne Grudem, "Submission and Subordination in the Trinity," November 2016, 68th Annual Meeting of the ETS, MP3 audio, https://www.wordmp3.com/product-group.aspx?id=534; and Millard Erickson, "Language, Logic, and Trinity," November 2016, *ETS National*, MP3 audio, https://www. wordmp3.com/details.aspx?id=24123. See also Bruce A. Ware, *Father, Son, & Holy Spirit: Relationships, Roles & Relevance* (Crossway, 2005).

34 Ware, *Father, Son, & Holy Spirit*, 151–153; Roger E. Olson, "Quick Post Re: Praying to Jesus?" *Patheos*, December 10, 2011, http://www.patheos.com/blogs/rogere-olson/2011/12/quick-post-re-praying-to-jesus/; Cheryl Schatz, "Jesus Unequal in Prayer?" *Women in Ministry*, December 21, 2007, http://www.strivetoenter.com/wim/2007/12/21/ jesus-unequal-in-prayer.

35 Phillip Carey, "The New Evangelical Subordinationism: Reading Inequality into the Trinity," *Priscilla Papers* 20, no. 4 (Autumn 2006): 42.

36 Kevin Giles, as quoted here: "Kevin Giles of ESS," *Reformation 21*, December 22, 2016, https://www.reformation21.org/mos/1517/kevin-giles-on-ess.

37 Giles, "Kevin Giles."

38 Piper, "'The Frank and Manly Mr. Ryle.'"

39 Matt. 28:1, 5–10; Mark 16:1–11; Luke 24:9–12; John 20:1–23.

40 John 20:17.

41 Luke 13:10–16.

42 See https://seedbed.com/was-paul-for-or-against-women-in-ministry.

43 Marg Mowczko, "There are Women Pastors in the New Testament," *Marg Mowczko*, May 9, 2021, https://margmowczko.com/women-pastors-new-testament.

44 The content that follows is also found in my chapter, "Human Flourishing: Global Perspectives," in *Discovering Biblical Equality: Biblical, Cultural & Practical Perspectives*, eds Ronald W. Pierce, Cynthia Long Westfall, and Christa L McKirland (IVP, 2021), 620–634.

45 Mimi Haddad, "Silent No More: Exposing Abuse Amongst Evangelicals," *CBE International*, July 21, 2016, https://www.cbeinternational.org/resource/silent-no-more-exposing-abuse-among-evangelicals.

46 See Jack Balswick, Judy Balswick, and Thomas Frederick, *The Family: A Christian Perspective on the Contemporary Home* (Baker Academic, 2021). See also Shuji G. Asai and David H. Olson, "Spouse Abuse & Marital System Based on ENRICH," https://app.prepare-enrich.com/pe/pdf/research/abuse.pdf accessed March 27, 2024. See also Mimi Haddad, "Human Flourishing: Global Perspectives" in *Discovering Biblical Equality: Biblical, Cultural & Practical Perspectives*, eds Ronald W. Pierce, Cynthia Long Westfall, and Christa L. McKirland (IVP, 2021), 620–634.

47 Steven Tracy, "Headship with a Heart: How biblical patriarchy actually prevents abuse," *Christianity Today*, last modified February 1, 2003. Available online at https://www.christianitytoday.com/ct/2003/february/5.50.html, accessed February 1, 2019.

48 Michelle Lee Barnewall, *Neither Complementarian nor Egalitarian: A Kingdom Corrective to the Evangelical Gender Debate* (Baker Academic, 2016).

49 Barnewall, *Neither Complementarian nor Egalitarian*, 63, 84–145.

50 "Table P-40: Women's Earnings as a Percentage of Men's Earnings by Race and Hispanic Origin," *United States Census Bureau*, accessed July 3, 2018, https://www.census.gov/data/tables/time-series/demo/income-poverty/historical-income-people.html.

51 Shannan Catalano, "Special Report: Intimate Partner Violence, 1993–2010," *US Department of Justice Office of Justice Programs, Bureau of Justice Statistics*, last modified September 29, 2015, https://bjs.ojp.gov/library/publications/intimate-partner-violence-1993-2010, accessed February 1, 2019.

52 Richard B. Hays, *The Moral Vision of the New Testament: A Contemporary Introduction to New Testament Ethics* (HarperSanFrancisco, 1996), 197. Barnewall's citation of Hays omits his clear affirmation of women's equality as biblical. See Barnewall, *Neither Complementarian nor Egalitarian*, 176.

53 See Elizabeth Beyer, ed., *Created to Thrive: Cultivating Abuse-Free Faith Communities*, https://cbeinternational.christianbook.com/created-thrive-cultivating-faith-communities-ebook/9781939971913/pd/119547EB?event=ERRCER1.

54 "What Americans Think About Women in Power," *Barna*, March 8, 2017, https://www.barna.com/research/americans-think-women-power.

55 See H. L. Johnson, *Pipelines, Pathways, and Institutional Leadership: An Update on the Status of Women in Higher Education*, American Council on Education, Higher Ed Spotlight infographic Brief, 2016 as cited by Karen A. Longman in her 2016 Pepperdine CCCU lecture, "Women in Leadership in Higher Education, Half the Sky: What's the Current Picture of Women in Leadership?" For more information see, https://www.acenet.edu/Documents/Higher-Ed-Spotlight-Pipelines-Pathways-and-Institutional-Leadership-Status-of-Women.pdf.

56 Emily Louise Zimbrick-Rogers, "'A Question Mark Over My Head': Experiences of Women ETS Members at the 2014 ETS Annual Meeting," *A Question Mark Over My Head: A Special Edition Journal of Christians for Biblical Equality*, 2015, 4–10, https://cbeinternational.org/wp-content/uploads/2015/12/ETS2015-web.pdf.

57 Amy Novotney, "Women leaders make work better. Here's the science behind how to promote them," *American Psychological Association*, March 23, 2023, https://www.apa.org/topics/women-girls/female-leaders-make-work-better. See also the Peterson Institute for Economics, "New research from The Peterson Institute for International Economics and EY reveals significant correlation between women in corporate leadership and profitability," *PR Newswire*, February 8, 2016, https://www.prnewswire.com/news-releases/new-research-from-the-peterson-institute-for-international-economics-and-ey-reveals-significant-correlation-between-women-in-corporate-leadership-and-profitability-300216273.html.

58 William Wan, "What makes some men sexual harassers?" *Pittsburgh Post-Gazette*, December 31, 2017, http://www.post-gazette.com/opinion/Op-Ed/2017/12/31/What-makes-some-men-sexual-harassers/stories/201712310300.

59 Barbara Roberts, "Bruce Ware teaches that a wife's lack of submission threatens her husband's authority, and he responds to this threat by abusing her," *A Cry For Justice*, August 22, 2016, https://cryingoutforjustice.blog/2016/08/22/bruce-ware-teaches-that-a-wifes-lack-of-submission-threatens-her-husbands-authority-and-he-responds-to-this-threat-by-abusing-her.

60 Wan, "What makes some men sexual harassers?"

61 Wan, "What makes some men sexual harassers?"

62 William Wan, "What makes some men sexual harassers? Science tries to explain the creeps of the world," *Washington Post*, December 20, 2017, https://www.washingtonpost.com/news/speaking-of-science/wp/2017/12/20/what-makes-some-men-sexual-harassers-science-tries-to-explain-the-harvey-weinsteins-of-the-world/.

63 "The Porn Phenomenon: The Impact of Pornography in the Digital Age," *Barna*, https://www.barna.com/the-porn-phenomenon.

64 Ruth Graham, "Why Southern Baptists are Furious Over a Sex Abuse Case in Kentucky," *New York Times*, November 7, 2023, https://www.nytimes.com/2023/11/07/us/baptists-abuse-kentucky.html.

SECTION THREE: THE COST OF PATRIARCHY

1 *Encyclopedia Britannica*, s.v. "patriarchy," accessed March 26, 2024, https://www.britannica.com/topic/patriarchy.

12 COLLABORATIVE LEADERSHIP: MORE KIN*DOM, LESS EMPIRE

1 "Global Gender Gap Report 2023," *World Economic Forum*, June 20, 2023, https://www.weforum.org/publications/global-gender-gap-report-2023/in-full/benchmarking-gender-gaps-2023.

2 "Global Gender Gap Report 2023."

3 Geoff Bennett and Shoshana Dubnow, "Southern Baptist Convention bans female pastors,

ejecting several churches in the process," *PBS News Hour*, June 15, 2023, https://www.pbs.org/newshour/show/southern-baptist-convention-bans-female-pastors-ejecting-several-churches-in-the-process.

4   "7 Christian denominations that don't allow women to serve as pastor," *The Christian Post*, August 14, 2023, https://www.christianpost.com/news/7-christian-denominations-that-do-not-allow-women-pastors.html.

5   "Zero-sum games" refer to competition where one party gains at the expense of another party. When that happens there really are no winners, as the outcome is always zero.

6   "Set-man thinking" is a theology seen often in churches where it is believed that God deals with people through a man, rather than through a group. Much of this thinking relates to the way God worked through Abraham, Isaac, Jacob, etc. This theology is faulty and dangerous because it is always lived out as a master-and-slave, teacher-and-student, over-and-under system of hierarchy (power and control), which is an empire model.

7   Antonio González, *God's Reign & the End of Empires (Kyrios)* (Convivium Press, 2012).

8   Read about the alliance between church and empire in "Christianity from the 16th to the 21st Century," *Encyclopaedia Britannica*, https://www.britannica.com/topic/Christianity/Christianity-from-the-16th-to-the-21st-century.

9   Joerg Rieger, *Jesus vs. Caesar: For People Tired of Serving the Wrong God* (Abingdon Press, 2018), XI.

10 See Travis Tomchuck, "The Doctrine of Discovery," *Canadian Museum for Human Rights*, May 11, 2023, https://humanrights.ca/story/doctrine-discovery.

11 See "Manifest Destiny," *History Channel*, November 15, 2019, https://www.history.com/topics/19th-century/manifest-destiny.

12 Paul D. Miller, "What Is Christian Nationalism?" *Christianity Today*, February 3, 2021, https://www.christianitytoday.com/ct/2021/february-web-only/what-is-christian-nationalism.html.

13 Joerg Rieger, *Christ and Empire* (Fortress Press, 2007), 2–3.

14 Joerg Rieger, *Jesus vs. Caesar*, 1.

15 Ruth Mace, "How did the patriarchy start—and will evolution get rid of it?" *The Conversation*, September 20, 2022, https://theconversation.com/how-did-the-patriarchy-start-and-will-evolution-get-rid-of-it-189648.

16 The Bible documents the influence of women in Jesus' ministry: Mary and Martha (Luke 10:38–42); Mary Magdalene, Joanna, and Susanna (Luke 8:2–3); and many women were involved in leadership in the early church. See Catherine Kroeger, "The Neglected History of Women in the Early Church," *Christian History*, vol. 7 (1, 17), https://christianhistoryinstitute.org/magazine/article/women-in-the-early-church.

17 See the archived Barna report, "Christian Women Today, Part 1 of 4: What Women Think of Faith, Leadership and Their Role in the Church" August 13, 2012, at https://www.barna.com/research/christian-women-today-part-1-of-4-what-women-think-of-faith-leadership-and-their-role-in-the-church, accessed December 10, 2023.

18 A. J. Willingham, "More women are aiming to become church leaders. Together, they could change American Christianity," CNN.com, July 30, 2023, https://www.cnn.com/2023/07/30/us/women-church-leadership-united-states.

19 *Merriam-Webster's Collegiate Dictionary* (2003), s.v. "collaborate."

20 See Isa. 58:12.

21 Matthew Henry and Thomas Scott, "Judges 4," in *Matthew Henry's Concise Commentary* (Logos Research Systems, 1997).

22 Inés Velásquez-McBryde, email exchange with author, December 14, 2023; shared with permission.

23 Timothy C. Geoffrion, *The Spirit-Led Leader: Nine Leadership Practices and Soul Principles* (Rowman & Littlefield Publishers, 2014), 130.

24 Saehee Duran, "Intentional Male Allies/Advocates: How Male Leaders Can Successfully Champion Female Ministers in the Assemblies of God U.S.A." (doctoral dissertation, Southeastern University, 2022), vii; available at https://firescholars.seu.edu/dmin/23/.

25 Inés Velásquez-McBryde, email exchange with author, December 14, 2023; shared with permission.

26 The term "phygital" is a combination of physical and digital spaces; the term was coined in 2007 by Chris Weil.

13 THE MAKING OF *THE MAKING OF BIBLICAL WOMANHOOD*

1 Danielle Strickland, "Burn Down the Patriarchy with Beth Allison Barr," *Right Side Up Podcast with Danielle Strickland*, February 28, 2022, podcast, https://daniellestrickland. substack.com/p/burn-down-the-patriarchy-with-beth-2fa#details.

2 Beth Allison Barr, *The Making of Biblical Womanhood: How the Subjugation of Women Became Gospel Truth* (Brazos Press, 2021).

3 See https://bfm.sbc.net/bfm2000/.

4 Beth Allison Barr, "Some Hope for Evangelicalism," *Patheos: The Anxious Bench*, August 4, 2021, https://www.patheos.com/blogs/anxiousbench/2021/08/some-hope-for-evange licalisms-future-black-womens-voices-and-a-church-called-tov.

5 Beverly Roberts Gaventa, *Our Mother Saint Paul* (John Knox Press, 2007).

14 MIND THE GAP

1 William Booth, *Orders and Regulations for Officers in the Salvation Army* (Headquarters of The Salvation Army, 1895).

2 Pamela J. Walker, *Pulling the Devil's Kingdom Down: The Salvation Army in Victorian Britain* (University of California Press, 2001), 2.

3 Walker, *Pulling the Devil's Kingdom Down*, 2.

4 Walker, *Pulling the Devil's Kingdom Down*, 2.

5 "The Salvation Army International Positional Statement: Sexism," May, 2019, https:// salvationist.ca/files/salvationarmy/Magazines/2019/July/IPS-Sexism.pdf.

6 Janet Munn, *Theory and Practice of Gender Equality in The Salvation Army* (CreateSpace Independent Publishing Platform, 2015).

7 Sue Swanson, "Report to The Salvation Army International Conference of Leaders," Toronto, Canada, July 2012.

8 Linda McKinnish Bridges, "Women in Church Leadership," *Review and Expositor* 95, no. 3 (August 1998).

9 Bridges, "Women in Church Leadership."

10 Patricia Hollis, *Women in Public, 1850–1900: Documents of the Victorian Women's Movement* (George Allen and Unwin Publishers, Ltd, 1979), 264.

11 Dale R. Baker, "Teaching for Gender Difference," *National Association for Research in Science Teaching (NARST)*, 1988, https://narst.org/research-matters/teaching-for-gender-difference.

12 Melinda Gates, "Gender Equality Is Within Our Reach," *Harvard Business Review*, September 26, 2019, hbr.org/cover-story/2019/09/gender-equality-is-within-our-reach.

13 "Global Gender Gap Report 2021," *World Economic Forum*, March 30, 2021, http://www3.weforum.org/docs/WEF_GGGR_2021.pdf.

14 John Hendra, "Speech by John Hendra on 'Feminization of Poverty in Rural Areas,'" *UN Women*, March 13, 2014, http://www.unwomen.org/en/news/stories/2014/3/john-hendra-speech-on-feminization-of-poverty.

15 Referred to as "mansplaining" and "gaslighting."

16 Nicholas D. Kristof and Sheryl WuDunn, *Half the Sky: Turning Oppression into Opportunity for Women Worldwide* (Vintage, 2010), p. xiv.

17 Sten Johansson and Ola Nygren, "The Missing Girls of China: A New Demographic Account," *Population and Development Review* 17, no. 1 (March 1991): 35–51.

18 Marie Vlachová and Lea Biason, eds., *Women in an Insecure World: Violence Against Women: Facts, Figures and Analysis* (Geneva Centre for Democratic Control of Armed Forces, 2005), vii.

19 UNFPA (United Nations Population Fund), "State of World Population 2000—Lives Together, Worlds Apart: Men and Women in a Time of Change," *UNFPA* (2000), chap. 3, https://www.unfpa.org/publications/state-world-population-2000.

20 International Labour Organization, "2016 Global Estimates of Modern Slavery," *International Labour Organization*, September 19, 2017, https://www.ilo.org/wcmsp5/groups/public/@ed_norm/@declaration/documents/publication/wcms_575605.pdf.

21 See "Achieve gender equality and empower all women and girls," infographic, *United Nations*, https://sdgs.un.org/goals/goal5.

See also, "Sustainable Development Goal 5: Achieve gender equality and empower all women and girls," *United Nations*, 2023, https://sustainabledevelopment.un.org/sdg5. The economic empowerment of women is a prerequisite for sustainable development.

22 Clara Julich, Grzegorz Trojanowski, Michelle K. Ryan, S. Alexander Haslam, and Luc D. R. Renneboog, "Who gets the carrot and who gets the stick? Evidence of gender disparities in executive remuneration," *Strategic Management Journal* 32, issue 3 (March 2011): 301–321, onlinelibrary.wiley.com/doi/10.1002/smj.878/abstract.

23 "Gender Equality," *Bill & Melinda Gates Foundation*, https://www.gatesfoundation.org/goalkeepers/report/2019-report/progress-indicators/gender-equality.

24 Balgis Osman-Elasha, "Women ... In The Shadow of Climate Change," *United Nations*, 2009, https://www.un.org/en/chronicle/article/womenin-shadow-climate-change.

25 Nicholas D. Kristof and Sheryl WuDunn, "The Women's Crusade," *New York Times*, August 17, 2009, www.nytimes.com/2009/08/23/magazine/23Women-t.html.

26 Nicholas D. Kristof, Sheryl WuDunn, and Melanie Verveer, "The Political and Economic Power of Women," speech presented as ambassador-at-large for global women's issues at the Center for International Private Enterprise, Washington DC, June 20, 2011.

27 "Global Gender Gap Report 2023," *World Economic Forum*, June 20, 2023, https://www.weforum.org/reports/global-gender-gap-report-2023/.

286 | NEED TO KNOW

28 Tomas Chamorro-Premuzic, "Why Do So Many Incompetent Men Become Leaders?" *Harvard Business Review*, August 22, 2013, https://hbr.org/2013/08/why-do-so-many-incompetent-men.

29 "The Salvation Army International Development Policy: Gender Equity," *Issuu*, https://issuu.com/isjc/docs/gender_equity/1?e=18664572/15220284.

30 See Iris Bohnet, "We can't get rid of bias—but we can disrupt it by design," *Evoke*, March 5, 2019, accessed October 5, 2019, www.evoke.org/articles/March_2019/Forward/Big_Ideas/disrupting_bias_by_design.

31 "Gender Equality," *Gates Foundation*.

32 See www.cbeinternational.org.

33 See www.amightygirl.com.

34 Eric Bock, "Awareness is Not Enough: Bohnet Discusses Gender Bias in the Workplace," *NIH Record*, April 14, 2023, https://nihrecord.nih.gov/2023/04/14/bohnet-discusses-gender-bias-workplace.

35 Jackson Katz, *The Macho Paradox: Why Some Men Hurt Women and How All Men Can Help* (Sourcebooks, 2006).

36 Jackson Katz, "Violence against women—it's a men's issue," TedTalk, November 2012, https://www.ted.com/talks/jackson_katz_violence_against_women_it_s_a_men_s_issue.

37 Walter Brueggemann, *Genesis: Interpretation: A Bible Commentary for Teaching and Preaching* (John Knox Press, 2010), 32, 34.

38 Marianne Schnall, "Madeleine Albright: An Exclusive Interview," *Huffpost*, June 15, 2010, https://www.huffpost.com/entry/madeleine-albright-an-exc_b_604418.

39 Paul Feinberg, "Remembering Martin Luther King Jr.'s 1965 UCLA Speech," *UCLA Anderson School of Management*, January 21, 2022, https://www.anderson.ucla.edu/news-and-events/remembering-martin-luther-king-jrs-1965-ucla-speech.

15 WHAT I NEED YOU TO KNOW (LORI ANNE THOMPSON)

1 Judith L. Herman, MD, *Truth and Repair: How Trauma Survivors Envision Justice* (Basic Books, 2023).

2 Judith L. Herman, MD, *Trauma and Recovery: The Aftermath of Violence—From Domestic Abuse to Political Terror* (Basic Books, 1997); and Judith L. Herman, MD, "Recovery from psychological trauma," *Psychiatry and Clinical Neurosciences* 52, no. S1 (September 1998): S105–S110, https://doi.org/10.1046/j.1440-1819.1998.0520s5S145.x.

3 See the CDC's "National Intimate Partner and Sexual Violence Survey: 2010 Summary Report," https://www.cdc.gov/violenceprevention/pdf/nisvs_report2010-a.pdf.

4 Wanda Lott Collins, "Silence sufferers: Female clergy sexual abuse," *Baylor University School of Social Work, Research and Application*, Spring 2009, https://www.baylor.edu/content/services/document.php/145861.pdf.

5 Victor I. Vieth, "What Would Walther Do? Applying Law and Gospel to Victims and Perpetrators of Child Sexual Abuse," *Journal of Psychology and Theology* 40, no. 4 (December 2012): 257–273.

6 Dictionary.com, s.v. "praxis," https://www.dictionary.com/browse/praxis.

7 Oxford Learner's Dictionaries, s.v. "praxis," https://www.oxfordlearnersdictionaries.com/definition/english/praxis?q=praxis.

8   Paulo Freire, *Pedagogy of the Oppressed*, translated by Myra Bergman Ramos (Herder and Herder, 1972).

9   Herman, *Truth and Repair*.

10 Herman, *Truth and Repair*.

16 DRESSING THE WOUNDS OF ABUSE

1   For information about abuse among clergy, see Diane Langberg, "Statistics," *Not In Our Church*, https://www.notinourchurch.com/statistics.html. Comparatively, for information about abuse in the workplace, see "In 2020, one in four women and one in six men reported having experienced inappropriate sexualized behaviours at work in the previous year," *Statistics Canada*, August 12, 2021, https://www150.statcan.gc.ca/n1/daily-quotidien/210812/dq210812b-eng.htm.

2   "What is harm?" *South Lanarkshire Adult Protection Committee*, https://www.adultprotectionsouthlanarkshire.org.uk/info/55/more_about_harm.

3   "Scores of priests involved in sexual abuse cases," *Boston Globe*, May 30, 2012, https://www.bostonglobe.com/news/special-reports/2002/01/31/scores-priests-involved-sex-abuse-cases/kmRm7JtqBdEZ8UF0ucR16L/story.html.

4   Sarah Pulliam Bailey, "Southern Baptist leaders covered up sex abuse, kept secret database, report says," *The Washington Post*, May 22, 2022, https://www.washingtonpost.com/religion/2022/05/22/southern-baptist-sex-abuse-report.

5   While there are multiple ways different anti-abuse disciplines refer to this concept (child abuse vs. intimate partner violence vs. sex offenders, etc.), the concept of the system around the acts of abuse remains across multiple disciplines. For further insight, consider this initiative: https://www.law.utah.edu/news-articles/new-initiative-studies-ecosystem-of-abuse.

6   See *Shiny, Happy People* on Amazon Prime; *Keep Sweet: Pray and Obey* on Netflix; the "Holy/Hurt" podcast by Hillary McBride; and @ReclaimingSelf.Therapy by Megan Von Fricken, LCSW on Instagram.

7   "Emotional Abuse," *Psychology Today*, accessed October 22, 2023, https://www.psychologytoday.com/ca/basics/emotional-abuse.

8   "What is Spiritual Abuse?," *National Domestic Violence Hotline*, accessed October 23, 2023, https://www.thehotline.org/resources/what-is-spiritual-abuse.

9   *Cambridge Dictionary Online*, s.v. "sexual abuse," accessed October 23, 2023, https://dictionary.cambridge.org/dictionary/english/sexual-abuse.

10 Petrina Coventry, "Why Does Power Abuse Persist?" *Business*, November 6, 2023, https://www.business.com/articles/psychology-of-power-abuse.

11 *Stanford Encyclopedia of Philosophy*, s.v. "exploitation," accessed October 3, 2022, https://plato.stanford.edu/entries/exploitation.

12 Members of dominant cultures: white, able-bodied, heterosexual, male, cisgendered, mid-aged, etc.

13 Intersectionality traditionally refers to the unique dynamics that develop when multiple systems of inequality come to bear. Intersectionality is certainly at play in our religious institutions, but there is also a compounding dynamic at play in abusive situations in our religious spaces. For example, what happens when you mix an imbalance of power with a disappointed, angry God? That's violent and spiritual abuse. Or when you mix sexual advances with religious authority? That's sexual and power abuse. Or when an elder board

decides they have the credentials to deny the definitions of abuse and use Scriptures on unity and gossip to silence dissent? That's spiritual and power abuse. See "What is Intersectionality," *Center for Intersectional Justice*, accessed October 23, 2023, https://www.intersectionaljustice.org/what-is-intersectionality.

14 I would define "resilience" as the capacity to withstand or recover from difficulty (juxtaposed with "fragility," which often responds with DARVO: Deny, Attack, and Reverse the Victim and Offender).

15 Layers of mistreatment include the ramifications of lack of representation in decision-making spaces, the disbelief of the stories of folks from the margins in our midst, the normalization of exploitation in our volunteer-based organizations, the denial of power and its dynamics, sexual misconduct, weaponized unity that silences victims, misapplied Scripture that retraumatizes survivors, etc.

16 "Modeling the Future of Religion in America," *Pew Research Center*, September 13, 2022, https://www.pewresearch.org/religion/2022/09/13/how-u-s-religious-composition-has-changed-in-recent-decades.

17 Jennifer Kuadli, "32 Shocking Sexual Assault Statistics for 2023," *Legal Jobs*, May 20, 2023, https://legaljobs.io/blog/sexual-assault-statistics.

18 Kate Gadinni, "A Large Number of Single Women Are Leaving the Church: Why?" *Relevant*, January 10, 2023, https://relevantmagazine.com/faith/church/why-are-so-many-single-women-are-leaving-the-church.

19 Colonization is defined in the Oxford Dictionary as "the process of settling among and establishing control over the indigenous people of an area" and in religious contexts is often rationalized in the name of evangelism. *Oxford Dictionary*, s.v. "colonization."

20 Tish Harrison Warren, "Why Pastors Are Burning Out," *The New York Times*, August 28, 2022, https://www.nytimes.com/2022/08/28/opinion/pastor-burnout-pandemic.html.

21 For more on the topic of religious institutions and narcissism, see Chuck DeGroat, *When Narcissism Comes to Church: Healing Your Community from Emotional and Spiritual Abuse* (IVP, 2020).

22 The "cost" can include, how out of our depth the leadership feels about handling a disclosure, how much work and/or expense it will take to properly investigate an allegation, what will happen to the accused leader if the claim is found to be true, what will happen in the organization if the leader's behavior requires consequences, etc.

23 For instance, a volunteer youth leader has no more spiritual right to abuse someone in our midst than one of our employees. The law binds the employee's behavior, but our Christian mandate binds even our volunteer's behavior. It is our legal responsibility to ensure our employee's behavior is safe; it is our biblical responsibility to ensure anyone in our midst with authority behaves safely.

24 Please never justify pressuring a survivor to share space with their abuser in the name of Matthew 18. At no point in the process of healing is a survivor biblically required to face their abuser. Period. If our theology is so small that we cannot imagine a path of healing more creative than a literal translation of this passage, we need to upgrade our mental image of God, God's work, and God's power.

25 God's principle of forgiving those who've harmed us is God's gift of liberation to the wounded party (offering them a path of freedom no longer weighed down by the perpetrator's choices). God's gift of liberation to the abuser is confession and repentance (offering them a path of freedom no longer weighed down by the shame of their choices). God does

not press past consent to impress either of these liberation principles upon Jesus-followers. And there is no spiritual precedent or authority for any human to do so either.

26 By "weaponized unity" I refer to the perversion of unity used to pressure survivors to remain silent or to coerce them to silently accept unjust responses to abuse in the name of protecting unity in the organization. Another example is implying that allies and advocates of survivors are harming the institution with their "gossip."

27 "What's an HR Audit and Why Is It Important?" *Walden University*, https://www.waldenu. edu/programs/business/resource/what-is-an-hr-audit-and-why-is-it-important.

17 THE BIBLE AND ABUSE OF GIRLS AND WOMEN

1 For more information, go to "Statistics," *National Coalition Against Domestic Violence*, https://ncadv.org/STATISTICS.

2 The first work of biblical scholarship to call attention to some of the horrific ways women are treated in the Bible was the classic *Texts of Terror* by Phyllis Trible (Fortress, 1984). (Fortress Press issued a fortieth anniversary edition in 2022.) For further examples and discussion of biblical texts related to the abuse of women, see Renita J. Weems, *Battered Love: Marriage, Sex, and Violence in the Hebrew Prophets* (Fortress, 1995); Cheryl Kirk-Duggan, ed., *Pregnant Passion: Gender, Sex, and Violence in the Bible* (Brill, 2003); Susanne Scholz, *Sacred Witness: Rape in the Hebrew Bible* (Fortress, 2010); and Rhiannon Graybill, *Texts after Terror: Rape, Sexual Violence, and the Hebrew Bible* (Oxford University Press, 2021).

3 See "Labor force participation rate for women highest in the District of Columbia in 2022," *U.S. Bureau of Labor Statistics*, March 7, 2023, https://www.bls.gov/opub/ted/2023/labor-force-participation-rate-for-women-highest-in-the-district-of-columbia-in-2022.htm.

4 Judges 19 bears some correspondence to the story of Sodom and Gomorrah (Gen. 19). Both episodes tell of a man who is a guest at a house; men of the town come to rape the guest; the host offers girls/women instead; the rapists remain intent on raping the guest who nonetheless remains safe. These stories are not about homosexuality, which is sexual attraction between two people of the same gender. Rape is a cheap weapon in war. The goal of the rapists is to shame the foreigner and therefore is unrelated to a loving, homosexual relationship. For further discussion, see Matthew Vines, *God and the Gay Christian: The Biblical Case in Support of Same-Sex Relationships* (Convergent, 2014), 59–75.

5 The Greek translation of the Hebrew Scriptures, called the Septuagint, states that the raped concubine does not move "because she was dead" *(hoti ēn nekra)*.

6 Trible, *Texts of Terror*, 64. See Matthew 26:26; Mark 14:22; Luke 22:19.

7 "Statistics," *National Coalition*.

8 A close translation of this verse in Hebrew reads: "Then King David heard these things and he was very angry." The mention of Amnon as the firstborn appears in the Greek Septuagint, not in the Hebrew.

9 For further discussion, see Ericka Shawndricka Dunbar, *Trafficking Hadassah: Collective Trauma, Cultural Memory, and Identity in the Book of Esther and in the African Diaspora* (Routledge, 2021).

10 See also Julie Faith Parker, "Hardly Happily Ever After: Trafficking of Girls in the Hebrew Bible," *Biblical Interpretation: A Journal of Contemporary Approaches* 28, no. 5 (2020): 540–556.

11   See Julie Faith Parker, *Eve Isn't Evil: Feminist Readings of the Bible to Upend Our Assumptions* (Baker Academic, 2023), 112–113.

18   WHAT I NEED YOU TO KNOW (DR. TAMMY DUNAHOO)

1   *Oxford English Dictionary*, s.v. "patriarchy."

2   Carolyn Custis James, *Malestrom: Manhood Swept into the Currents of a Changing World* (Zondervan, 2015).

3   Susanne Bruckmüller and Nyla R. Branscombe, "How Women End Up on the 'Glass Cliff,'" *Harvard Business Review*, Jan–Feb 2011, https://hbr.org/2011/01/how-women-end-up-on-the-glass-cliff.

4   See Beth Allison Barr, *The Making of Biblical Womanhood: How the Subjugation of Women Became Gospel Truth* (Brazos Press, 2021).

5   Michael Gryboski, "Rick Warren shares 3 Bible passages that changed his mind on women pastors," *Christian Post*, March 9, 2023, https://www.christianpost.com/news/rick-warren-explains-what-changed-his-mind-on-women-pastors.html.

6   See for example, Graham Joseph Hill, *Holding Up Half the Sky: A Biblical Case for Women Leading and Teaching in the Church* (Cascade Books, 2020).

19   PAIN IS AN INVITATION

1   Rob Dixon, *Together in Ministry: Women and Men in Flourishing Partnerships* (IVP, 2021). This work explores and questions the phenomenon of women's opportunities being limited in ministry settings due to the oppressive impact of fear-based rules and habits intended to protect male leaders from sexual sin, such as "the Modesto Manifesto" and the "Billy Graham Rule."

2   Susan Muto and Adrian van Kaam, *Commitment: Key to Christian Maturity* (Epiphany Press, 2010), 144.

3   Darren Shearer, "Why Most Churches in the U.S. Are Businesses," *Theology of Business Institute*, https://www.theologyofbusiness.com/why-most-churches-are-businesses; Harriet Sherwood, "Religion in US 'worth more than Google and Apple combined,'" *The Guardian*, September 15, 2016, https://www.theguardian.com/world/2016/sep/15/us-religion-worth-1-trillion-study-economy-apple-google.

4   Muto and van Kaam, *Commitment*, 27.

5   Aaron White, "The Creative Way Down: Surrender Course," Week one, *Infinitum*, https://infinitumlife.teachable.com/p/creative-way-down-surrender.

6   Muto and van Kaam, *Commitment*, 147.

7   Muto and van Kaam, *Commitment*, 147.

8   Muto and van Kaam, *Commitment*, 144.

9   Shared with permission from Hugh Walker, MDiv, MFT, Clinical Supervisor Adult Addictions, St. Joseph's Care Group, Thunder Bay, Ontario, Canada.

10 Jerome S. Bernstein, "Spiritual redemption or spiritual bypass," chapter in *Living in the Borderland* (Routledge, 2005), 148.

11 Original written addition from Hugh Walker.

12 Kristen Kobes Du Mez, "Toxic masculinity in evangelical culture is crucial to Trump's success," in an interview with Chris Karnadi of *Faith and Leadership*, October 22, 2020, https://faithandleadership.com/kristin-kobes-du-mez-toxic-masculinity-evangelical-culture-crucial-trumps-success.

20 EQUITABLE MULTICULTURAL SPACES

1 Robert P. Jones, *The Hidden Roots of White Supremacy and the Path to a Shared American Future* (Simon & Schuster, 2023), 299–300.

2 Adrian Pei, *The Minority Experience: Navigating Emotional and Organizational Realities* (IVP, 2018), 39.

3 Robert Chao Romero and Jeff M. Liou, *Christianity and Critical Race Theory* (Baker Academic, 2023), 51.

4 Pei, *The Minority Experience*, 102.

5 Christena Cleveland, *Disunity in Christ: Uncovering the Hidden Forces That Keep Us Apart* (IVP, 2013), 139.

6 Michael O. Emerson and Christian Smith, *Divided by Faith: Evangelical Religion and the Problem of Race in America* (Oxford University Press, 2000).

7 Christina Edmondson and Chad Brennan, *Faithful Anti-Racism: Moving Past Talk to Systemic Change* (IVP, 2022).

8 Dr. Twyla Baker (@indigenia), "A group of my Indigenous colleagues and I put voice to a feeling we've all experienced at multiple points in our journeys, and I wanted to get it down before I lost it," Twitter, January 22, 2019, 5.24 pm, https://x.com/Indigenia/status/10877 62882983538689?s=20.

21 FROM "THEM" TO "US"

1 See "Poverty deepens for women and girls, according to latest projections," *UN Women*, February 1, 2022, https://data.unwomen.org/features/poverty-deepens-women-and-girls-according-latest-projections.

2 "Poverty and Shared Prosperity 2022: Correcting Course," *The World Bank*, 2022, https://www.worldbank.org/en/publication/poverty-and-shared-prosperity.

3 "PAWSSD Chapter 2," *United Nations*, https://www.un.org/development/desa/dspd/world-summit-for-social-development-1995/wssd-1995-agreements/pawssd-chapter-2.html.

4 See "Poverty Rate by Country 2024," WorldPopulationReview.com, https://worldpopulationreview.com/country-rankings/poverty-rate-by-country.

5 See Andrew Peer and Sevil Omer, "Global poverty: Facts, FAQs, and how to help," April 4, 2023, *WorldVision.org*, https://www.worldvision.org/sponsorship-news-stories/global-poverty-facts.

6 "40 million in modern slavery and 152 million in child labour around the world," *International Labour Organization*, September 19, 2017, https://www.ilo.org/global/about-the-ilo/newsroom/news/WCMS_574717/lang--en/index.htm.

7 See "Human Trafficking (HT)," *IATA*, https://www.iata.org/en/programs/passenger/human-trafficking.

8   Wikipedia, s.v. "performative activism," paraphrased.

9   See https://ethicalstorytelling.com/.

22 THE HOLY WORK OF RESISTANCE

1   Kat Armas, *Abuelita Faith: What Women on the Margins Teach Us about Wisdom, Persistence, and Strength* (Brazos Press, 2021).

2   See Judy L. Glanz, "Exploration of Christian Women's Vocational Ministry Leadership and Identity Formation in Evangelical Churches on the West Coast," SPCE, vol. 17 (2).

3   Martin Luther King Jr., "'The Birth of a New Age,' Address Delivered on 11 August 1956 at the Fiftieth Anniversary of Alpha Phi Alpha in Buffalo," *Stanford University*, accessed December 11, 2023, https://kinginstitute.stanford.edu/king-papers/documents/birth-new-age-address-delivered-11-august-1956-fiftieth-anniversary-alpha-phi.

4   See "Guatemala," *The Center for Justice & Accountability*, https://cja.org/where-we-work/guatemala.

5   Emily Kaplan, "'Las Abuelas': How a Group of Sexual Slavery Survivors in Guatemala Won a Historic Legal Victory," *Ms. Magazine*, April 28, 2022, https://msmagazine.com/2022/04/28/guatemala-rape-women-war-sexual-assault-violence.

6   Kaplan, "Las Abuelas."

7   Billy Graham, "What's 'the Billy Graham Rule'?" *Billy Graham Evangelistic Association*, July 23, 2019, https://billygraham.org/story/the-modesto-manifesto-a-declaration-of-biblical-integrity.

8   Rob Dixon, *Together in Ministry: Women and Men in Flourishing Partnerships* (IVP, 2021), 127.

9   Halee Gray Scott, "To More Than a Few Good Men: Don't Give Up on Working with Women," *Christianity Today*, December 6, 2017, https://www.christianitytoday.com/ct/2017/december-web-only/dont-give-up-working-with-women-billy-graham-pence-rule.html, cited in Dixon, *Together in Ministry*, 126.

10   Adam Grant and Sheryl Sandberg, "Madam CEO Get Me a Coffee," *New York Times*, February 8, 2015, https://www.nytimes.com/2015/02/08/opinion/sunday/sheryl-sandberg-and-adam-grant-on-women-doing-office-housework.html.

11   Kim Elsesser, "Women Do More Office Housework—Here's How to Avoid It," *Forbes*, June 14, 2023, https://www.forbes.com/sites/kimelsesser/2023/06/14/women-do-more-office-housework-heres-how-to-avoid-it/.

CONCLUSION

1   See Ryan P. Burge, "With Gen Z, Women Are No Longer More Religious than Men," *Christianity Today*, July 26, 2022, https://www.christianitytoday.com/news/2022/july/young-women-not-more-religious-than-men-gender-gap-gen-z.html.

2   Franklin Leonard, @franklinleonard, X (formerly Twitter), October 10, 2015, 5:35 pm, https://twitter.com/franklinleonard/status/652885246220734464?lang=en.

Words Create Worlds

Want to buy bulk copies of
Need to Know?

By purchasing bulk copies from us, you are not only getting a better price per book, but you are also helping us to:

- ✅ Invest in training and equipping the church through insightful resources
- ✅ Support and publish authors from the global church
- ✅ Give voice and platform to emerging authors

Unlock Imagination. Release Potential.

Made in USA - Kendallville, IN
16699_9781955142571
11.11.2024 2037